Fire in His Bones

Endorsements

One of my professors liked to extend his metaphors and often likened Babylon to the dead, organized church, and Zion to the place of anointing. He said one time that Babylon was on a flat plain and words shouted on a flat plan seem to fall out of your mouth and to the ground—but Zion, this mountaintop place of the abiding of the presence of God produced words that echoed for miles. Words spoken from the presence of God appear to be such that the listeners are literally pulling the words out of the mouth of the preacher.

Pastor Wilkerson was such a preacher. His sermons have an echo that elevates them from the realm of the ordinary to this heavenly place where the words are carried on the wings of the Holy Spirit and straight into the human heart. I have met few men whose words are so empowered by the Spirit of God.

Audiences pulled the words from him, and the words resonated in their hearts, transforming their lives as instruments of God. I have met many people who can trace the turning point in their lives to a single Dave Wilkerson sermon.

Perhaps he was the inspiration for these verses.

My Jesus make your words a part of me
All fresh and vibrant, power leaping bright
Cause them to bless, to burn, to purify
Then cast me yonder flaming, through the night
Jesus Mighty Archer cast me
Cast me flaming through the night

My Jesus cast me where the lonely are
And where the hungry waste away and die
Cold hearts are waiting for the warming fire
And waiting in thy quiver, Lord am I
Waiting there are they my Jesus
Here my Jesus, here am I

Jim Palumbo, President: EvangAlliance, Inc.

One of my life's greatest privileges and honors has been to serve as Brother Dave's interpreter from English to French and to speak with him at conferences all over the world. I had a front-row witness to the power, anointing, and conviction of the Holy Spirit doing a deep work in thousands as he preached the Word.

Charles Spurgeon wrote that if a message is truly from God, it will impact all people all over the world, in every context and culture, and it will still be true a hundred years from now. Such are the messages of David Wilkerson. They have transformed millions of lives over decades, and they will continue to do so until our Lord's return. His sermons are as profound, Christ-centered, and life-giving today as the day they were first preached.

As you open your heart, you will experience again the fullness of these eternal truths. The Word of God is not bound by time, and though Pastor David is now with our Lord, he still speaks powerfully to our generation.

Claude Houde, Senior Pastor: New Life Church, Montreal, Canada, Chairman: French-World Theological Institute, President: Christian Association for the French-Speaking Nations

It is amazing how David Wilkerson's messages always penetrate my heart like he had first-hand knowledge of the wrestling of my soul. This knowledge came from his frequent feasting on the Word of God and through fervent prayer. What he penned was birthed by the Holy Spirit. The result was messages that were timely and relevant—spiritual nourishment for the soul.

Roger Jonker, Chief Operating Officer and Vice President: World Challenge

DAVID WILKERSON

WITH GARY WILKERSON
& ADÉLE BOOYSEN, DMIN

FIRE
IN HIS
BONES

A Collection of the
Fifty Most Powerful Sermons
of David Wilkerson

NASHVILLE

NEW YORK • LONDON • MELBOURNE • VANCOUVER

Fire in His Bones

A Collection of the Fifty Most Powerful Sermons of David Wilkerson

Published in New York, New York, by Morgan James Publishing in partnership with World Challenge Press

Proudly distributed by Ingram Publisher Services.

ISBN 9781636980072 paperback
ISBN 9781636980089 ebook
Library of Congress Control Number:
2022941562

Cover & Interior Design by:
Christopher Kirk
www.GFSstudio.com

Morgan James PUBLISHING

Builds

with...
Habitat for Humanity®
Peninsula and
Greater Williamsburg

Morgan James is a proud partner of Habitat for Humanity Peninsula and Greater Williamsburg. Partners in building since 2006.

Get involved today! Visit MorganJamesPublishing.com/giving-back

Table of Contents

Acknowledgments

A book about a preacher with fire in his bones could not be effectively compiled without a group of people with fire in their bones, people who believe we live in a generation that needs a clear and uncompromising word from God.

Thank you to Karen Anderson who helped get this project started and kept us all focused and to David Hancock who gave oversight to the work. Thank you to Adele Booysen who took the messages of David Wilkerson and turned them with great skill and heart into what you see on these pages. Also, thank you to Jason Staples who helped with editing and checked the content for accuracy. Tara Cooper was stellar as proofreader.

A special thanks to my executive assistant and daughter, Annie Holloway. Without you, this project would not have begun, been developed or be in readers' hands right now. I'm very proud of you and how God is using you to touch many lives.

—Gary Wilkerson

Foreword

Twenty-six hundred years ago, the Hebrew prophet Jeremiah had the Word of the Lord come to him in wave after wave, crashing up his heart, his soul, his very bones. The message was heavy and urgent. Jeremiah described it as a fire shut up in his bones, burning so intensely that he could no longer hold it back.[1]

Fast forward to the 1950s in rural Pennsylvania, and we see another man of God—David Wilkerson. A prophet? Yes, but much more. A husband, a father, and a pastor whose heart and soul were also being burdened with a call from the God of heaven: "Go to New York City. It is urgent. The youth are dying there, killing each other. You must tell them that Jesus loves them and died for their sins!"

On a street corner in Brooklyn in 1958, I heard one of the first of many sermons Dave preached in New York. He was crying out in that hostile environment, talking about something that was strange and foreign to me, saying that there was a God in heaven, and his Son, Jesus, came to earth because he loved us.

The fire in Dave Wilkerson's bones brought a message that caused a reaction in my bones: disbelief, anger, and rejection.

A violent teenaged gang leader who had suffered such abuse from the hands of my witchcraft-practicing parents, I could not accept this message at first. But like a boxer pounding the rib cage of his opponent, Dave kept pounding away: "Nicky, Jesus loves you! You can kill me and cut me into a thousand pieces, but each piece would cry out that Jesus loves you!"

---

1 Jeremiah 20:7–9

The book of Hebrews tells us that the Word of God is living, active, and sharper than a sword. That Word divides asunder, cuts and separates, our innermost parts.[2] On that day in Brooklyn, I experienced the power of the Word of God from the mouth of a man of God.

In *Fire in His Bones*, you will hear the heart and passion of David Wilkerson crying out to a lost and sinful generation to repent and turn to the living God. You will read and re-live timeless messages from a tender shepherd pleading with the flock to trust the Lord, to believe God's Word, to allow the Holy Spirit to fill them with a passion and a burden for the lost.

Many people might wonder how Dave's messages could be so powerful and effective. You can learn preaching techniques in seminary. You can be taught how to put together a sermon. But nothing can match the anointing of the Holy Spirit on a person's life. When the Spirit of the living God breathes on you and speaks thunderous words that penetrate to your very bones, well, then it is impossible to keep them in.

That was the case with Dave. The kind of impact and response to his teaching can only come from a position of brokenness before the Lord.

I remember a time right after my best friend in the gang, Israel, and I got saved. We were staying in the same room with Dave, and early one morning, Dave woke us up to join him for a time of prayer. We headed to a chapel and after five minutes, Israel and I fell fast asleep. When we woke up two hours later, Dave was still praying!

Dave Wilkerson was a man who was constantly on his knees, yearning to hear God's voice for his family, for his church, for his generation, and for future generations.

Dave was an extremely generous man who wasn't attached to earthly things. He founded Teen Challenge and built that powerful ministry over many years. Then, one day, Dave turned Teen Challenge over to another ministry and went on to write more books and travel all over the world to preach.

God spoke to Dave, telling him to return to New York City and open a church in the "heart of Babylon"—Times Square. It was there, at Times Square Church, that Dave preached hundreds and hundreds of sermons that were transcribed for the *World Challenge Pulpit Series* newsletters. Each month, for years and years, hundreds of thousands of people around the world read Dave's powerful messages.

---

2   Hebrews 4:12

Dave never forgot about those on the streets, though. Until the day the Lord called him home, Dave had a heart for the lost. He was a gifted businessman and a faithful steward. God blessed the ministry of World Challenge and continues to do so. World Challenge has the heart of David Wilkerson and supports many ministries around the world—including Nicky Cruz Outreach—and has a strong burden to reach the poor, including orphans and widows, as well as those bound by drugs and violence.

On that hot summer day in 1958 in the ghetto of Brooklyn, God had ordained a divine encounter between Dave and me. For the past sixty-plus years, our stories, our lives, our ministries, and our families have been connected for one holy purpose: to reach the lost with the message of Christ.

Scripture talks about another Hebrew prophet, Elisha, whose words were powerful and fire filled. When Elisha died, he was buried in a cave, but that wasn't the final chapter of this prophet's amazing life. The Bible tells the story of a time when some enemies of Israel were invading the land during another burial. When the friends of the dead man saw the hordes coming toward them, they quickly buried the body in Elisha's tomb. Amazingly, when the dead man's body touched Elisha's bones, the dead man came back to life and stood upright on his feet![3]

With the release of these fifty sermons, I believe future generations of believers can benefit from a fire that cannot be shut up. When you read these sermons, they will touch you and bring forth life to your bones and to your situation.

Though Dave and his precious wife, Gwen, have gone on to be with the Lord, the Word of God in these messages will bring hope and encourage you in these dark times.

God is still faithful and an all-consuming fire![3]

Nicky Cruz
President: Nicky Cruz Outreach

---

3   Hebrews 12:28–29

Introduction

The life-giving preacher is a man of God
whose heart is ever athirst for God,
whose soul is ever following hard after God,
whose eye is single to God,
and in whom by the power of God's Spirit
the flesh and the world have been crucified,
and his ministry is like the generous flood of a life-giving river.
~ EM Bounds

The very first sermon I remember hearing my father preach was when I was about six years old. He took me with him to a large arena where thousands of mostly young people gathered. The place was overflowing, and kids were sitting on the floor. He invited many of them to come sit up on the stage with him to make room for others.

I remember sitting backstage, looking out as the crowd sat in memorized silence as my father spoke. At the end of his message, hundreds responded to his call for salvation. They were throwing their drugs and needles on the stage as they were convicted of sin and called to a new hope of life in Christ.

At six years old, I decided what I wanted to do with my life. I wanted to be a preacher. I wanted to speak words of life that helped others live. Of course, at six,

I did not fully understand the fullness of my decision, but I made it and have been preaching my whole life.

Later, while I was in Bible college, my father came to preach to our student body. I remember another student coming up to me after Dad finished preaching and telling me that my father's message was not homiletically sound. That student wanted polish and procedure matching the scholar's books.

I believe my father was so immersed in the word of God that his messages were, in fact, solidly Biblical. But being polished was not his priority. Dad wanted to see God's power be manifested, he wanted chains to be broken in sinners' lives, he wanted captives to be set free, he wanted spiritual awakening in a lost generation. And through sheer dependency on the Holy Spirit, he saw that which he most deeply desired.

My father was no dry academic, nor was he a people pleaser. He was a man with fire in his bones. And he was used mightily in bringing miracle transformation to drug addicts and gang members. Later, my father was a large part of what was called the Jesus Movement and later the Charismatic Movement, bringing life to dead churches and dried-up Christians.

Dad seemed to be able to keep his pulse on the heart of what God was doing. This kept his preaching pertinent, practical, and timely for the hour in which he lived.

Later in life, I traveled full time alongside my father as we preached in over seventy nations to more than 100,000 pastors and leaders.

From spending countless hours with Dad, I can assure you…

his preaching was filled with power because his life was filled with power,

his preaching was filled with love because his heart was filled with love,

his preaching was filled with zeal because his soul was filled with passion for the lost,

his preaching was filled with wisdom because he spent hours a day studying God's Word,

his preaching was filled with the Holy Spirit because he spent hours a day in prayer, crying out to God for a holy visitation.

More than once, I heard him backstage crying out to God, "I need a word!" That desperate plea was not for a message that would entertain or tickle ears or draw big crowds; that cry was that he would have a word from God, not from his own ideas or his own abilities to craft and proclaim.

It has been over a decade since my father's passing. I miss him, and I miss his preaching. Many others have echoed the same sentiment. That is why, on the fiftieth anniversary of his founding a preaching ministry called World Challenge, we have put together fifty of his most impactful sermons over those fifty years.

These are diverse sermons. Some are thunderous calls to repentance and holiness; others are a gentle wooing to know God's love and tender grace. Some were preached at his evangelistic events, others at Times Square Church in New York, and several from the pastors conferences conducted by World Challenge. All these sermons have been condensed.

We trust and pray that these timely, enduring messages will revive your heart, will call you into greater passion for Jesus, and will encourage you in your walk with God. These messages have touched my heart, and I truly believe they will do the same for you.

A writer and a preacher that both my father and I greatly respected and read often is Charles Spurgeon, a nineteenth-century Englishman. The following are four important things Spurgeon suggested we remember about reading, and these are things to remember as you read this valuable book.

1. **Earnestly desire godly books.**

   Referring to 2 Timothy 4:13, Spurgeon said this of Paul: "He was inspired, and yet he wants books! He had been preaching for thirty years, and yet he wants books! He had seen the Lord, and yet he wants books! He had a wider experience than most men do, and yet he wants books! He had been caught up into the third heaven and had heard things that it was not lawful for a man to utter, and yet he wants books! He had written a major part of the New Testament, and yet he wants books!"

2. **Renounce light literature.**

   "Give yourself to reading. You need to read. Renounce as much as you will all light literature, but study as much as possible sound theological works, especially the Puritan writers and expositions of the Bible."

3. **Godly books drive us to the Bible.**

   "Visit many good books but live in the Bible. All human books grow stale after a time—but with the Word of God the desire to study it increases, while the more you know of it the less you think you know. The Book grows upon you: As you dive into its depths you have a fuller perception of the infinity which remains to be explored. You are still sighing to enjoy more of that which it is your bliss to taste."

4. **Read deeply more than broadly.**

"Master those books you have. Read them thoroughly. Bathe in them until they saturate you. Read and reread them…digest them. Let them go into your very self. Peruse a good book several times and make notes and analyses of it. A student will find that his mental constitution is more affected by one book thoroughly mastered than by twenty books he has merely skimmed.

"*Little learning and much pride comes from hasty reading.* Some men are disabled from thinking by their putting meditation away for the sake of much reading. In reading let your motto be 'much, not many.'

"Give yourself unto reading. The man who never reads will never be read; he who never quotes will never be quoted. He who will not use the thoughts of other men's brains proves that he has no brains of his own. You need to read."

This book meets Spurgeon's criteria. It will be of great value to you because it is, indeed, a godly book. It is not light literature. It will drive you to the Bible. And it can be read and reread to take you deeper into the things of God.

With you in Christ,
Gary Wilkerson
President: World Challenge Inc.

Part 1

"Prophesy to the Bones"

A Collection of Prophetic Messages

"Again, [God] said to me, 'Prophesy to these bones, and say to them, "O dry bones, hear the word of the Lord! Thus says the Lord God to these bones: 'Surely I will cause breath to enter into you, and you shall live. I will put sinews on you and bring flesh upon you, cover you with skin and put breath in you; and you shall live. Then you shall know that I *am* the Lord.' "

Ezekiel 34:4–6

1

The Vision

*My father preached this message in 1973. Much of it has been fulfilled,
the rest of it is right at the door. These warnings are to prepare us
as a bold, uncompromised, and pure church of Jesus.*
~ Gary Wilkerson

God has compelled me to share with you a vision to warn the church of an upcoming persecution of all Spirit-filled believers. For months, I tried to shake it off, but I could not. I have only had two such visions in my life. The first was when God took me to the streets of New York. Every facet of that vision has been fulfilled.

I have been afraid to share this vision for fear that I would be called a fanatic. But the same Holy Ghost that prompted me years ago to share the story of *The Cross and Switchblade* imparted this vision to be shared with you.

In this vision, I saw five terrible calamities coming to America and the world.

First, I saw a worldwide recession caused by economic confusion. There are only a few more flourishing years followed by an economic recession that will affect the lifestyle of every wage earner in the world. The world's economists will be unable to explain what is happening. Large and trusted corporations will go bankrupt, as will many churches.

One of the clearest messages I have ever received from God in my life is this: "Use the next few good years left to prepare for financial crises. Get your house in order because hard times are coming."

Second, I saw nature having labor pains. There will be supernatural signs and changes that men[4] will not be able to explain. Some disasters that we are witnessing now are mere labor pains. These will become more frequent and more intense the closer we get to the birth of the Kingdom of God.

I saw major earthquakes coming to the United States. I saw worldwide famine, especially in China, India, and Russia. I saw the world's food supplies completely dwindle, and millions starving. I saw tornadoes, hailstorms, floods, and hurricanes pound the earth with such intensity and violence that all of mankind will have to admit that the world is under supernatural siege.

Third, I saw a flood of filth and a baptism of dirt in America. I heard God saying that he will pour abominable filth upon America—triple-X rated movies on cable television, R-rated movies on network television. Our newsstands will be flooded with pornographic filth. But then there will be a successful campaign against such smut. The Supreme Court will rule against pornographers, and the nation will return to its former moral standards. But then, the floodgates will swing open and fill the earth with vomit out of hell.

Fourth, I saw rebellion in the home, the greatest problem being youth's hatred toward their parents. Children will turn against their parents with a passion, and parents will die a thousand deaths at the hands of children who have learned to despise their hypocrisy. Children and their parents will live under the same roof, but it will be like enemies living under a truce. This was the clearest vision I have ever seen in my life.

Fifth, I saw a persecution madness against Spirit-filled Christians who love Jesus Christ.[5] The Holy Spirit prompted me to share more with you regarding what I saw coming in the way of persecution.

1. **I saw an hour of persecution coming such as mankind has never seen before.** This will be a persecution of true believers, and it will rise like a

---

4   Throughout this manuscript, when David refers to *men,* he is referring to *humankind*—
    including women.
5   John 15:19–20; 2 Timothy 3:12

many-headed monster out of the sea. It will start slowly, subtly, coming at a time when religious freedom appears to be at a peak, then it will spread to the entire world.

2. **I saw the formation of a Super World Church Council consisting of a union between liberal ecumenical Protestants and the Roman Catholic Church.** They will be joining to create one of the most powerful religious forces on earth. It will start as a cooperative charities program, and it will end in a political union. It will be spiritual in name only.

    While this visible Super Church gains political power, the true body of believers will grow tremendously in spiritual power. This power will come from persecution. The persecution will drive these Christians closer together and closer to Jesus Christ. The Holy Spirit will bring together all people of our faith and walks of life.

    Next, there will be persecution of charismatic Catholics. Charismatic Catholics will face the most grievous persecution of all. High-level political pressure will be placed on priests to put the fire out. It will begin as a slow trend but will gather momentum and all Catholics in this movement will eventually face persecution from within their church.

3. **I saw persecution through a media struggle.** There is at present tremendous freedom for preaching the gospel on radio and television. But watch out. Persecution and harassment are already beginning. The Super Church Council will attempt to establish a kind of screening board and will have the final authority on all religion in the media. No program will be aired without their approval.

    I saw Satan trying to bog down these programs and stations in red tape legal proceedings. Satan will use every tactic at his disposal to remove all Christ-centered programs from the media.

    There will be persecution coming from Hollywood and from television comedies. These shows will become bolder and bolder and will poke fun at Christ and all true Christians. Comedy writers will strike to put down sacred traditions.

4. **I saw persecution through the taxation of churches.** There will be attempts to tax churches and church-related organizations. The Internal Revenue Service will become one of the most powerful weapons against the church.

5. **I saw three distinct ways the devil will try to undermine Christian education.** Christian schools and colleges and universities will not escape the coming hour of persecution. They will face political harassment, red tape, acute financial problems, and federal and state aid will come with more and more strings attached.

   There will be an almost unexplainable spirit among students of apathy, unrest, and disrespect for leadership. And the faculty will be infiltrated by teachers and professors who will become unwitting tools in the hands of Satan to undermine the foundations of faith and leadership.

6. **I saw the Jesus Revolution going sour.** The Jesus Revolution will become a revolting movement. It will stagnate, and undisciplined followers will return to their drugs, their free sex, and their old ways of life. Persecution will separate the sheep from the goats, and only fully surrendered disciples will be left standing when the fog clears.

   The time is soon coming when it will no longer be popular to be a Jesus person. A day will come when Bibles will be plucked from believers' arms and ripped apart by a laughing crowd of mockers. The harassment will eventually become so violent and widespread that young Christians will either harden themselves and stand up and witness against it, or crumble before it and deny their faith. And this is what persecution is all about.

7. **I saw a spiritual awakening coming behind the Iron and Bamboo Curtains.** While the free nations are experiencing this wave of persecution, those who had previously lived under religious persecution will enjoy a limited time of freedom.

8. **I saw a gossip war being waged against true believers who refuse to indulge in the freedoms of the new morality.** They will be the target of the most vicious, malicious gossip of all time. Their every motive will be questioned, every statement examined. Pastors will face the most malicious gossip of all. There will be innuendos, lies, and false statements floating around that are from the very pit of hell. Not a single true minister of the gospel will be immune to the gossip war, but this war will also be aimed against every true believer.

When I received this vision of calamities, it so frightened me I was just so transfixed before God, and it kept me up night after night. I asked the Lord about all these things. How are we going to do all that we are supposed to do when so many will be forsaking you? Do we turn this whole world over to the devil and just let him have his way? Do we just give up?

How can a Christian remain sane? How can we keep our fortitude? How can we be objective? The Holy Spirit gave me just five little words in response: **God has everything under control.**

When it looks like nature is out of control, remember that God's Word clearly predicted it would happen. Child of God, in these days to come, the Holy Spirit would say to you, "Do not fear the fury of nature. God is still King of the flood, and you look upon those floods, earthquakes, and hurricanes, and you say to yourself, 'That is my God talking. He is calling, and he is saying, "Get ready." '

Even the devil is under his control. As with Job, God may permit him to touch everything around you. But you hear it, Satan cannot possess you or rob you of your faith in God. The Bible says, "Resist the devil and he will flee from you."[6] Does that suggest a victorious devil? Never! God has everything under control, and we are under his control. So, we are not afraid of the devil.

In Paul's letter to Timothy, he encourages him, "God has not given us the spirit of fear, but of power and of love and of a sound mind."[7] No matter how things look in this world, no matter how dire this warning, rest assured all things are still working together to everyone who loves God, called according to his purpose.[8]

No matter what happens, nothing can harm you.

---

6   James 4:7
7   2 Timothy 1:7
8   Romans 8:28

2

The Last-Days Deception

One of the most difficult things for any of us is to see ourselves as we really are—as others see us and as God sees us. We are quick to judge others and slow to judge ourselves, blind to our real spiritual condition. In fact, we hardly know ourselves. And even when God gives us a glimpse into who we are, most of us are not ready to see the truth.

How about you? Are you blind to your spiritual condition, like the Laodiceans in Revelation? They were believing a great lie about themselves, saying, "We are rich, increased with goods and have need of nothing."[9]

The Laodiceans had sat under the preaching of the apostle Paul.[10] He had instructed them to humble themselves and to examine themselves. "Let the word of Christ dwell in you richly in all wisdom, teaching, and admonishing one another in psalms and hymns and spiritual songs,"[11] he had said. This was Paul warning them, **"Let the Word change you. Let it judge you. Let it convict you so that you do not stand before God deluded one day."** But in Revelation, we find out that God did not find them living this way.

The Laodiceans were not the first to have such a twisted view of themselves. We can likewise look at numbers within our churches and believe if we are growing in

---

9   Revelation 3:17
10   Colossians 4:15
11   Colossians 3:16

attendance, we are flourishing. Yet we, like the Laodiceans, are blind to our spiritual condition and how God sees us.

The Lord says of these believers in Laodicea, "You do not know it, but you are wretched. You are miserable, you are poor, and you are blind, and you are naked. What a shocking indictment from God himself. You are blind to your spiritual condition. You are not what you claim to be. You are hiding your real feelings. You are not as righteous as you think you are. You are not seeing the truth about yourself."[12]

I believe God can easily say the same of us.

You may have heard truths that were intended by the Holy Ghost to get down into the very root of your problem to change you. But rather than allowing the Spirit to change you, you harden your heart and decide the word is for somebody else.

＝＝ ＝＝

The apostle Paul in his letter to the Romans talks about boasting in God knowing his will, being "confident that you yourself are a guide to the blind, a light to those who are in darkness, an instructor of the foolish, a teacher of babes, having the form of knowledge and truth in the law. You, therefore, who teach another, do you not teach yourself? You who preach that a man should not steal, do you steal? You who say, 'Do not commit adultery,' do you commit adultery? You who abhor idols, do you rob temples? You who make your boast in the law, do you dishonor God through breaking the law?"[13]

What a terrible indictment to hear that you are a teacher, lecturing people about their sins yet you have not seen your own heart. **You can clearly see all that is wrong with others, yet you fail to see those shortcomings in your life.**

Could it be that you are projecting your shortcomings onto others?

＝＝ ＝＝

The prophet Isaiah tells of a people who plant a tree, water it, and watch it grow. And then they cut down the tree to warm themselves and bake some bread over the fire. From the rest of the wood, they carve a god and worship it.[14]

---

12 Revelation 3:17–19, paraphrased
13 Romans 2:19–23
14 Isaiah 44:14–17

Of them, Isaiah says, "They do not know nor understand; for [God] has shut their eyes, so that they cannot see, and their hearts, so that they cannot understand. And no one considers in his heart, nor is there knowledge, nor understanding..."[15]

Can you imagine you could be so blind to your spiritual condition that you could spend years nurturing a tree only to suddenly chop it down, cook on some of it, and use the leftovers to carve from it a god for yourself? You know what that says? **You can be blind and not know it.**

There are so many areas you can be blind to and not even see it—gossiping, unhealthy relationships, being prejudiced against people with a different background than yours. And then, being convicted by the Holy Ghost and the Word of God, you break down weeping, confessing before the Lord that you are broken. Because of the grace of God, the Word has found its mark. It has cleansed you.

If, after all this time, God's Word has not moved you to repentance, you can be sure that there is a hardness in your heart. Everybody can see it. Everybody knows it but you. It will finally come to light when you stand before the judgment of God and he tells you, "I know you not."[16]

Oh God, help us!

═ ═

So when there has been a word from the very hand of God—a cleansing word—ask God, "Lord, would you give me ears to hear and eyes to see? Melt my heart. Do not let me be hardened. Break in me what needs to be broken; expose in me that which needs to be exposed."

Without such a willingness to be shaped by God, you can grow bitter and not even know it.

═ ═

James warns us to "be doers of the word, and not hearers only, deceiving yourselves. For if anyone is a hearer of the word and not a doer, he is like a man observing his natural face in a mirror; for he observes himself, goes away, and immediately

15   Isaiah 44:18
16   Luke 13:25; Matthew 7:23

forgets what kind of man he was. But he who looks into the perfect law of liberty and continues in it, and is not a forgetful hearer but a doer of the work, this one will be blessed in what he does."[17]

When the mirror of God's Word is held before you, do you walk away unchanged? Or do you examine yourself before the Lord and invite God to deal with you, to speak to your heart, and to change you?

Proverbs speaks of being instructed, being willing to learn and to be shaped, in these words, "Take firm hold of instruction, do not let go; keep her, for she is your life."[18]

Life depends on being willing to learn, yet how easy it is to let go of this until it is too late. Like the person caught in adultery, who says, "How I have hated instruction, and my heart despised correction! I have not obeyed the voice of my teachers, nor inclined my ear to those who instructed me."[19]

Perhaps you have also wondered at times, "Why did I not take heed?"

Allow the Word of God to soften your heart so you can do the will of the Father. This is why Jesus warned us, "Not everyone who says to Me, 'Lord, Lord,' shall enter the kingdom of heaven, but he who does the will of my Father in heaven. Many will say to me in that day, 'Lord, Lord, have we not prophesied in your name, cast out demons in your name, and done many wonders in your name?' And then I will declare to them, 'I never knew you; depart from Me, you who practice lawlessness!' "[20]

Jesus said there will be *many* who had done mighty works in his name yet he will not allow them entrance into heaven. But he is also saying, "When I speak to you, listen and obey what I ask you to do. If you set your heart to obey, I will give you the strength to do it."

Oh God, search our hearts.

God is merciful. He is kind. But he also means what he says.

══ ══

God gave me a vision years ago, and it was scary. In fact, I could not have handled it lest God had given me one phrase at the end of the vision. God said,

---

17 James 1:22–25
18 Proverbs 4:13
19 Proverbs 5:12–14
20 Matthew 7:21–23

"When you preach this, make sure you tell the people, 'This God has everything under control.' "

When I finally preached on the vision it was so heavy. But when I said, "God has everything under control," the place came alive. Finally, there was some hope.

But having seen all these things that are coming, that was all I talked about. I got consumed by the message. I became so critical that a dear friend of mine finally stood up and said, "David, that is enough! I cannot stand being around you anymore. You have taken all my faith, all my hope. You discourage me!"

At first, I was offended. Who did he think he was? I warned him that his business might fail, and he would be glad I had warned him. I was stewing.

When my wife Gwen and I talked about it and I asked her if she heard what my friend had said, she told me, "I heard, and he is right."

I went to prayer and God showed me my friend was indeed right. For months, God showed me how arrogant I had gotten. "Yes, I have shown you these things, but not to bring despair," God told me. "You have to preach both to warn *and* to bring in hope."

If you want to know your spiritual condition, ask the Lord to show you where you have been deceived. God will speak to you. When the mirror of God's Word is held before you, you may be surprised—even shocked—at what God shows you. But if you soften your heart and listen, you will walk away a changed person. From there, walk not in your own strength, but with God.

3

A Fire in My Bones

God had given Jeremiah a harsh message for Jerusalem, warning of the city's destruction.[21] When Pashur—the governor of the chief priests at that time—heard Jeremiah prophesying about the destruction of the city, he was incensed. Pashur sent for Jeremiah and had him put in stocks[22] right at the gate of the temple where everybody could see his humiliation for a full twenty-four hours.

God had spoken to Jeremiah, clearly giving him the message for Jerusalem, yet here he was locked up, humiliated, and in pain.

Agonized, Jeremiah cried out to God, "Lord, you deceived me, and I was deceived!"[23] He goes on to complain that he has become a public joke, that he hears people whispering to denounce him as a prophet. Jeremiah wishes to no longer speak of God's message nor to mention God's name. Nevertheless, he knows he cannot do that as God's Word is like a fire in his bones, and he is tired of trying to hold in that fire.[24]

Here was a man who could not doubt he was called. God had spoken to him very clearly. Even from before birth, Jeremiah had been ordained to be a prophet to

---

21 Jeremiah 19:15
22 Jeremiah 20:1–3; Stocks were like a wooden yoke. A person's neck was put in the yoke, and then their hands were twisted, and their entire body was contorted.
23 Jeremiah 20:7, paraphrased
24 Jeremiah 20:7–9

the nations. God had told Jeremiah that he knew him even before the earth was created. God had a plan for his life and had sanctified Jeremiah in his mother's womb, creating him to preach the gospel.[25]

Even so, Jeremiah objected that he was too young. God responded telling Jeremiah not to say he was not worthy to do the work for which he had been created. "For you shall go to all to whom I send you, and whatever I command you, you shall speak," God told Jeremiah, adding, "Do not be afraid of their faces, for I am with you to deliver you."

And with that, God reached out, touched Jeremiah's mouth, and said, "I have put my words in your mouth."[26]

God had given Jeremiah specific orders. He had given Jeremiah his heart so he could speak God's words. And this man was totally obedient to the call of God.

The Lord told Jeremiah, "Gird up your loins, rise up, speak to the people all that I command you. Do not be afraid of any man's face. Do not be afraid of anything that man can do. Do not be dismayed by them lest I dismay you before them."[27]

Again and again, God's message to Jeremiah is straightforward.

- **Gird up your loins.** God is essentially saying, "I have called you from the womb.[28] I have given you a word, and I have made you a promise. I will be with you."[29]
- **Do not be afraid.** "As long as you live, I am with you. No demon can touch you, no enemy can touch you, nobody can prevail against you. So, rise up, and in faith do as I have commanded you."
- **Do not be afraid.** "Do not worry about anything that man can do. Do not pay attention to their frowns or their smiles. Do not think about flattery; do not think about anything but one divine purpose—to speak my mind."
- **Speak what I tell you to speak.** "I am with you now as you speak my words, as you obey me and give me your confidence and your trust. I will never put you to shame. I will be with you everywhere you go and everything you do."

---

25 Jeremiah 1:5
26 Jeremiah 1:5–9
27 Jeremiah 1:17 KJV
28 Jeremiah 1:5
29 Jeremiah 1:5–9, 19

- **I will give you the words when it is needed.** "Throw down idolatry, build up the believers. But if you are not going to trust what I told you, if you are not going to take me at my word, if you are not going to believe that I am with you, if you do not believe I am faithful, if you will live in doubt and fear, I will have to let your flame go out. I will have to let you be dismayed."
- **Still, I will defend you.** "I have made you an impregnable city with iron pillars and brass walls against society, against kings and priests, and against all the people. They shall fight against you but not overcome you, for I am with you."

This not only is God's message to Jeremiah. It is God's message to every believer. "I am with you. I have made you a defended city. There are pillars holding up the walls, and there are brass walls around you. Be not afraid."[30]

Every follower of Christ has a mandate from God. We are to speak the words God lays on our hearts, on our lips. Speak God's words on the job, speak it in the home, speak it wherever you go.

God will give you the words to speak. If you are praying at home and on your face before God, by the time you go out in public God will have already given you his words to speak. In your times before the Lord, God will plant his words in your soul so they can bear fruit in your conversations, if only you tune your heart to his.

Jeremiah reached a low point in his ministry the night Pashur had him put in stocks, though. Here was a godly man, a caring man, yet he was tortured. So, Jeremiah complained to the Lord saying, "You have deceived me, and I was deceived. You are stronger than I am, and you have prevailed. I'm in derision daily and everyone mocks me."[31]

The word deceived here means seduced. What this prophet is saying cannot be sugarcoated. He is saying, "God, you called me. You anointed me. You said I was called from my mother's womb. I do not understand this kind of pain and mockery and derision that I am going through now. You never told me about this!"

---

30 Jeremiah 1:18–19, paraphrased
31 Jeremiah 20:7 KJV

In other words, Jeremiah is saying God has opened him up to derision, to being exposed. Angry, Jeremiah declares, "God, I do not understand. You have opened me up to mockery, and I have ended up a failure! I am nothing but a foolish, humiliated man."

Perhaps you can imagine what Jeremiah went through that night of torture. I can relate, and maybe you can too. Perhaps you are going through your night of torture, a painful and humiliating situation.

There was a time in ministry when the devil tried to destroy the church God had called me to plant, a time when the enemy tried to destroy the ministry. I know the pain Jeremiah felt going through a night of confusion. You say things that you never thought you would say.

Perhaps you find yourself saying, "Enough, God! I cannot go on. I am not going to live this Christian life anymore. I had it easier when I was in the world…"

When Jeremiah complained, God did not correct him. He did not rebuke him, because God saw Jeremiah's heart. He saw the fire burning within. I believe God was saying, "This is my man. He is just letting off a little steam. He is angry because I am doing something new in him. But he will come out of the fire with a faith that cannot be shaken."

Once Jeremiah was released the next day, he had even more fire in his bones. He would not be intimidated. And like Jeremiah, God brought me out of the dark night with glory!

God's eyes roam to and fro throughout the earth so he can show himself strong on behalf of those whose hearts are loyal to him.[32] God himself will bring you out of whatever it is you are going through. I do not know what you may be going through but here is what the prophet Jeremiah said.[33]

"I will not make mention of God," he said. "I will no longer speak his name." And then he comes to his senses. "But God's Word was in my heart like a burning fire shut up in my bones; I was weary of holding it back, and I could not."

---

32   2 Chronicles 16:9
33   Jeremiah 20:9

That is why I could not quit. That is why you cannot quit. That is why Jeremiah could not quit—because he had a fire burning in his bones... and you have a fire burning in your bones.

God made you a promise. God spoke to you. He called you from the womb. You simply must remember God's promises and believe. Faith will carry you through.

God says you are not going down. You are not going to quit. If you allow, God will add the fuel of faith, and you will see him consume all your doubts and sins, for our God is a consuming fire.[34]

Tell him, "Jesus, I cannot fight this. I know the word you have given me is a fire, and I know you abide in me, and you lay hold of that word." Then you go to the Bible, and you start taking God at his word. That is the secret of the covenant. That is the secret of the overcoming life.

I do not know what your battle is, but I do know God's voice. And God says, "I have made you a walled-in city with brass walls and impregnable gates. I made you a promise, and I will never fail you. I will give you the words."

Receive God's words. Stand on it. **Do not let the devil shake you.**

---

34 Hebrews 12:29

4

Getting Ready for the End of All Things

God showed the apostle Peter that he would soon take him home.[35] But before he would be taken, the Holy Spirit gave him a word for the church, that false prophets shall bring damnable heresies. They will preach covetousness—materialism. They will despise the laws of the land. They will be presumptuous, self-willed, and corrupt. Scoffers will come, filled with lust. They will mock the message of the coming of Christ. And many shall follow them.[36]

Peter also warned that the end—the great day of the Lord—will happen suddenly. It will come like a thief in the night. "The heavens will pass away with a great noise, and the elements will melt with fervent heat...," he declared. "Both the earth and the works that are in it will be burned up. Therefore, since all these things will be dissolved, what manner of persons ought you to be in holy conduct and godliness...?"[37]

We see the handwriting on the wall. But how do we prepare for these tumultuous end-time events? We want to know in some detail how we will survive such frightful times. What about employment, housing, food, clothing?

Amazingly, Peter gives no advice about physical preparations. He says nothing about where to put your money, about a housing crisis, about global warming, or inflation.

---

35 Peter 1:14
36 1 Peter 4:7–8
37 2 Peter 3:10–12, paraphrased

Truth is, Peter had experienced poverty. He traveled about picking grain from farmers' fields.[38] He knew about sleeping under stars.[39] He lived without a job, with just one change of clothes, one pair of sandals.[40] He had no money except what he found in the mouth of a fish.[41] Yet Peter had experienced the Lord's faithfulness.

Instead, Peter focuses on the preparation of the heart. He focuses on character. He challenges you to consider what is in your heart, what you are becoming. Peter says God will take care of all your physical needs—but are you preparing spiritually?

Even Jesus left us very little advice about physical preparations for the end times. He warned his disciples of wars and rumors of wars, of famines, earthquakes, and persecution. He spoke of floods of iniquity that would cause the love of many to grow cold.[42]

But Jesus said little about the loss of houses, loss of jobs, about safe havens, or how to survive an economic crash. Rather, Jesus said, "Therefore do not worry, saying, 'What shall we eat?' or 'What shall we drink?' or 'What shall we wear?'... For your heavenly Father knows that you need all these things."[43]

$$\equiv\equiv$$

Under the prompting of the Holy Ghost, Peter warns, "But the end of all things is at hand; therefore be serious and watchful in your prayers."[44] Stay calm. Do not panic. Stay in prayer. Control your stress through prayer.

Peter also encourages the church above all things to fix our minds on Christ.[45] Above all your concerns about survival, this one thing should be your focus in these end times. This is the message of a dying apostle: "I give you the most important word from God's heart—as if this were my last message... Keep fervent in your love one for another—because love covers the multitude of sins."[46]

---

38 Mark 2:23
39 Matthew 8:20
40 Mark 6:8–9
41 Matthew 17:27
42 Matthew 24:4–31; Mark 13; Luke 21
43 Matthew 6:31–32
44 1 Peter 4:7
45 1 Peter 1:13
46 1 Peter 4:8, paraphrased

In light of the greater mercy God has shown you, in light of God's unconditional forgiveness of all your past sins, in light of his covering your past, in light of his being so compassionate, long-suffering with you, you must reach out with fervent mercy to those who have sinned against you, forgiving as if they had never sinned against you.

A brother once wrote to me: "Pastor Dave, you have faithfully warned us about the economic holocaust you see coming. Surely the same Spirit of God who showed you the things to come will show you how we are to survive. A good God would not warn us then not tell us what to do to make it through the storm. Please give us a word."

Another man wrote, "I feel cheated. I asked you for financial advice about where to invest my money and how to save my family when another depression comes. You told me to go to prayer, ask the Holy Spirit for direction. I feel cheated. You gave me the same old theological cop-out. I need specific answers."

What I am sharing here is the Word of the Lord. Peter was a godly man, and the Holy Spirit has shown us through him what God said. Peter was specific in saying that the first and most important preparation is to get your heart ready. **If you do not deal with your heart, all other preparations are in vain.**

The end of all things is near, Peter said, so stay calm. Get on your knees. And above all else, practice unceasing mercy and love among your brothers and sisters. And forgive and cover their sins.[47]

Who hurt you? Who sinned against you? Who spread gossip about you? If you do not forgive and cover that sin, you are like the man forgiven a great debt who then went out and choked a man who owed him a few dollars.[48]

You may say, "I have no bitterness. I have pure love for all my brothers and sisters. I never expose the sins committed against me. So, Peter's admonition gives me very little edification. It does not apply to me."

But Peter's message here has everything to do with the future of the church. It has to do with God getting his church ready for the latter-rain outpouring of the Holy Spirit prior to the Lord's coming.

---

47 1 Peter 4:8
48 Matthew 18:23–35

Satan knows God has revealed in the prophets that in the latter days, the Holy Spirit will once again fall on a prepared people.[49] The latter rain is promised to be greater than the former.[50] The type has to do with two types of rain in Israel. The spring rain was called *former* or the *first* rain. And just before harvest in the fall came the *latter* rain.

Moses told Israel there could be no harvest without a latter rain. "Then I will give you the rain for your land in its season, the early rain and the latter rain, that you may gather in your grain, your new wine, and your oil."[51]

The prophet Zechariah also saw this outpouring of the Spirit in the last days. "Ask the Lord for rain in the time of the latter rain. The Lord will make flashing clouds; he will give them showers of rain, grass in the field for everyone."[52]

Similarly, Joel declared, "Wake up, church! This is that which had been prophesied. It is beginning to rain. The Lord is making bright clouds. The Spirit is preparing for the last great harvest."[53]

Satan knows this, and he is determined to hinder the harvest. He has released a furious attack on the church, trying to bring discord. Even God's people are overwhelmed by the darkness covering the world. Fear has fallen on every nation. People feel helpless. Courts make laws against the will of the people. Stress is causing all kinds of sicknesses. Sin has been downgraded and hell has been discarded.

Along with this, many ask the question: Does this generation go out with dysfunctional families and dead, dry churches withering away as Israel did in the Old Testament? Not according to the prophets. They say that God will arise in the darkness.[54] He will rain down the Holy Spirit.

The prophet Haggai stood before people who were downcast because they were looking back at the past glories of the old temple. The present temple seemed insignificant. "Who is left among you who saw this temple in its former glory? And how do you see it now? In comparison with it, is this not in your eyes as nothing?"[55]

---

49 Joel 2:28
50 Joel 2:23
51 Deuteronomy 11:14
52 Zechariah 10:1
53 Joel 2:21–27, paraphrased
54 Isaiah 60:2, Isaiah 9:2
55 Haggai 2:3

Do you see God's work these days as nothing compared to Pentecost and past revivals as nothing? God said, "My Spirit still remains with you; I am with you, so fear not. ... The glory of this latter house shall be greater than of the former, saith the Lord of hosts: and I will give peace, saith the Lord of hosts."[56]

Peter was there when the Spirit fell at Pentecost. He knew the Spirit came upon a people who were all in one accord! Mercy was flowing in and through them.[57]

Think about those gathered who had sinned against God. Peter had blasphemed. James and John sinned against the apostles, professing to be greater than them. **They were all forgiven.**

This is why Peter focused on these issues. He knew these things had to be cast out, lest the Spirit be hindered.

Beloved, with a spirit of unforgiveness and attempts to disrupt, demon forces will come with fury to hinder the outpouring.

Do not hinder the latter rain on your house. Holy Spirit, rain down.

---

56   Haggai 2:5, 9, paraphrased
57   Acts 2:43–47

5

Everything Will Change in Just One Hour

In just one hour the world will change, John warns us.[58] He confirms what Paul had said about the destruction that will come from the hand of the Lord. "When they say, 'Peace and safety!' " Paul warned, "then sudden destruction comes upon them."[59]

Through the prophet Isaiah, God also speaks of a time when he will turn everything upside down. "Behold, the Lord makes the earth empty and makes it waste, distorts its surface, and scatters abroad its inhabitants. … The land shall be entirely emptied and utterly plundered, for the Lord has spoken this word."[60]

Isaiah does not name the city, but he does say there will be sudden destruction that will change everything, that the city gates—the exits and entrances—will be devastated.[61]

John also says the merchants will weep and wail and cry because no one is buying their merchandise. There are sellers but no buyers.[62]

We do not know when this will happen, but the hour will come when the whole world will change. And it will be beyond our ability to cope with this cataclysmic event.

---

58 Revelation 18:8, 10, 20
59 1 Thessalonians 5:3–4
60 Isaiah 24:1, 3
61 Isaiah 24:12
62 Revelation 18:11

You may say, "Why the warning? What is the purpose of that? Why do you not just wait until it happens? Why put this burden upon us?"

Remember what Jesus said when he foresaw the destruction of Jerusalem. He said the city was going to burn to the ground. "And now I have told you before it comes, that when it does come to pass, you may believe," he said.[63]

So, when there is panic all around you, you will be able to say, "My God warned me."

Even though nobody wants to hear a message of destruction, we cannot ignore this warning.

Here is why I believe the prophet Isaiah is talking about our day. First of all, there is a growing number of prophets warning of an apocalyptic moment coming. Those are not just church prophets. I am talking about experts such as scientists. God can use them to deliver prophecies too just like God used Assyria as a razor to shave his people,[64] and just like God spoke through King Cyrus, a heathen, saying, "Cyrus is my shepherd, and he is doing my bidding."[65]

The second reason why I believe we can assume that Isaiah's warning speaks to our generation is that God moves through judgment; he acts when the cup of violence overflows. And there is no greater violence in the sight of God than the violence of pedophiles.

All over the world, children are being taken and trafficked—even sold on the Internet—and sent to brothels. Children are abused and babies are aborted, their blood crying from the ground.

What are we doing? Getting hardened to the news? Does it not move us anymore? I can tell you, it moves the heart of God. How long do you think God will endure? How long do you think God will put up with this?

When God moves, all of this will change, and it will change rapidly. Sudden destruction, when it comes, will change the church. There will be a great shaking as though God takes an olive tree and shakes it.[66]

---

63 John 14:29
64 Isaiah 7:20
65 Isaiah 44:28, paraphrased
66 Isaiah 17:6; 24:13

God says, "I will shake everything that can be shaken. I will turn everything upside down."[67]

===

Isaiah speaks of a time of cataclysmic devastation, of a time that will be so incredibly dark, a time of fire.[68] In the middle of that, what will be happening in the church? Apostasy will change things overnight. Everything that we see that is wrong in the church will change—and in the house of God, there will be a revival.

I am not a prophet; I am a watchman. I watch what is happening around us, and I read God's Word. If God speaks through his Word, I believe it, and I preach what God says. **The Bible says that in the middle of this time of devastation, a song will rise.**

"When it shall be thus in the midst of the land among the people, it shall be like the shaking of an olive tree, like the gleaning grapes when the vintage is done. They shall lift up their voice, they shall sing; for the majesty of the Lord they shall cry aloud from the sea. Therefore glorify the Lord in the dawning light…"[69]

Did you get it? In the middle of the fire God will have a people who are not in a panic, people who will praise the majesty of almighty God. He said in the fires you will sing. "From the ends of the earth have we heard songs…"[70]

What does Isaiah say we will hear? Not weeping, not murmuring, not groaning, not complaining, not agonizing. **You will hear a song coming from the church in every nation. And this song will be coming at the darkest time.**

I believe that something will also happen among our youth, especially students who are going to schools and colleges where they are robbed of their faith. Ungodly teachers and professors have had our young people as prisoners for years, bombarding them until they have no faith left.

But in the hour when everything will change, when the world is shaking and trembling and everybody is awakened, those teachers and professors will be looking for somebody to give them a word. Prosperity preachers will be turning to their Bibles, looking for something to say to the people who will be asking, "Why did you not warn us?"

---

67   Hebrew 12:27, itself interpreting Haggai 2:6
68   Isaiah 24
69   Isaiah 24:13–15
70   Isaiah 24:16

That hour of change will not be the end of the world. The Bible talks about a future beyond that shaking.[71] Individuals will change, your life focus will change. No longer will you obsess about your problems and adversities. Other than that which is of the Spirit, of love, and of Christ, everything else that may have once been dear to you will no longer have value. Things that you held dear will vanish.

And out of the chaos of that hour, the antichrist will come. The antichrist cannot come to power until there is chaos.[72]

As for idols, this great cataclysmic event will bring them down. They will be crushed to stone.[73] Even idols like sports will no longer be talked about. Do not get me wrong: I am a football fan, but millions of dollars are spent on sports while people are starving. That will change.

The events will be no respecter of persons. After the shaking, we will all be on equal footing. Isaiah says, "And it shall be: as with the people, so with the priest; as with the servant, so with his master; as with the maid, so with her mistress; as with the buyer, so with the seller; as with the lender, so with the borrower; as with the creditor, so with the debtor."[74]

Whether presidents, world leaders, or those living in poverty, all will face the same struggles, the same conditions.

Are you ready for some comfort? The apostle Paul offers encouragement. To the church in Thessalonica, he says, "But you, brethren, are not in darkness, so that this day should overtake you as a thief"[75] He compels us to comfort one another, saying, "For God did not appoint us to wrath, but to obtain salvation through our Lord Jesus Christ, who died for us, that whether we wake or sleep, we should live together with him. Therefore comfort each other and edify one another, just as you also are doing."[76]

---

71 Hebrews 12:26–27
72 2 Thessalonians 2:3–12
73 Isaiah 27:9
74 Isaiah 24:2
75 1 Thessalonians 5:4
76 1 Thessalonians 5:9–11

Paul is talking about some destruction, but he is also talking about a time when we will be with the Lord. Therefore, he encourages us not to tremble as the world does but instead to speak to one another saying, "Live or die, we belong to the Lord. We are headed for eternal life in Christ."

As you watch the news and listen to what is happening to the economy, remember God is speaking—not to make you afraid but to prepare your heart. This is also why Paul says to put on the breastplate of faith.[77]

—— ——

I do not live in fear, nor do I allow a fear of death to have dominion over me. Likewise, you cannot have freedom until you comfort yourself with the Word of God saying, "Whatever happens, bless God[78]. Even if I die, I will simply pass from death unto life. Therefore, I do not live in fear; I do not live in bondage."

I have a secret song in my heart. It may simply be David Wilkerson's thoughts, but I have this feeling today just as I had before 9/11. God spoke to us, telling us not to be afraid. At that time, the Holy Spirit moved in Times Square Church and in other congregations. God warned us. At that time, sometimes for up to fifteen minutes, we sat in silence before the Lord.

In the hour when everything will change, things will be different. There will not be silence. There will be singing and shouting and praising of God to encourage the body and strengthen their spirit. The saints of God will be quickened by the Holy Ghost.

—— ——

If you are afraid of what lies ahead, ask the Holy Spirit to relieve you of that fear. Ask the Spirit to fill you so you too can live with a song in your heart.

---

77 1 Thessalonians 5:8
78 Job 1:21, paraphrased

6

Are You Ready for the Coming Storm?

I saiah prophesied that God will one day rise up and shake the whole earth, and when that time comes, God will shake the earth as if it were an olive tree, till every bit of fruit falls. He carries on saying that the entire earth shall appear to be a mere cottage when God begins his shaking.[79]

Several other prophets concur with Isaiah's words—Ezekiel, Joel, and Haggai all talk in different ways about God shaking the nations. The writer of Hebrews echoes these prophecies, saying that God will not only shake the earth but also heaven, that only those things which cannot be shaken may remain.[80]

We cannot deny this truth: God will shake everything so that he alone is revealed as the only unshakable power.

$$==$$

Just as any loving parent gently shakes their sleeping child when it is time to wake up, God has been gently shaking the church to wake us up. When we do not wake up immediately, the shaking becomes a bit firmer and more serious.

I believe this is exactly what God is doing to America *and* the world.

---

79   Isaiah 24:13, 18–20
80   Ezekiel 38:20–23; Joel 3:16; Haggai 2:6–7; Hebrews 12:26–27

When the Lord says, "I will shake the earth," he means it. He will shake our economy, our education system, our government—everything we put our confidence in.

I had a very vivid recurring dream about the president of the United States—which president, I do not know—looking out the window of the Oval Office, shaking his head in disbelief and saying, "How did it happen? What went wrong?"

No one could explain America's collapse to him. That is the way it will be when God does his shaking: No one will be able to explain it.

⸗

When the storm comes, I wonder how many Christians will be able to stand. How many will have the foundation of faith necessary to endure?

The Lord gave me a revelation of Jesus's parable of the builders from Matthew 7. "Therefore," Jesus says, "whoever hears these sayings of mine, and does them, I will liken him to a wise man who built his house on the rock: and the rain descended, the floods came, and the winds blew and beat on that house; and it did not fall, for it was founded on the rock.

"But everyone who hears these sayings of mine and does not do them will be like a foolish man who built his house on the sand: and the rain descended, the floods came, and the winds blew and beat on that house; and it fell. And great was its fall."[81]

What house is Jesus referring to us building? It is our walk with him. We are building a foundation of getting to know Christ, of understanding his ways. And Jesus is saying that **the only thing that will hold up in the coming storm is what is established on a rock foundation.**

This parable is about obedience. Jesus is describing a lifestyle of total, absolute obedience to his Word. *That* is a rock-solid foundation!

Jesus himself is our Rock. But that is not the full meaning of *rock* as it is used in this parable. Just as water sprang and flowed out of the rock in the wilderness,[82] when we live in obedience, there is a spring that flows from the motives of our hearts.

---

81   Matthew 7:24–27
82   Exodus 17:1–7

If the spring is not pure, everything that flows out of it will be polluted. That type of obedience—when we obey due to a sense of legalism—makes God weep. It is a cold, technical formality, based on the fear of consequences.

The sad truth is that **many Christians obey God only because they are afraid to go to hell.** Having no genuine desire to please him, they fear their Father's wrath.

Jesus showed us an example that was very different from that. He did everything out of pleasure for his heavenly Father.[83] The rock upon which Jesus built was a life of obedience. The desire to please his Father was the spring from which his obedience sprung.

Desiring to do what pleased his Father, Jesus shut himself up in prayer on the mountaintops, in quiet places, often all night long. When he prayed, "Not my will, but yours be done,"[84] Jesus was essentially saying, "Father, what do you want? What will bring you pleasure? What can I do to fulfill the desire of your heart?"

Oh, to be like Jesus.

On the other hand, the person who builds his house on sand does so only for show. It is a temporary lifestyle. He reasons he will live in that house for a few years then sell it and leave the problems to someone else. It is only a facade with no real foundation!

Such a person does not believe a storm is coming. They do not want to think that things will get hard.

That is the way the world deals with eternity: They simply do not think about it.

Tragically, even some Christians try to put eternity out of their minds. They do not want to believe that one day they will stand before the Lord and answer for everything they have said and done.

———

I had a horrible, vivid dream about hell. I was on one side of a veil that was impassable. Yet I saw people on the other side walking around, moving yet going nowhere. Among them were people I knew, people I thought were Christians.

In this dream, these people were with someone who represented the one thing or person they desired most here on earth. They had gotten the very thing they had

---

83 John 8:28–29
84 Luke 22:42

thought they wanted, but now it brought such terror and torment to their soul, they were weeping, living in endless torment.

The thing that frightened me most about the dream was that I shouted to them, "Let me pray so you can get out!"

But they looked at me and answered, "You cannot help us." Then they turned and walked away.

I woke up, trembling and crying out, "Oh, God! If that is what hell is like, let me never fail to warn the people. There *is* a hell—it is real!"

Jesus talks about something similar right before the parable of the builders, declaring, "Not everyone who says to me, 'Lord, Lord,' shall enter the kingdom of heaven," he said, "but he who does the will of my Father in heaven. Many will say to me in that day, 'Lord, Lord, have we not prophesied in your name, cast out demons in your name, and done many wonders in your name?' And then I will declare to them, 'I never knew you; depart from me, you who practice lawlessness!' "[85]

I call these people "In the name of Jesus" people. They will stand before God's throne and say, "Lord, we did many wonderful works in your name..." But the tragic truth is, they built their houses upon sand.

Many great works have been done by those who have never been intimate with Christ. They cried, "Lord, Lord!" throughout their lives, coming to God for relief, for power, for rewards. Yet these people never stopped long enough in his presence to get to know him.

There are entire ministries and churches about which this is true. They use God's name without knowing him. They certainly are busy for God, but they do not obey him with a love that flows from enraptured hearts.

If you say you are a Christian—that you love Jesus, that your house is built upon a rock, that you walk in obedience to the Lord—yet you neglect him day

85 Matthew 7:21–23

after day in prayer, then you do not know him. Your house is built on sand, and when the hard times come it will collapse.

You cannot get to know Jesus by going to church alone. You have to have a day-by-day, hour-by-hour conversation with the Lord. That way, you get to know him, you grow to love him, you desire to know what pleases him.

And when you know God in this way, you see the Lord with arms outstretched saying, "Come to me and receive life, receive strength. I will carry you, no matter what you go through."

A life built upon the rock is a life of passionate love for Jesus. The more you love him, the easier it is to know what pleases him as you serve and obey him. You will no longer care what the world says about you. You can answer, "I have heard from my Father, and I am doing the good pleasure of his heart!"

This kind of obedience naturally flows when your heart is enraptured with Jesus.

If you say you love Jesus, how can you go throughout the week without spending time in his Word? How can you not yearn to get alone with him in prayer? How can you *not* have a time of pouring out your heart in love before your Father, praising and worshipping him, seeking to learn what pleases him? These are foundational to obedience!

I urge you to **get to know Jesus's words. Memorize them. Live them.** Try beginning with the Sermon on the Mount.[86]

==

God's commandments are not a heavy burden laid upon you. On the contrary, obeying them becomes easier the more you grow to love him. *That* is building your house upon the rock.

Then, when the storm comes, you can stand unafraid. Because you are living a life marked by lovingly obeying Jesus, nothing will move you—not even a fierce shaking from on high.

86 Matthew 5–7

7

Sodom's Sister

God has been waging a war for a very long time. It is a war against pride. Wherever he finds pride, he strikes at it until he destroys it. God takes pride so seriously that, according to Ezekiel, God destroyed Sodom with fire and brimstone due to their pride, their prosperity, and their neglect of the poor.[87] **All sin emanates from pride.**

Ezekiel equates pride with an utter rejection of dependence on the Lord and turning to confidence in the flesh and human ability. He said, "That is pride, that you will not acknowledge me as being the one who delivers. You will not acknowledge me; you trust in your armament. You trust in your ability to accomplish it and you have turned aside from acknowledging my power and my strength."[88]

Pride goes before destruction.[89] Before bringing Edom down, God warned them, "The pride of your heart has deceived you, you who dwell in the clefts of the rock, whose habitation is high; you who say in your heart, 'Who will bring me down to the ground?' Though you ascend as high as the eagle, and though you set your nest among the stars, from there I will bring you down."[90]

---

87   Ezekiel 16:49
88   Psalm 146:3–10 and Isaiah 28–29, paraphrased
89   Proverbs 16:18
90   Obadiah 1:3–4

Likewise, God warned Israel, "The lofty looks of man shall be humbled, the haughtiness of men shall be bowed down, and the Lord alone shall be exalted in that day."[91]

Even of Babylon, the nation with its great armies, God said, "Call together the archers against Babylon…. Repay her according to her work; according to all she has done, do to her; for she has been proud against the Lord, against the Holy One of Israel."[92]

══ ══

A proud nation is a nation that says, "We neither need nor want God in our education system. We do not want him mentioned in our courts. We do not want any public prayers to him, and never mention the name of Christ." A proud nation declares, "Who needs God to fight our battles? We are a superpower!"

Pride of a nation comes when they scoff at prophets and watchmen who warn of coming judgment. Pride refuses to believe there is a God in heaven who will smite with anger those who turn against him.

Most tragic of all, pride comes when we ignore all the warnings of history of how God has dealt with past nations. This is the indictment of the prophet Ezekiel against Judah. He pointed to the history of Sodom and Samaria, two cities like Jerusalem that fell under the judgment of God.[93]

Judah did not learn from history. They did not heed the prophet's warnings.

══ ══

The Bible says that Samaria turned their back on God, they did not fear the Lord. They killed their babies at the bellies of foreign deities.[94]

Judah witnessed the Assyrian army coming and, for three years, they besieged Samaria.[95] They watched as the whole population was taken captive, and they

---

91 Isaiah 2:11
92 Jeremiah 50:29
93 Ezekiel 16:44–63
94 2 Kings 17:7–18
95 2 Kings 17:5–6

watched them be carried away. They saw the judgment of God on their neighbor. Yet, Judah learned nothing from it.

Then there was Sodom. Even in Ezekiel's time, they were the epitome of evil. When God could no longer endure the corruption of Sodom, he sent fire and brimstone, destroying a proud and prosperous people in a single day.

Ezekiel came to Judah and accused Judah of being worse than Samaria and more corrupt than Sodom.[96] But Judah had been God's nation, God's chosen people.

What God is saying is that Sodom and Samaria were proud. "They committed abominations before me, therefore I removed them." To Judah, God says, "You have witnessed this. You have seen past judgments. You have seen how I work; you know my ways. Now, look at yourself. You consider Sodom the epitome of sin rejection of God. But you have justified them by your sins."[97]

God is saying, "You now are the epitome of sin and rebellion. Do not talk to me about Sodom. Do not talk to me about Samaria. Your sins are twice as wicked. Your sins are greater, Judah. You had the temple. You had the Scriptures. You had the prophets, you had the law, you had Moses, and you had the example of my judgment on others before you."

== ==

Ezekiel's word to Judah has horrible, tragic implications for the United States of America because America has become the sister of Sodom and Samaria.

Though Sodom had no Scriptures and no prophets, America has been inundated with the gospel. Bibles, books, media, pastors, teachers, evangelists, prophets, and watchmen across the land are warning and pleading for repentance. Even Nineveh repented at the preaching of one prophet,[98] yet America has mocked countless watchmen and prophets.

Sodom's great sin that precipitated judgment was pride, but there is a kind of pride that neither Sodom nor Samaria could have been guilty of. It is a sin that can only be committed by those living in the last days—meaning us.

96 Ezekiel 16:47, 51
97 Ezekiel 16:51–52, paraphrased
98 Jonah 3:5–9

Ours is not a sin against greater light; it is a sin against him who says he is the Light.

Four hundred years after Ezekiel tried to warn Judah to humble themselves, God sent his Son as the Redeemer, he sent him to break every chain, to set every prisoner free—everybody bound by sexual sin, addictions of all kinds, even pride.[99]

Through Christ, God gives us this free offer and all he asks of us is that we believe, that we trust him, and let his Spirit live in us so we can live in peace and victory.

Yet in the epitome of pride, the United States and many nations have rejected the Light, saying, "We do not need God." Instead of accepting God's mercy, we seek to cast him out of our society. That is blasphemous pride.

You cannot tell me that God will not judge a nation that makes it unconstitutional to utter his name in schools and public buildings.

There are two words that will help you to understand what is going on in the United States and around the world. These two words are *Christ* and *antichrist*. There is a spiritual war that began when Jesus was born, and it will not end until Armageddon.[100] When God gathers all the armies of the world to one place, and God the Father destroys all the armies and makes them a footstool of his Son.[101] The final spiritual war—a holy war—will be between Christ and the antichrist.

The apostle John said, "By this you know the Spirit of God: Every spirit that confesses that Jesus Christ has come in the flesh is of God, and every spirit that does not confess that Jesus Christ has come in the flesh is not of God," he said." Of the latter, John said that it is the spirit of the antichrist, which is a religious movement that "is now already in the world."[102]

Furthermore, Paul said that in the last days there will be a great falling away.[103] We will witness it more and more. There will be a battle that is spiritual in nature, and it will continue.

99   Isaiah 61:1; Psalm 146:7–9
100 Revelation 16:16
101 Referring to Psalm 110:1, cited of Jesus in Luke 20:43; Acts 2:35, 7:49; Hebrews 1:13, 10:13
102 1 John 4:2–3, paraphrased
103 1 Timothy 4:1; 2 Thessalonians 2:3

What are we to do as a church? What are we to do as God's people? We are to wake up.

I believe God's anger is against the backslidden church. He will judge his house because that is where judgment begins. The Bible makes it clear that God will try everything to get the church's attention. He even sends wake-up calls. These wake-up calls get increasingly more severe. Then finally, the last thing God will do—he did it to Judah—is to break the economy. He said, "I am going to take away your supply of bread."[104]

God will bankrupt every denomination that has turned against the virgin birth of Jesus Christ, every denomination that is preaching that Jesus Christ is not God in the flesh. God will cut off their money and they will go bankrupt.

I am already getting letters from all over the United States from people who have been disappointed by the wealth and prosperity gospel, saying things like, "I was misled, and now my daughter has cancer, my husband lost his job, and they offer me no hope. All they tell me is that I have a lack of faith."

I tell you, God will bankrupt that whole scene. They will be running for the hills.

We have received a wake-up call to get serious.

As for the final spiritual war, do you need to get ready to be a martyr? No! Christ already died for us, and in that one death, he conquered all the religions of the world and all the powers of hell. **You do not have to die for Jesus; he died for you and for the whole world.**

Oh, there will be martyrs. There will be those who will pay with their lives, but there will be no merit in any man's death. The Bible says, "If you give your body to be burned at the stake and do not have love, it amounts to nothing."[105]

104 Ezekiel 4:16
105 1 Corinthians 13:3, paraphrased

Those who follow Jesus Christ are the only ones who have a resurrected leader, and he already won the war. That is why he said, "Now when these things begin to happen, look up and lift up your heads, because your redemption draws near."[106]

Jesus said he will be coming with his armies.[107] He said every eye shall behold him and every knee shall bow before him—every world leader and every spiritual leader worshipped in other religions will all bow before Christ, declaring that he is King of Kings, Lord of Lords.[108]

We have nothing to fear. If God created us out of the dust of the earth, can he not protect us? Will he not keep his children who love him?

Live or die, we are the Lord's.

---

106 Luke 21:28
107 Revelation 19:11–14
108 Revelation 1:7; Romans 14:11 (quoting Isaiah 45:23); Philippians 2:10; Revelation 17:14; 19:16

8

The Towers Have Fallen,
but We Missed the Message

On Tuesday, September 11, 2001, the twin towers of the World Trade Center in New York City were destroyed. Days later, as I looked out the window of my study in our thirtieth-floor apartment, huge clouds of smoke were still smoldering from the ruins. They rose from the rubble and drifted out over the Hudson River, passing above the Statue of Liberty.

I wept at the sight of the utter devastation. I pleaded with God for mercy. Mercy for the grieving families who had lost loved ones. Mercy for the workers still digging through the rubble, hoping to locate survivors but finding only body parts and corpses. Mercy for the police officers, firefighters, and volunteers who wept openly over the indescribable horrors they saw.

Our church was allowed to set up a relief tent at ground zero of the disaster. Ministry leaders and volunteers from our congregation worked around the clock, helping to feed and encourage the weary workers.

Six weeks before the disaster, the Holy Spirit had warned our pastoral staff that a calamity was coming. Our hearts were stirred to intercede concerning the prompting of the Spirit. We held congregational prayer meetings four nights a week. From the very beginning, each meeting was marked by an awesome stillness that settled over the congregation. For hours, we sat in the Lord's presence, often without a sound, followed by soft weeping and heartrending repentance.

When the calamity struck, the nation was asking, "Where is God in all this?" We were right to ask this question. We need to understand where God is in a calamity such as that of 9/11. And while we heard opinions from media experts and politicians, their rhetoric sounded the same. There was no real understanding of the meaning of the destruction.

Meanwhile, many theologians were saying, "God had nothing to do with these disasters. He would not allow such awful things." **Nothing could be further from the truth. This kind of thinking is causing our nation to rapidly miss the message God wants to speak to us through the tragedy.**

To understand where God was in the events, we have to trust his Word. He knows the thoughts of all human beings—including every ruler, despot, and terrorist.[109] But God does not only watch what is happening. *He has everything under control.* Nothing on the face of the earth takes place without God's knowledge of it, his permission for it, and, at times, him being behind it.[110]

God delivered a message to America and the world through the events of 9/11. I wept and grieved over this awful calamity. I sought the Lord in prayer and through his Word. And I experienced grief that is even deeper than the mourning for innocent people dying. If we turn a deaf ear to what he is loudly proclaiming, then much worse is in store for us.

The prophet Isaiah and the apostle Paul speak directly to what we experienced. Paul makes it clear, "Now all these things happened to them as examples, and they were written for our admonition, upon whom the ends of the ages have come."[111]

At the time that Isaiah prophesied, God had been dealing patiently with Israel for about 250 years. The Lord had sent "light afflictions" upon his people, calling them to repentance.[112] He was trying to woo them out of their brazen idolatry and

---

109 1 Chronicles 28:9; Psalm 94:11; Isaiah 66:18; Ezekiel 11:5
110 Isaiah 45:5–12; 10:5–15
111 1 Corinthians 10:11
112 2 Corinthians 4:17, derived from 2 Kings 17:13–23

back into his blessing and favor. All of the prophets throughout the years had spoken to Israel the same essential word: "Humble yourselves."[113]

Scripture says, "They served idols...yet the Lord testified against Israel and against Judah, by all of his prophets, every seer, saying, Turn from your evil ways, and keep my commandments and my statutes." Still, God's chosen nation rejected his call to repentance. "They would not hear, but stiffened their necks."[114]

These people mocked the prophets who called them to humility. Instead, they "followed idols, became idolaters...they left all the commandments of the Lord their God...and sold themselves to do evil in the sight of the Lord...Therefore the Lord was very angry with Israel."[115]

God sent wake-up calls to Israel. The Lord's first wake-up call to Israel came as an invasion by Assyria. This archenemy attacked two Israelite provinces, Zebulun and Naphtali. Fortunately, the attacks were limited to these two points, but the damage was substantial.[116]

God was clearly speaking to his people, but they still missed the message. So, God sent a second wake-up call. This one was severe. The Assyrians would invade Israel, and the Syrians and the Philistines combined forces and attacked them from two sides.[117]

Still, the people had boasted that they would rebuild, so these attacks came as strong warnings to God's people. The Lord wielded enemies as an instrument of warning to Israel, calling the nation to repent.[118] God charged a coalition of Israel's enemies to chasten his chosen people. The Lord was warning Israel, "You have lifted yourself up with pride. Now I am about to bring you down. I will allow you to be destroyed by your enemies."[119]

Did Israel repent after this horrifying attack? Did the rulers hear God speaking through the awful calamity? No. Israel's reaction was just the opposite. The people's initial fear quickly gave way to a flood tide of national pride.

Once the attack died down, the Israelites regained their confidence. Arrogantly, they declared, "The bricks have fallen down, but we will rebuild with hewn stones;

---

113 Jeremiah 13:18; Deuteronomy 8:2–3
114 2 Kings 17:12–14
115 2 Kings 17:15–18
116 2 Kings 15:29; Isaiah 9:1
117 Isaiah 9
118 Isaiah 10:5–6
119 Isaiah 9:12, paraphrased

the sycamores are cut down, but we will replace them with cedars."[120] They were saying, in other words, "These calamities are not from our Lord. They are unfortunate disasters that cannot be explained. Being a mighty nation, we will build everything back bigger and better. We will come through this disaster stronger than ever."

Israel refused to heed God's warning.

==

Does that sound familiar? We tend to give lip service to God, but we continue our slide into the mire of immorality.

When a nation is under divine correction, it will react in one of two ways. It may humble itself and repent, as Nineveh did.[121] Or it may give lip service to God, but then turn inward to its own strength to rise above the correction, as Israel did.

We face the same danger Israel did. We could easily miss God's message to our nation. Deep in my spirit, I heard the Lord saying, "I have prospered you, yet you have persisted in worshipping idols of gold and silver. I have endured your shameless sensuality, your mockery of holy things, your shedding of innocent blood, your tireless efforts to remove me from your society.

"Time is running out for you. I have sent you prophet after prophet, watchman after watchman. You have been warned again and again. Yet still you will not open your eyes to your wicked ways. Now, **I have struck you in hopes of saving you.** I want to heal your land, to destroy your enemies, to bring you back into my blessing. But you do not have eyes to see it."

==

If God would not spare other nations that have outlawed him, why would he spare America? He will judge us as he judged Sodom, Rome, Greece, and every other culture that turned its back on him.

---

120 Isaiah 9:9–10
121 Jonah 3:5–9

God is a God of compassion, though. He feels grief and sorrow over death, saying through the prophet Ezekiel, "I take no pleasure in seeing you suffer and die. That is why I am pleading with you: Turn from your sin and live."[122]

God weeps over those calamities that befall the innocent. He is said to "bottle the tears of his saints."[123] Yet, at times, God's justice and righteousness cause him to restrain his pity; he is forced to carry out his righteous judgments.

What will happen to America if we reject God's call to turn to him? What will happen if abortions continue and fetuses are used for research, if we rebuild all things bigger and better, only to enrich ourselves more, and if we rely on our armed forces for power rather than on God?

Isaiah describes what happens to a nation that rejects God and boasts of its greatness: "For wickedness burns as the fire...They shall mount up like rising smoke. Through the wrath of the Lord of Hosts, the land is burned up, and the people shall be as fuel for the fire."[124]

Devouring fires will rise to the heavens. Darkness will cover the land. The economy will be hit with a staggering blow. And there will be disunity in the nation, in communities, in neighborhoods, in families. In a desperate fight to survive, people will look out only for themselves.

I was given a prophetic message in 1992 that was more severe than what we saw in 2001. Indeed, if America rejects God's call to turn back to him, we will face the same judgments Israel faced. The nation's economy will collapse, and violence will erupt. Fires will consume our cities, and tanks will rumble through the streets.

---

122 Ezekiel 18:31–32, paraphrased
123 Psalm 56:8, paraphrased
124 Isaiah 9:18–20

Perhaps you wonder, as I have, "Can any of this be avoided?" Absolutely! I believe we will be given a reprieve if our president proves to be like Josiah, a king who sought the Lord with all his heart.[125]

Pray that God would give our president the same spirit that Josiah had—to tremble at his Word.[126]

Pray also that our nation repents and turns back to the Lord.

And most of all, pray for your own heart. **"Lord, let me tremble not at the disasters, but at your Word. I want to hear your voice in all of this. Cause me to turn wholly to you."**

---

125 2 Kings 23:25
126 2 Kings 22:15–20

9

The Great and Final Apostasy

R ecently, as I was reading Ezekiel 16, I felt the grief of God concerning a
church that has turned away from its beginnings. The passage contains a
parable with dual application—first to Israel and now to the church in
the last days.

The church was birthed in holiness, in adherence to the Word of God. The
church was planted in New Testament power, in the purity of Christ and the righteousness of God. This was preached with power, fire, and authority.

The church took root first in Israel, and it grew to be a tree that spread its
branches. Those branches are now called denominations within the body of Christ.
Most of these denominations were founded by praying men of God.

I think of John Wesley, the founder of the Methodist Church, for example. In
his lifetime, Wesley preached hundreds of thousands of times. He would get up at
five in the morning and head out on horseback, holding street meetings for coal
miners by six.

Wesley prayed for hours every day. God shook England under this man's preaching. He was a man of righteousness. After John Wesley died, there were pastors who
came to the United States and established Methodist Bible schools and churches.

They had pastors who rode on horseback all over Kentucky, Tennessee, and
all through the Midwest. They held revival meetings—called camp meetings—and
people came from miles around. Thousands would cry out to God, "God, forgive

my sins. God, move mightily." And God moved mightily, indeed. There was such conviction at these meetings that people fainted.

Years later, in 1906, there was the founding of the Pentecostal movement in Los Angeles. There was a little church on Azusa Street in downtown Los Angeles that had a Black pastor named William J. Seymour. Just a few people came together at his church to pray for America.

One night, as Seymour and others were praying, the Holy Spirit fell upon that little group. People were trembling under the Spirit of God, and they spoke in tongues. The news spread, and soon people from all over Los Angeles came and experienced such power and conviction.

God began to move in that little church. It was not long before people came from other states—even from other countries—compelled by the stories of what was happening in that little chapel. As Seymour preached, thousands would fall on their knees and repent of their sins.

Out of the original roots of Wesley and Seymour came a great harvest of godly, righteous men and women. But over the years, many a church born from camp meetings of the Midwest and the little church on Azusa Street have forgotten their roots. They have forgotten their beginnings.

=====

God sent Ezekiel to his people because they had turned and apostatized.[127] Ezekiel said, "Now then, O harlot, hear the Word of the Lord!"[128] God's anger had been stirred. He had been provoked by a people who had turned against their God, a church that had turned against its beginnings.

We see the same with some of our nation's universities. Harvard and Yale were started as Bible schools. Princeton and Columbia were started by pastors. But now, as far as I am concerned, these have all become ungodly colleges. They have become apostate schools.

The same goes for Christian colleges and seminaries all over the United States. Many are fighting to keep the inroad of apostasy from invading their schools. But it has become a losing battle because professors who no longer believe the truth the

---

127 *Apostasy* refers to the rejection of the truth once believed and proclaimed.
128 Ezekiel 16:35

schools had been founded on are coming into these schools. They no longer talk about the cross, no longer believe in the divinity of Jesus Christ. They justify every kind of sin and no longer believe there is a hell.

You see it all over the world. On my last trip to England, they were closing Church of England campuses all over the country. They were selling those churches as nightclubs. There is a darkness coming down over that country and all over Europe. So few go to church. Yet that is where John Wesley came from. That is where countless hymns were penned. But now, Europe has turned from its roots.

Through Ezekiel, God said, "Look, this was the iniquity of your sister Sodom: She and her daughter had pride, fullness of food, and abundance of idleness; neither did she strengthen the hand of the poor and needy."[129]

What is the number one sin named? Pride. God is essentially saying, "**The pride of my apostate church is far worse than that of Sodom.** Sodom did not sin like you have sinned. They did not have the Light. But you? You knew me! I found you. I saved you. I called you. I put righteous robes on you. I sanctified you. I blessed you and spread you all over the world. And then? You played the harlot."

$$\equiv\equiv$$

There is something worse than a perverted gospel. Worse than a perverted gospel is a gospel of half-truths, a watered-down gospel. Such a gospel proclaims, "Just believe and get saved." It says nothing of repentance. Nothing of godly sorrow. Nothing of turning from your sins. Nothing about taking up your cross and following the Lord.

The prophet Isaiah warned of this, saying "Now go, write it before them on a tablet, and note it on a scroll, that it may be for time to come, forever and ever: That this is a rebellious people, lying children, children who will not hear the law of the Lord; who say to the seers, 'Do not see,' and to the prophets, 'Do not prophesy to us right things; speak to us smooth things, prophesy deceits. Get out of the way, turn aside from the path, cause the Holy One of Israel to cease from before us.' "[130]

These days, people do not want to be corrected, nor do they want to be convicted.

---

129 Ezekiel 16:49
130 Isaiah 30: 8–11

Ezekiel said, "They have not distinguished between the holy and unholy, nor have they made known the difference between the unclean and the clean."[131] In doing so, they strengthen the hands of the wicked.[132]

$$===$$

What will it be like when we stand before the throne, when we stand before Christ and the books are opened?[133] I cannot bear the thought of me preaching a diluted gospel so as to not offend people simply to keep the crowds coming, the money flowing, and every seat filled. But when I stand before God, there will not be blood on my hands; I have proclaimed to you the whole gospel of Jesus Christ.

A diluted gospel is no gospel at all. Ezekiel calls it untempered mortar. He called it whitewash.[134] When a storm comes and God blows against those whitewashed walls, they will not stand. **The Lord will blow against those walls of cheap grace, of a cheap, costless, inoffensive gospel, and he will blow them down.**

When that day comes, there will be those who will say, "Do not worry, all things continue as they were from the foundation of the world. This will all blow over; be at peace."[135] What willful ignorance!

In the midst of the fire, when the vials of wrath are being poured out upon the earth, those who have been hardened will blaspheme God; they will not repent of their sins.[136]

But something else will also happen. God said he will cause the apostasy to stop. "I will make you cease playing the harlot, and you shall no longer hire lovers," Ezekiel said.[137] In other words, you are not going to give yourself over to this apostasy anymore. He said, **"I will save you—not by your covenant but mine."**[138]

I believe God is speaking to the church, reminding us that in the midst of the most frightful times, when the judgments are falling, God will move in grace and mercy. "In the midst of this judgment," God essentially said, "I will cause you to

---

131 Ezekiel 22:26
132 Jeremiah 23:14
133 Revelation 20:12; Daniel 7:10
134 Ezekiel 13:10; 13:10 ESV
135 2 Peter 3:4
136 Revelation 16:9, 11, 21
137 Ezekiel 16:41
138 Ezekiel 16:59–63, paraphrased

cease from playing the harlot. And I will do this for the sake of my name—not because you are good, not because of your prayers."

God said that while there will be those who are blaspheming and hardening their hearts, he will find every backslider, everyone who has ever known his name, and he will remove the apostasy from their hearts. He will do so despite their perversions.

"Nevertheless, I will remember my covenant with you in the days of your youth," God said, "and I will establish an everlasting covenant with you. Then you will remember your ways and be ashamed..."[139]

That is forgiveness; that is repentance.

== ==

Jesus came to a world and to a people who would turn against him, who would crucify him. He came as an act of mercy and grace—not because you or I deserved it but because of his covenant.

And when Christ returns, God will wake up every backslider who has ever known Jesus but turned away from their roots. He will wake up every person who has been in a church where they had known the fire of God, where they had known the Word of God, where they had walked in the Spirit but had drifted away.

When God wakes you up, he will cause you to draw near. God will cause you to look at your idols and realize those have failed you. Then you will look to Jesus who will give you a new heart—a heart of flesh, not of stone, a heart of repentance and humility.[140] He will give you a heart of worship so you can join the angels around the throne, singing, "Worthy is the Lamb who was slain to receive power and riches and wisdom, and strength and honor and glory and blessing!"[141]

When he breaks open the seals, may God find you facedown before his throne.

139 Ezekiel 16:60–61
140 Ezekiel 36:26
141 Revelation 5:12

10

Preparing for Hard Times

From the hours I have spent with the Lord, I believe the times ahead will be worse than any of us know. Not everyone wants to hear this message, but I know I have been appointed to be one of God's watchmen. And as a watchman, if I do not sound of the trumpet and warn the people, their blood is on my hands.[142]

When I talk about the times ahead, people tend to take one of two approaches. They either ignore the reality that things will get worse, or they prepare by buying supplies and moving to the countryside as preppers.

I believe we should be prepared, but we are to prepare God's way. When you prepare God's way, you do not need any extra money, you do not need to leave your home, you need not stockpile anything, nor do you need a private source of water or guns.

I had warned our church three or four years before the war in Iraq that there would be 500 fires burning in the Middle East. Nobody thought much of it. But then, when the Iraqi forces retreated from Kuwait in 1991, they set the oil wells on fire, causing more than 600 fires in the region.

I have been able to see these things since I was a child and had written down the things God would show me since I was a teenager. Recently, I have been seeing

---

142 Ezekiel 33:1–9

New York City on fire. In my mind's eye, there were riots, troops, and tanks in our streets—not only in New York but in cities all over the nation.

I began to see the grocery stores being mobbed and having only a few days of food supplies while mobs were out of control, looting.

Thinking of so many people who live from paycheck to paycheck, hardly able to pay their rent, barely having enough to get tokens for the subway, I asked the Lord what I was to tell these people. "Do you want us to stockpile food?" I asked God.

God mildly and lovingly rebuked me. "You are looking at it from your point of view—not mine," I heard him say. Then God started showing me things.

The only trustworthy preparation for hard times is in the *heart*, not the body. If you set your heart to seek God with everything in you, saturating your heart with the Word of God, relying on the transforming work of the Holy Spirit, growing passionately in love with Jesus, you are better prepared for the coming storm than those who have a year or two's supply of food piled up.

The children of Israel were told to stand by and be ready to leave at any moment.[143] They were headed for hard times. They were leaving from the security of Egypt where they had food, yet they were slaves. In the wilderness ahead, there was no water, no food, and no resources.

Still, Moses did not give them any instructions to stockpile or to build wagons and load them down with food to last the duration of the journey ahead.

Instead, Moses gave them these spiritual instructions:[144]

Get secured by the blood. They were to kill a lamb and sprinkle that blood on their doorposts.[145] As long as that blood was applied and sprinkled on the doorpost, they and everyone in their homes were safe.

Eat the lamb. They were to feast.[146] That lamb pointed to Jesus Christ who would, years later, shed his blood. When you and I take communion today, we remember that Jesus offered his body for our salvation. And when we feast on the Word of God, we grow spiritually strong for the wilderness experience to come.

The Word of God is the food you are to store up in your mind and your soul until you are so strong in faith that nothing can shake you. What are you feasting

---

143 Exodus 12:11
144 Exodus 12:1–27
145 Exodus 12:3–7
146 Exodus 12:8–9

on? Do not tell me that God should give you a plan of survival if you are wasting your time in front of your television and computer.

Be ready to go.[147] In other words, do not be tied down to this world. Keep your eyes focused on eternal things. The Israelites had just enough dough in their kneading troughs to last a day or two and then it would be gone. The Lord was inviting them to trust him.

***

There are countless people who have put their *eternal* destiny in the hands of the Lord, but they have not put their *earthly* destiny in the hands of the Lord.

Why is it so hard for you to put your earthly destiny—what you eat, wear, and the roof over your head—in God's hands?

If all you are doing is to prepare physically, you are in trouble. Some say to have a thirty-day supply of food ready, and some say to have supplies for a year or two. But what if this thing lasts ten years or more?

If Jesus tarries, where are you going to get a place to store all that?

I am not against any preparation. What I am saying is that if you are preparing your spirit, if you are dealing with your sin issues, if you are building up your faith, *then* you are ready.

You are ready for any privation. You are ready for troubled waters, you are ready for persecution, crop failure, drought, shortages, sickness, and trials of all kinds. **Most of all, you are ready for the coming of the Lord and the wedding feast of the bride.**[148]

***

God has made an everlasting covenant to keep and protect those who keep their hearts set on him. In God's first covenant with Abraham, he said, "Do not be afraid, Abram. I am your shield, your exceedingly great reward."[149]

---

147 Exodus 12:11, 33–34
148 Matthew 22:1–14
149 Genesis 15:1; At that time, Abraham's name was still Abram. During the second covenant (Genesis 17:1–8), he changed his name to Abraham.

In other words, God would not only protect Abraham, but he would also be his paymaster. Everything he needed was going to come from God's hand. Everything.

God was essentially telling Abraham, "I am going to protect you, take care of all your physical needs. All you have to do, Abraham, is walk before me righteously, put your trust in me, and love me with all your heart."

This covenant extended to Abraham's son, Isaac, and then to Isaac's son, Jacob. It finally extended to the seed of Abraham.[150] Everyone walking with Jesus Christ by faith is the seed of Abraham.

Are you trusting Jesus as Lord and Savior? Do you belong to Christ? Are you his by faith? Then you are the seed of Abraham. **God's covenant with Abraham to be his shield and protector pertains to you.**

There are certain conditions to the covenant, though. The Bible tells us, "And now, Israel, what does the Lord your God require of you, but to fear the Lord your God, to walk in all his ways and to love him, to serve the Lord your God with all your heart and with all your soul, and to keep the commandments of the Lord and his statutes which I command you today for your good."[151]

Yes, God is your friend, your kinsman-redeemer, but he is also the almighty God, creator of heaven and earth.

As for the hard times ahead, keeping God's covenant promise in mind, you can trust him to drive all fear from your mind for he will keep his covenant. Not only will you have food to eat; God will bless you and take care of you in every way.[152]

You may think, "I know about all these promises, of God's keeping power, of him being my shield and my protector. Both my earthly and eternal destiny are in God's hands. I know he will take care of me. But what about the martyrs?"

---

150 Psalm 105; Romans 9:8
151 Deuteronomy 10:12–13
152 Deuteronomy 30:15–16; 11:13–23

The writer of the letter to Hebrews says, "Still others had trial of mocking and scourging, yes, and of chains and imprisonment. They were stoned, they were sawn in two, were tempted, were slain with the sword…They wandered in deserts and mountains, in dens and caves of the earth. And all these, having obtained a good testimony through faith, did not receive the promise, God having provided something better for us, that they should not be made perfect apart from us."[153]

When you read this passage, you may ask, "Where was God's shield? These believers were cut in two!"

Until you wrestle with this, your faith will not stand. And the reality is that until Jesus comes, there will be much more of this suffering.[154]

God judges nations not just for their wickedness but because they touch the apple of his eye—people who are closest to his heart.[155] Those are people who have a strong testimony of intimacy with Christ. Of them, the Bible says they chose not to be delivered, choosing a better resurrection.[156] And for them, martyrdom is a gift, just as it was for Paul who was chosen to suffer as a testimony to many.

If this has you worried, this battle is not for you. But if God does choose you, while you may think you will fail when being tested, rest assured that when the time comes, God will give you the mercy, the grace, and the power to prevail, just as he has done with martyrs in the past.

Martyrs are God's chosen people. For them, suffering becomes a gift from God. They are like the Hebrew children who said, "We know God is able to deliver us but if not, we trust him."[157]

And on the day when we gather around God's throne, they will be the ones who will be closest to his heart. But take heart—God still loves the fainthearted like me and you. His covenant still stands.

---

153 Hebrews 11:36–40, paraphrased
154 Revelation 6:9
155 Zechariah 2:8
156 Hebrews 11:35
157 Daniel 3:17–18, paraphrased

There is no need to worry. With Paul, we can say, "For if we live, we live to the Lord; and if we die, we die to the Lord. Therefore, whether we live or die, we are the Lord's."[158]

Even so, Lord Jesus, come quickly.[159]

---

158 Romans 14:8
159 1 Corinthians 16:22 Aramaic translation, Revelation 22:20, paraphrased

II

Why the World Hates Christians

Not long before Jesus's arrest and crucifixion, he told his disciples, "I have chosen you. I have ordained you to bear lasting fruit—fruit that would withstand the judgment day when we are all called to give an account before the throne of Christ."[160]

When the Bible says Jesus has ordained you to bear fruit, I take that to mean it is Christ doing his work through you. You are commanded to evangelize, to make disciples and train them, but you are not the one causing others' lives to change. **Lives are changed because of Christ being at work in you and through you.**

There are many Christians who say they are followers of Christ, but they are not. They bear no lasting fruit.

Jesus warned the Pharisees, "Woe to you, scribes and Pharisees, hypocrites! For you travel land and sea to win one proselyte, and when he is won, you make him twice as much a son of hell as yourselves."[161]

In other words, Jesus was telling them, "You have made what you consider to be a convert. You got some kind of a confession from him and you have got him to attend your church. This person looks the part and even says the right things. But the message you preach has no power to change a single life. Your motives are not

---

160 John 15:16–17, paraphrased
161 Matthew 23:15

55

right, and you have caused your so-called convert to stumble—he was going to hell before you talked to him, and now he is twice as damned as before."

This condemnation extended to the Pharisees. Jesus cried hypocrisy, and it is worth paying attention. These are scholars of God's law he was talking to. Still, Jesus said they are so set on building up their synagogues that they would go to extremes to make converts. **To them, it was about the headcount, not the conversion of hearts.**

I wonder what Jesus would say when he sees that same spirit with churches that measure success by the number of bodies they can pack into a service rather than lives being transformed. Some megachurches have godly shepherds who preach the gospel. And just like at Times Square Church, they see thousands of lives transformed. But even at our church, there are some members who call themselves Christians, yet they are not truly converted.

Some folks worship another Jesus, one they made up to fit their idea of what they prefer in a Savior. Folks like those harden their hearts and are unwilling to be convicted by the Holy Ghost.

And in the same way, at some churches, the message is toned down to please people. The pastors preach less than the entire gospel. I tremble to think it possible that any preacher of the gospel could make converts two-fold children of hell.

Jesus gave a scathing rebuke to the religious scribes, saying that they were shepherds who loved the praises of men, who loved to sit in high places and be recognized by leaders and by politicians, who wanted to be accepted.[162] But if you are looking for acceptance, if at work you so desire the approval of colleagues that you hide your light under a bushel, you are not living according to the gospel.

In the same way, a church praised by the world is foolishness. There is no such thing as a church that is truly preaching and working under the guidance of the Holy Ghost that is loved and accepted by the world. It is simply not impossible.

This is why Jesus warned his disciples, "If you were of the world, the world would love its own. Yet because you are not of the world, but I chose you out of the world, therefore the world hates you."[163]

---

162 Luke 20:46–47
163 John 15:19

I was greatly influenced by the writings of a man called George Bowan, a missionary in India from 1848–1879. Bowan warned of the coming of a Protestant antichrist, saying that the antichrist will be the influence of society being brought into the church—its ways, its methods, and its morals, infiltrating the church.

Bowan said the time will come when this antichrist may take his throne, and you will know that time has come when the Protestant church is no longer persecuted. When that time comes, Jesus will no longer be seen as Lord, and the ways of the world will have taken over. Such a church is loved and accepted by the world.

To that church, Jesus said, "Woe to you when all men speak well of you, for so did their fathers to the false prophets."[164] But Jesus also encouraged his followers, declaring, "Blessed are those who are persecuted for righteousness' sake, for theirs is the kingdom of heaven. Blessed are you when they revile and persecute you, and say all kinds of evil against you falsely for my sake."[165]

In other words, the closer you get to the mission of Christ, the closer you get to preaching the gospel, the more hated and the more despised you will be by the world. And *that* is a blessing.

Jesus said, "If the world hates you, you know that it hated me before it hated you."[166] In other words, as a committed, transformed believer, you will be hated because of your mission to share the gospel. You will be marked. You will be persecuted at work *and* at church.

What is your mission as a witness for Jesus Christ? It is more than just going out and telling people Jesus loves them. **Your mission is to take from ungodly men that which is dearest to their heart—their self-righteousness.**

164 Luke 6:26–27
165 Matthew 5:10–11
166 John 15:18

You come to translate people out of the kingdom of darkness into a kingdom of light. They are confused, thinking the kingdom of light is bondage and suffering. They think you want to take away their freedom. And they do not like that.

Some of those people are ones who come to church and call themselves Christians. There are millions of people filling church pews thinking they are in God's good graces, and week after week they hear sermons that comfort them.

But then we come along and preach repentance and life change, that self-made integrity is not acceptable to God. We preach the blood of Christ and the separation from the world. We talk about submission and obedience to the Word of God. Those are messages they do not want to hear.

In more than fifty years, I ministered to some of the hardest, wickedest sinners on the face of the earth. To drug addicts, alcoholics, and prostitutes. I also ministered to church people, and those who have been going to church all their life are harder to reach than anybody on the street. **They are hardened to the gospel because they have an image of Christ that they have conjured up for themselves, one who makes wonderful promises but has no rules for them to abide by.**

This is why you cannot do this work in your own strength. Through the Holy Ghost, Christ has to do his work through you.

———— == ————

Jesus once said, "The world cannot hate you."[167] But as you saw earlier, he also said the world *will* hate you on account of him. Here is the differentiator: When you are of the world, the world cannot hate you because the world does not hate its own.

When you follow the example of Jesus, you will become like him—meek, gentle, and kind. You genuinely care about people. There is no reason for people to hate you for that, is there? Still, they do. If you are fulfilling your mission, the world will hate you, and they will persecute you.

The more you live according to the ways of the cross, the greater will be your hunger for Jesus. The greater your hunger for Jesus, the more you will speak the truth and fulfill the divine purposes and the ministry that God has ordained for his church. And the more you speak the truth, the more the world will hate you.

---

167 John 7:7

You will know what it is like for people to be condescending toward you, to look down at you. They will talk behind your back. They will say things to you that are hurtful. But there will be even greater persecution than that.

Many Christians will lose their jobs on account of their faith. You will be hated because you represent Jesus, and you are coming against everything the world believes to be right—everything that they have tried to earn, everything that they stand for and what they call their hope. You are taking that hope from them.

It is imperative that you understand that. The mission for which you have been called is a difficult one. But God is strengthening the church and when you come into God's house and fellowship with brothers and sisters, you know you have the same spirit. They tell you, "Welcome home. Here is where you are loved."

Which is why it is so important to gather as the body of Christ, not only to *receive* love but also to *give* love. You have a role to play in building up the body as it goes back out into the world to face persecution and trials.

So, keep your eyes on Jesus, the author and perfecter of your faith,[168] living a life of surrender every day.

---

168 Hebrews 12:2

12

The Cup of Trembling

The prophet Isaiah speaks not only to his time; he speaks to our generation, more so than all the other prophets. And according to Isaiah, God's people have drunk from a cup of trembling.[169]

He originally wrote this message to the children of Israel who were in captivity in Babylon. They lived in a troubled and chaotic time. This message was not only for his time, though. Every nation would be drinking from this cup of iniquity which Isaiah describes to have four elements—four great fears from which Isaiah's generation had drunk. And these are the very mixtures facing the whole world today.

The fear of survival is the first element of intoxication in this cup of trembling.[170] This is a fear of survival due to the chaotic state of the world. And it came upon the people—even God's people were sharing this fear. Evidently, they were acknowledging the rumors that the Persians were coming, and the Persians would eventually bring Babylon down. They had remembered being driven out from Jerusalem when they were children.

The second element in the cup is the lack of leadership.[171] There were no leaders, no guides, no princes. Meanwhile, there were false prophets who were in it for personal gain, saying there was going to be peace and prosperity.

---

169 Isaiah 51:17
170 Isaiah 51:13
171 Isaiah 51:18

The third element in the cup of trembling is the fear of calamities and terror on all sides.[172] Isaiah does not list in detail what those calamities were, but history shows what a desolate time it was.

The overwhelming fear of losing their children to the Babylonian system is the fourth element of intoxication in this cup of trembling.[173] God had allowed this because of the idolatry and sensuality of that generation. Their children would wind up on the streets.

And in the midst of all this is a cry coming up from the people of God. "Awake, awake, put on strength, O arm of the Lord! Awake as in the ancient days, in the generations of old."[174]

This cry comes from the remnant in Babylon. They were not given into the spirit of the age. They were seeking God. Still, they were walking in fear, drinking of this cup. It is a mixture of wine that the Lord said the wicked shall drink of.[175] These are God's people in the midst of chaos. They go on raising up an accusatory prayer. "Are you not the one who dried up the sea, the waters of the great deep; that made the depths of the sea a road for the redeemed to cross over?"[176]

It is a cry for God to wake up—as if God were asleep. God has already promised his arm is not short,[177] and he does not slumber, nor does he sleep.[178]

We are no different. We can talk about how Jesus fed the multitudes and raised the dead, but when it comes to our everyday life, when it comes to believing God when the doubts and fears come moving in about mortgages and the state of our children, we start drinking from the cup of fear, anxiety, despair, and worry.

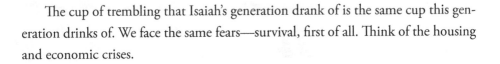

The cup of trembling that Isaiah's generation drank of is the same cup this generation drinks of. We face the same fears—survival, first of all. Think of the housing and economic crises.

---

172 Isaiah 51:19
173 Isaiah 51:20
174 Isaiah 51:9a
175 Psalms 75:8
176 Isaiah 51:10
177 Isaiah 59:1
178 Psalm 121:3–4

Through Moses, God said, "If a nation would honor me, I will set you above all the other nations. I will bless you and blessings will overtake you. Your enemies will be defeated before your eyes. The Lord will open to you his good treasure. You shall lend to nations, and you shall not borrow. You shall be the head and not the tail."[179]

God essentially said, "Let me tell you what happens to nations when you deny my word and put me out of your society."

Next, there's the lack of leadership. Every election year we hear the same promises being made. I grieve for all the young people today. If I had to vote today, I would write Jesus on the ballot. I cannot see one that I would vote for.

No matter if it is a Democrat or a Republican, no one has a clue. They do not know what to do with the economy. They do not know what to do with healthcare. It is all far beyond them. Tell me of any politician—any man or woman on the face of the earth—who has the answers. Truth is, there is no leadership. Only King Jesus, only God can save us.

Then there is desolation, famine, and terrorism in the cup of trembling. In Africa alone, countless numbers are dying from starvation, ethnic wars, and terrorism. God is on the move, saying, "Now, will you listen to me? Now can I get through to you?" That is precisely what God is doing through these events.

Finally, there is the fear of the loss of our children. Our college campuses are drowning in alcohol and drugs. Crystal meth is sweeping the world and these meth labs are in homes all over the United States. Even in the nicest schools, there are hardly any juniors or seniors who do not smoke pot, drink, and have sex.

Folks, this is the fear that is sweeping America. If you are not careful it will get into your heart and it will overwhelm you. You will drink the dregs of the cup.

As for the cry for God to awake, God comes right back and says, no, no, no—*you* wake up! *You* stand up.[180]

There are some people I know who have drunk so much from the cup of trembling that they have drunk the very dregs. They say I cannot handle one more problem. I have even heard ministers say they are on the brink of just walking away from everything.

---

179 Deuteronomy 32:2–13, 28:13, paraphrased
180 Isaiah 51:17

God says, "No. You stand up." He has made a provision. "Therefore please hear this, you afflicted, and drunk but not with wine. Thus says your Lord, the Lord and your God, who pleads the cause of his people: 'See, I have taken out of your hand the cup of trembling, the dregs of the cup of my fury; you shall no longer drink it.' "[181]

God calls himself a God who pleads the cause of his people. It is as if God says "No, I am not asleep. I am the same God who parted the Red Sea. I am the God who raises the dead. I have made provision for you to never drink from the cup of trembling. This was not meant for you."

No matter how the conditions are, no matter what happens in our personal lives, in the nation, or in the world, God never intended his people to live in fear. God will come and deliver us from fear, to live without fear all of our lifetime.[182]

There will be pangs of fear. There will be those sudden things that come on us and, naturally, we will fear. But with what is coming in the days ahead, you will have to have the kind of faith within you with which you can stand strong.

That is why you have to come to the house of the Lord, to hear the Word and be encouraged. According to Paul, we have all been given a measure of faith,[183] but that faith has to be expanded, it has to be fed, it has to be nourished. How do you do that? By reading God's Word. "Faith comes by hearing, and hearing by the Word of God."[184]

God had said to Israel, "I AM will deliver you."[185] In the same way, God will deliver *you*. This is an everlasting covenant.

God is not going to come down supernaturally and suddenly remove all the fear from your heart, though. What I have seen work in my life is to get up every day and lay hold of two or three promises of God's keeping grace.

God instructed me to keep my eyes on the resurrection of Jesus Christ. When I wake up in the morning, even when the news is worse than ever, in the midst of it I can say, "I have committed everything, live or die, to the Lord. I am the Lord's."

181 Isaiah 51:21–22
182 Luke 1:74–75, paraphrased
183 Romans 12:3
184 Romans 10:17
185 Exodus 3:11–14, paraphrased

Ask the Holy Ghost to strengthen you. And when the fears come and go, stand up and proclaim the Word of God. Say it out loud:

> Lift up your eyes on high, and see who has created these things, who brings out their host by number; he calls them all by name, by the greatness of his might and the strength of his power; not one is missing.
>
> Why do you say, O Jacob, and speak, O Israel: 'My way is hidden from the Lord, and my just claim is passed over by my God'? Have you not known? Have you not heard? The everlasting God, the Lord, the Creator of the ends of the earth, neither faints nor is weary. His understanding is unsearchable. He gives power to the weak, and to those who have no might he increases strength. Even the youths shall faint and be weary, and the young men shall utterly fall, but those who wait on the Lord shall renew their strength; they shall mount up with wings like eagles, they shall run and not be weary, they shall walk and not faint.[186]
>
> Through the power of his Word, allow God to deliver you from the cup of trembling.

---

186 Isaiah 40:26–31

13

The Capacity to Be Stirred

S ome of the most neglected truths in all the Bible are found in Revelation 2 and 3. There, John captures messages to seven churches, including the church in Sardis:

"I know your works, that you have a name that you are alive, but you are dead. Be watchful, and strengthen the things which remain, that are ready to die, for I have not found your works perfect before God. Remember therefore how you have received and heard; hold fast and repent. Therefore if you will not watch, I will come upon you as a thief, and you will not know what hour I will come upon you."[187]

Here is the soxlemn word of Jesus dictated from the throne room, yet you will rarely hear a sermon on this passage. Why? I believe these chapters contain the antidote against apathy within the church, and the devil does not want this message preached.

In Revelation 1, Christ appears in a vision to John. Christ is walking, looking like a burning fire. There is a two-edged sword coming out of his mouth. He appears among seven burning candlesticks. He has seven stars in his hands. The seven stars are seven angels of the seven churches, and the seven candlesticks are seven churches.

Jesus commands John to send letters to these churches and the under-shepherds, the angels of the church.[188] As the guardians of the church, God would hold them responsible for the state of their church.

---

187 Revelation 3:1–3
188 Henceforth referred to as pastors.

For the church of Ephesus, the pastor was told, "You have left your first love, you have fallen into apathy and you must repent."[189]

To the pastor in Pergamos, God said, "You have allowed false doctrine, a worldly Nicolaitan spirit is at work in that church."[190]

The pastor in Thyatira was told, "An ungodly Jezebel spirit has overcome you; you are not dealing with sin in your house."[191]

God said to the pastor at Laodicea, "You and your people are becoming indifferent, lukewarm, prosperous. You are lukewarm, having no fire, no spiritual hunger, and no spiritual growth."[192]

Keep in mind, this is Christ speaking, and he is burning with love for the church. He is not angry at the churches or their pastors; he simply urges them to wake up and deal with their issues. Why then are these chapters rarely taught? I believe it is because the enemy has dropped a spirit of apathy like a cloud over the church.

Jesus warned that there would be another gospel coming. The message that is being preached today is a message without a cross, a message without sacrifice, a message without a hell or a devil, a message devoid of the judgment seat of Christ or a throne of judgment. What is being preached is a soothing, quiet message of prosperity and goodness.

Unwilling to be convicted by the Word of God, multitudes are falling victim to this false gospel. They allow their hearts and minds to be robbed of truth, to be taken captive by a message that never mentions sin, conviction, or the day you will stand before the judgment throne and give an account for all you have done.

In the process, the church has been robbed of the capacity to be stirred. Today, if the message of God's judgment were to be preached in many a church, most of the congregation would walk out. The rest would sit there with their hands folded, unmoved. Only a few—a remnant—would be moved to blush at the depravity of their sins and respond with a heart of repentance.

---

189 Revelation 2:4–5, paraphrased
190 Revelation 2:5, paraphrased
191 Revelation 2:20, paraphrased
192 Revelation 3:15–16, paraphrased

As for the letter to the pastor of Sardis, it shook me. This church was once known for its charity, good works, and the apostolic presence of Christ. But Jesus warns them that the spirit of death had moved in among them.

Still, Jesus has hope for this church, declaring, "You have a few names even in Sardis who have not defiled their garments..."[193] To this faithful remnant, Jesus says, "Be watchful, and strengthen the things which remain, ... for I have not found your works perfect before God. Remember therefore how you have received and heard; hold fast and repent."[194]

God is warning you and me. I believe Jesus is saying, **"You have settled into a comfort zone. You have rested on your achievements. The Father has prospered and blessed you, but now you have no fire, no zeal. You have a sense that you have arrived."**

God forbid that happens to the lampstand churches around the world today, that we would be so wrapped up in doing our own thing, thinking we have arrived and that we can enjoy God's presence without any commitment.

===

The prophet Haggai had a strong message for the church. The children of Israel had been delivered from Babylon and sent back to Jerusalem to rebuild the house of God. God wanted a place where he could visibly manifest his presence so people could go to the temple and see evidence of God moving. Lives would be changed before their very eyes.

The prophet Haggai says they had started right. They had begun to build the temple, but they became discouraged. So, Haggai tells Zerubbabel, "You say this is not the time to build, that we do not have the time to build the house of the Lord. Is this the time for you to hide in your nice houses and my house is being neglected?"[195]

Speaking through Haggai, God says, "Your wages go into a bag with holes."[196] What he is saying is that you had dreams but those were in *your* interest, and because you had neglected *God's* interests, God would blow it all apart.

---

193 Revelation 3:4
194 Revelation 3:2–3
195 Haggai 1:2–4, paraphrased
196 Haggai 1:6, paraphrased

Haggai goes on to say, "I called for drought, and you end up dry."[197] In other words, "You end up not being satisfied—nothing you purchase or do brings you any satisfaction."

＝＝＝

Rest assured, God is not against you and me being blessed. If you put God's kingdom and his work first, if you get back to building the house of God instead of putting your interests first, God says, "I will bless your going out and your coming in. I will bless you in the field; I will bless you in the city. I will bless your store; I will bless your house."[198]

It is true that, sometimes, when a nation is stricken with a perfect storm, it impacts both the just *and* the unjust. But you may also need to examine your heart in light of what the prophet Haggai said.

What he is saying, in effect, is that you wind up in terrible debt, and there is misery with it. You cannot get ahead. You strive and strive, yet you cannot keep your head above the water.

Why? This is what God said through the prophet, "Because my house lays neglected."

The Lord spoke to me, saying "Do not think this cannot happen to you, Dave, if you neglect the prayer closet, if you neglect my Word, if you neglect giving what belongs to me."

God, I want the zeal of God to eat up my soul until I die. **I want a fire in my bones. The older I get, the more I want to be on fire for God.**

That is what God wants of his church—a greater fire and zeal in his house, and a greater love that spreads from among us.

＝＝＝

The Bible also says, "Then they obeyed the voice of the Lord their God, and the words of Haggai the prophet, and the people feared the presence of the Lord." And then, Haggai prophesied, "'I am with you,' says the Lord."[199]

---

197 Haggai 1:11, paraphrased
198 Deuteronomy 28:3–6, paraphrased
199 Haggai 1:12–13, paraphrased

The Lord stirred up the spirit of Zerubbabel and the spirit of all the remnant of the people.[200] Being stirred, they came and did work in the house of the Lord their God. They left their houses for a season.

God said, "But seek first the kingdom of God and his righteousness, and all these things shall be added to you."[201] You take care of my house and I will take care of your house. I will take care of your children. I will take care of your budget.

Haggai continues, "Consider now from this day forward... from the day that the foundation of the Lord's temple was laid—consider it: Is the seed still in the barn? As yet the vine, the fig tree, the pomegranate, and the olive tree have not yielded fruit. But from this day I will bless you."[202]

You may not see it right away, but God has determined and he has commanded a blessing on you from the day that you made a commitment and heard the voice of the Holy Ghost.

If that happens to be today that you make a decision, declaring, "I am coming back, Lord, to your interests, whatever it costs me," then from this day, God will bless you.

God did that for his people who responded to Haggai's warning. God began to bless his people. That God is the same yesterday, today, and forever.[203] God does not change.

The moment you and I set our hearts again afresh to sing with Holy Ghost gusto, not to come dragging ourselves into the house of God but coming with expectancy, having prayed and sought God, he commits to bless us.

≡≡

Do you pray for your church? Do you pray for the pastors? Do you pray that the fire of God will always be burning in your church? **May your children know and see and experience the manifestations of the presence of Christ in his house as you bring down his glory through your commitment.**

---

200 Haggai 1:14
201 Matthew 6:33
202 Haggai 2:18–19
203 Hebrews 13:8

14

A Time to Weep and a Time to Fight

Nowadays, nobody seems to know what is going on in the world. God will not leave his church without answers, though. God does not leave his people in the dark.

My father and grandfather—both preachers—taught me that if you want to know the patterns of God's movement, if you want to know his nature and what he will do in the future, look at what he has done in the past, for Jesus is the same yesterday, today, and forever.[204]

Despite all that is going on in the world, what an amazing God we have who has everything under control. The only way we can make it through these uncertain times is to study God's Word, to flood our minds with the truth, with the promises of God.

With all that is going on, have you begun to doubt God's goodness? Are you allowing the news to drag you down?

The Bible warns in the last days of scoffers who will come.[205] This is what is happening all over the world. People who were once examples of faith are being shipwrecked in their faith.

Perhaps you think that would never happen to you. Paul said, though, "Let him who thinks he stands take heed lest he fall."[206]

---

204 Hebrews 13:8
205 2 Peter 3:3–4
206 1 Corinthians 10:12

There will be many who will say, "God is not answering my prayers. Things are getting worse, even when I fast and pray." There will be a testing of your faith such as the world has never seen. But God is still with you; he is still faithful. When you stay rooted in his Word, you will hear God speak like I do.

=== ===

Look at the example of David, how he reacted to a calamity. He had been running from Saul and he went down to Gath.[207] That was an act of disbelief. David allied himself with the Philistines. This was *so* far from the will of God. Still, David joined the Philistines and anticipated the invasion of Israel.

Some of the captives of the Philistine army recognized him, though. They said, "Isn't that the one who killed our giant? What is he doing here? Send him home."[208]

So, David and his entire battalion were asked to leave. They headed to Ziklag, a three-day journey. But the Amalekites had invaded Ziklag, kidnapped the wives, the children, and the cattle, and burned the city down. There was nothing left but smoldering ashes.

How did David and his men react? After all, these were hardened soldiers. Nevertheless, these men wept until there were no more tears left. They were so bitter that they spoke of stoning David.[209]

Now, my beloved friends, there is a time to tremble and a time to weep. David did not stand there before that calamity and say, "Well, God is God. Things happen."

Tell that to 600 men who have lost everything. Simply telling them to trust God would not help. David turned to Abiathar, the priest, asking him what to do. But Abiathar could not help David. He had no word for him.

David insisted on having a word from God, a word that would sustain him after losing everything, so he asked Abiathar for an ephod to help him determine what God was saying.[210]

---

207 1 Samuel 21:10
208 1 Samuel 29:3, paraphrased
209 1 Samuel 30:6
210 An ephod was a garment made of fine linen that was worn by the high priest (Exodus 28:4) and by the priests (1 Samuel 22:18). The ephod was worn over other garments and was decorated with precious stones (Exodus 28:6–12). The Urim and Thummim were fastened to the ephod and were used for guidance when critical decisions needed to be made (Ezra 2:63, Nehemiah 7:65, Judges 20:18–28).

Using the ephod, David inquired of the Lord. God told David to go and that he would recover everything. Go where? He did not know who it was that burned down his city, let alone where to find them.

There was much they could never get back, and there would be a time of living in tents. But God never failed them. David and his men never went without a meal. Still, David's men blamed him as their commander, and they had stones ready to kill him.

══ ══

We are like that, aren't we? When we face calamities, we look for somebody to blame. You cannot see the troubles in the world today and not tremble or weep—especially when it affects your family. So, you look for someone to blame.

Instead of allowing things to get out of joint, the writer of Hebrews encourages us to encourage ourselves in the Lord. "Therefore, strengthen the hands which hang down, and the feeble knees, and make straight paths for your feet, so that what is lame may not be dislocated, but rather be healed."[211]

This is exactly what David did. When doubts and fears came to his men—their faith failing despite having seen victory after victory, despite having seen God's provision—David encouraged himself in the Lord.

I believe the Lord is telling us today to be careful. Be careful that your faith does not get lame or that you get out of joint. If you have been battling fears, it is normal. God understands that.

How do you do that? You go to the Scriptures. Get alone with God. Inquire of the Lord and, like David, encourage yourself in the Lord. Also, be part of your local church so you can get your spirit built up. Go where the Word is preached so it can become life in you, so it can bear fruit in you. Do not let it just be words that leave you unchanged.

The messages you hear at church can quickly fade in the face of life events. The joy you experience worshipping with others can fade quickly. So, root yourself in the Word of God. Read Psalms 34 and 121—memorize these psalms until these verses take life in you.

---

211 Hebrews 12:12–13

Encourage yourself in the Lord. Then, when you go to the house of God, God will affirm that which he has been saying to you in private. This way, you will be able to withstand any storm.

<hr>

As for David, after inquiring of the Lord, he set out in some direction because he had a voice behind him saying, "This is the way, walk in it."[212]

David was out probably half a day's journey from where he started when someone brought him a half-dead Egyptian slave. "Who are you?"[213] David asked the man. I imagine God must have been smiling as he waited for David to see that this was his deliverance—a half-dead Egyptian!

After they gave the man water and fed him, the Egyptian told him that he had been a servant to one of the Amalekites—the very people who had destroyed Ziklag. But when this servant got sick, they left him behind.

In exchange for a promise not to turn the man over to his master, the man agreed to take David and his army right to the enemies. So, they put him on a horse, and he led them right to the Amalekites.[214]

<hr>

Whatever crisis you are facing today, God will deliver you. He has a million ways in which he can do that—including through a half-dead Egyptian. God *will* deliver you even though he will not tell you how. If he were to tell you, you would probably not believe him.

I have seen that in the way God has answered some of my prayers. In the 1970s, we had no money to run the Teen Challenge drug center in Brooklyn, NY. We were broke. So, we did the only thing we knew to do—we fasted and prayed. We did not call anybody; we did not get nervous.

When I went to the Teen Challenge center, I found a check for $25,000 on my desk. It had been sent by a missionary living in Mongolia who had written books.

<hr>

212 Isaiah 30:21
213 1 Samuel 30:11–13
214 1 Samuel 30:13–16

He was in his eighties. He wrote, "I have heard about your work, and God told me to send you my life savings."

If you had told me there was a missionary on the other side of the world who had been writing books for years, and God was going to speak to him in prayer someday and he would send me $25,000, I would have laughed at you.

Yet God has a way.

You will get through these trying times. Even if it does not seem like it, God has everything under control.

David declared in the Psalms that God had "brought me out into a broad place; he delivered me because he delighted in me."[215]

As for you? You have something better than an ephod. You can hear the voice of the Lord through the Holy Spirit who abides in you and delights in you.

The Holy Spirit is the full expression of God's love through Christ. There could be no greater expression that God can give us but that he would send the Holy Ghost on a mission to comfort you in a time of trouble, and to direct you when you have no direction.

He will love and keep you because you are bone of his bone and flesh of his flesh.[216] Live or die, whether the mountains fall into the sea,[217] no matter how the world shakes when everything is shaken, one thing is sure—**God delights in you. He will *not* fail you.**

215 Psalm 18:19
216 Genesis 2:23
217 Psalm 46:2

15

There Is Power in the Presence of God

Allow me to tell you a bit about the story of Abraham. Abraham was looking for a bride for his son, Isaac, so he sent a servant to the area where he had been raised.[218]

The servant desired to fulfill his master's wishes, yet he could not see how he could accomplish this task. He questioned Abraham, "What if I cannot find a young woman who is willing to travel so far from home?"

Abraham stood firm. "The God of heaven, who took me from my father's house and my native land, solemnly promised to give this land to my descendants... he will see to it that you find a wife there for my son." So, despite his doubts, , the servant went, looking for God to do the supernatural and provide a wife for Isaac.[219]

What if I cannot...? Whatever it is you are trusting God for, oftentimes following that very request is this question, *"What if I cannot get the healing that I need? What if I cannot find that spouse that I am longing for? What if I cannot find that ministry where I long to serve? What if a position never opens up? And if it does, what if I cannot do the work?"*

218 Genesis 24:1–4 NLT
219 Genesis 24:7 NLT

There are two ways to look at this question. The first one is filled with fear, doubt, unbelief, uncertainty, anguish, stress, and striving. It is borne in fear and doubt. *What if you do not come through?* Run from that kind of attitude. Run to the presence of God, into the arms of God.

The second way to look at this question can be a cry of a desperate soul. "God, I cannot have a child," Hannah cried.[220]

"God, if your presence does not go with us," Moses declared, "then we are not going."[221]

These are cries of faith. They are cries for God to rend the heavens and come down,[222] a declaration, "We cannot do this ourselves. We do not have the power or the strength, but God does. God can do the impossible."

$$\equiv\equiv$$

I believe the next great move of God in the church will be a massive move among young adults. God is about to move mightily in this generation.

The Bible says, "Where sin abounded, grace abounded much more."[223] There has not been a generation that has been so filled with unbelief and doubt as among young adults. They are leaving the church en masse, leaving Christ behind, not believing in anything.

Yet there is still a longing for the supernatural. They spend hours every day playing video games because they get to enter a fantasy world. What they do not know is that **in Jesus Christ there is something far better than a fantasy!**

I picture a day where thousands of young men and young women are crying out to God day and night—a true move of God, a last-days outpouring of the Spirit.[224] This generation will cry out, "No more dead, dry religion. We want life in the Spirit! We want the glory of God to fall on the church and on our lives."

I believe this generation will not only see the glory of God in church services; they will see the glory of God in their businesses, on the streets, at football games, when they are shopping.

---

220 1 Samuel 1:10–11, paraphrased
221 Exodus 33:15, paraphrased
222 Isaiah 64:1
223 Romans 5:20
224 Joel 2:28–32

Perhaps you are part of that last-days, Jacob generation who will be used mightily by the Lord. And perhaps you are asking that same question Abraham's servant asked, "What if I cannot?"

Do not ask that question in doubt. Ask it in yearning.

Abraham's response to his servant was powerful. "The Lord, in whose presence I have lived, will send his angel with you and will make your mission successful,"[225] he declared. **Abraham had confidence in the mission because he had been in the Lord's presence.**

If God is going to do something supernatural in your life—if you are going to see an outpouring of the Holy Ghost in your life, the chains of addiction broken, your marriage healed—it will be through this one thing that Abraham found. **The miraculous will come from dwelling in the presence of the Lord.**

By spending time in the presence of God you can get the clearest revelation on the direction for your life. And you can find freedom from whatever is holding you captive. Spending time in God's presence is not about finding favor with God, though. Instead, what you will find is a foundation of grace upon which you can build your faith.

Faith comes from spending time in God's presence. Abraham had faith because he had heard God. He heard God because he was in his presence.

Truth be told, waiting in God's presence is no easy task. There have been things in my life that I have had to wait for. There have been promises God shared with me years ago and I only saw them come to fruition thirty years later. **Some things take time. Some happen instantly.** Whichever way, the joy is that we get to wait in his presence without wanting for anything.

Abraham walked with God, and he was constantly meditating on the Lord, even when he was caring for his cattle, whatever it was, he was living in the presence of

---

225 Genesis 24:40 NLT

God.[226] As a result, he had great faith, declaring, "God will send his angel with you and will make your mission successful."[227]

I love the confidence Abraham had because he had been in the presence of the Lord. **Because he walked with God, he got a word from the Lord. And when he got a word from the Lord, he could hold on to it.**

The same can be true for you—as you spend time with God, dwelling intimately with him, God will send his Spirit with you, and he will make your mission successful. He will break the chains that hold you captive and fill you with confidence from the Holy Ghost.

$$\equiv\equiv$$

What happened when the servant went to the land of Abraham's upbringing where he was supposed to find this wife for Isaac? He prayed, "O Lord, God of my master, Abraham, please give me success on this mission."[228]

The servant had seen Abraham's passion for the presence of the Lord, and he desired to have the kind of faith that his master Abraham had. In essence, he was declaring, "If it works for Abraham, it can work for me!"

Faith like that of Abraham is contagious. That is why I like to surround myself with men and women of faith, who have bold confidence, who spend time in the presence of the Lord, and who come out with a word from the Lord. You can have that same kind of faith, just like the servant had. Remember, scripture says God shows no partiality.[229]

"Before I had finished praying in my heart," he said, "I saw Rebekah coming out with her water jug on her shoulder."[230] I do not know about you, but that is the kind of faith I want, where before I am even done praying, God answers.

---

226 Based upon the statement that Abraham *lived* with God. Genesis 24:40a NLT.
227 Genesis 24:40b NLT; based upon the outpouring of the Holy Spirit in the New Testament, I believe as the New Testament Church, we can say God will send his *Holy Spirit* with you, and his Spirit will make your mission successful.
228 Genesis 24:42 NLT
229 Deuteronomy 10:17; Acts 10:34
230 Genesis 24:45 NLT

Because of the shift in faith, this guy went from saying, "What if I cannot...? I do not know if I have what it takes..." to seeing God answer his prayer even before he was done praying.

God in his sovereignty is already working to answer your prayer even before you start praying. We can see this in the response of Rebekah's brother Laban: "The Lord has obviously brought you here, so there is nothing we can say."[231] Laban acknowledged that the Lord had obviously been orchestrating the encounter.

May that be true for you. May it be obvious that God has already accomplished on earth that which you have been praying for, whether for a person or a cause. May that which you are praying for respond to your faith, respond to you having been in the presence of God, having received supernatural power so that even while you are praying—or even before—God will be orchestrating the events around you so that the person you are praying for, or the city you are praying for responds, "What else can we do except say yes to the things God has for us? It is so obvious that God is moving."

May this realization change the way you pray for your children, the way you pray for the sick. James says when you lay hands on the sick they will recover. They will be healed.[232] He does not say *some might* be healed. Praying with such confidence comes from being in God's presence. And in his presence, God begins to speak and you can confidently go, knowing God is already at work.

But the enemy often tries to delay God's work. After having declared that it was obvious that God had ordained the meeting, Laban tells the servant to wait, to let Rebekah spend some days at home.[233]

Having faith like that of Abraham, though, the servant has boldness, clarity, and uncompromised vision for the mission he had been sent on. "Don't delay me," he declared. "The Lord has made my mission successful; now send me back so I can return to my master."[234]

I believe the servant finally understood that God had already given him success on the mission to which he had called him through Abraham.

---

231 Genesis 24:50 NLT
232 James 5:14–15
233 Genesis 24:55 NLT
234 Genesis 24:56, 58 NLT; They solved the matter by asking Rebekah what she wanted to do, to which she said, "I will go."

The same goes for you. This is a "now" word from heaven! **This is not just a story from the Old Testament. This can be the reality in which you live as you spend time in the presence of the Lord,** hearing from God, and walking in the confidence of knowing what God shows you.

You too can live without the excuse of "What if I cannot...?"

Part 2

"Dry Bones"

A Collection of Messages on the Holy Spirit

"So I prophesied as I was commanded; and as I prophesied, there was a noise, and suddenly a rattling; and the bones came together, bone to bone. Indeed, as I looked, the sinews and the flesh came upon them, and the skin covered them over; but there was no breath in them.

Also He said to me, 'Prophesy to the breath, prophesy, son of man, and say to the breath, "Thus says the Lord God: 'Come from the four winds, O breath, and breathe on these slain, that they may live.' " So I prophesied as He commanded me, and breath came into them, and they lived, and stood upon their feet, an exceedingly great army."

Ezekiel 34:7–10

16

Raised From the Dead

As Christians, we believe in the resurrection of Jesus Christ. We also believe that we will be resurrected when Jesus comes again. We will be raised into his presence with incorruptible bodies.

In his letters to the churches in Corinth and Thessaloníki, Paul also speaks of a God who raises the dead, speaking of men and women who had passed away.[235]

I have found, though, that there are men and women who appear dead, who have no real life, being dead in trespasses and sins. They need to be raised from the dead even before their hearts stop beating. They need the Holy Spirit.

Jesus said he would send the Holy Spirit as our Comforter.[236] The Spirit of God is the one who brings this resurrection power to raise us out of our deadness.

When you are dead in sin, you eventually become lifeless, you become bored with the sins the deeper you go. The apostle Paul said, "Yes, we had the sentence of death in ourselves, that we should not trust in ourselves but in God who raises the dead, who delivered us from so great a death, and does deliver us; in whom we trust that he will still deliver *us*..."[237]

---

235 1 Corinthians 15:12–58; 1 Thessalonians 4:13–18
236 John 16:7
237 2 Corinthians 1:9–10

There is a story behind what Paul was saying. Paul went to Ephesus where they were worshipping the goddess Diana. The silversmiths were making fortunes selling little replicas of the goddess Diana.

When Paul came on the scene, he cried out, "Your god is not really a god. That is a false god. There's only one God and his Son lived and died on this earth."[238]

The merchants stirred up the mobs, and they took Paul and they bound him, getting ready to kill him. Paul thought it was all over when he wrote, "We were burdened beyond measure, above strength, so that we despaired even of life."[239]

Have you ever felt that way, being pressed beyond your power, despairing of life? When Paul did and called out to God, God delivered him. That is when he wrote to the church in Ephesus, essentially saying, "I was resurrected from the dead. He took me out of the grave. I was dead. I stared hell in the face and death in the face and God redeemed me—God resurrected me."[240]

I believe with everything in me that there is a resurrection power that we can experience today. Yes, there is a final resurrection at the return of Christ,[241] but Paul is not speaking only of that. He is talking about what God does here on earth in the here and now.

That is what happens when Christ is preached and God by his Spirit touches lives.

When that person surrenders to Christ, they experience being resurrected from the dead.

There was an alcoholic laying on the street, and somebody said, "There is a church two blocks away." So, he staggered in and heard the truth about the love of Jesus Christ and the mercy of God for sinners, that no matter what you have done, no matter what you have committed, no matter how deep you are into it, there is a Savior who saves and gives you a new life, that "old things are passed away; behold, all things have become new."[242] He was raised from the dead, from the grip of sin on his life.

---

238 Acts 19:26, paraphrased
239 2 Corinthians 1:8
240 Loosely referring to Ephesians 2:5–6
241 1 Thessalonians 4:13–18
242 2 Corinthians 5:17

The same goes for the pastor who emailed me saying, "Pastor Dave, I quit the ministry and left my church because I did not see any results. I fell so deep into sin that my wife and children left me. I lost everything and had nothing left to my name. I gave up." He felt like he had a death sentence on his life.

"But then one day in my despair and my darkness," he told me, "I got down on my knees and I said, 'Oh God, I have sinned against you. I have grieved the Holy Spirit. Is there any hope for me?' "

One tear came, then another. The Holy Spirit came, and the Lord restored him. God healed him. He had been away from his wife for nearly two years, I believe. He got up from his knees, a changed man. He began to worship the Lord anew.

He and his wife were reconciled, and now they are working with our Teen Challenge team in California.

***

And there was a young man who emailed me saying, "Pastor Dave, I was about to kill myself. I had lost everything. I had no hope. I tried every sin. I tried every possible way to find peace. So, I took my pistol, put it to my head, and then I prayed these words: 'God, if you love me and you are real, you had better stop me or I am dead.' And a little still small voice said, 'Go to your mailbox.' "

This young man put the gun down, went to the mailbox, and there was a package. Somebody had sent him a copy of *The Cross and the Switchblade*.

He read the whole thing and started weeping. "God if you can save Nicky Cruz, a Mau Mau gang leader, you can save me," he said. "That boy is on fire for God!"

What is that but resurrection from the dead?

***

I can tell you countless stories of marriages being restored, of life being breathed back into families and individuals.

There was a young lady who had spent at least ten years trying to find peace. She was spending her nights dancing at the Roseland Ballroom. But then one day, evidently empty, searching, and seeking, she walked into Times Square Church. I was preaching—what, I do not know—and she thought I was a psychic!

"He is reading my mind!" she thought. At the end of that service, she walked down the aisle and gave her life to Christ. What a testimony she is for the Lord.

That sounds like Paul's testimony in his letter to the church in Ephesus. "And you he made alive, who were dead in trespasses and sins; you walked in the lust of your flesh, you fulfilled the desires of your flesh and mind; and by nature you were children of wrath, just as the others," Paul writes. "But God, who is rich in mercy, and because of his great love with which he loved us, even when we were dead in sin, he has raised us up together with Christ and made us sit together in heavenly places."[243]

There was a young girl named Cookie Rodriguez from one of the gangs here in New York City. She was on heroin, and she was prostituting herself to support her habit. Someone encouraged her to come to one of my meetings where she sat in the balcony. Cookie had never cried in her life. She was so hardened and bitter.

Halfway through my message, a number of young people were being stirred by the Holy Spirit. To the right and left of her, according to her testimony, those around her were crying. But not Cookie. She tried to cry but no tears would come. She cried out, "Oh, please God, make me cry! If you make me cry, I will give you my life." One tear came. Then another. Then a river.

Cookie went on to develop homes for drug-addicted prostitutes. She has written a book and last I talked to her, she was preaching all through Texas, on fire for God.

God had an appointment with her the day she walked into the meeting—a divine appointment.

I am not encouraging you to embrace a new religion. You can find religion anywhere, and self-made religious organizations are springing up everywhere. But this? It is about getting a new life.

---

243 Ephesians 2:1–6, paraphrased

Christ is reaching out by his Holy Spirit more than ever, reaching out to the walking dead, those who are seeking meaning in their accomplishments, in their possessions, and in their positions.

On the surface, everything looks fine. Yet, the cry that comes from the board rooms, from Wall Street, from the bars is, **"Is this all there is to it? Is this the only thing there is? Is this life?"**

There is so much more to life.

God has created you with a need for him. If you do not know God, you will experience emptiness. You will know that something is missing.

This is why so many turn to alcohol. This is why so many turn to drugs.

───────

God says, "Therefore, if anyone is in Christ, he is a new creation; old things have passed away; behold, all things have become new."[244]

And he makes it clear, "You did not choose me, but I chose you."[245] **God chooses *you*.**

In his mercy, God reaches out to you who are beyond feeling, who give yourself over to your lusts. But you can be resurrected. You can be changed. You can come into a new life.[246]

You are not reading this by accident. God has a divine appointment with you. You cannot get away from the Holy Spirit once he has you on his radar. **The Lord is not *chasing* you; he is *wooing* you.**

The Holy Spirit offers you hope, new life, and resurrection from the dead. Today, acknowledge you are a sinner, that you need help. Do not put this off any longer.

---

244 2 Corinthians 5:17
245 John 15:16
246 Ephesians 4:18–23

17

A Fresh Baptism of the Holy Ghost

When God breathes the breath of his Spirit, everyone knows he has come. Luke, the author of Acts, writes, "Suddenly there came a sound from heaven, as of a rushing mighty wind."[247] According to this verse, God's breath came at Pentecost with a sound from heaven. Luke says this sound was mighty, rushing, filling the whole atmosphere.

Something else also happens when the Holy Spirit comes—he shakes up everything in sight. At Pentecost, the religious rulers in Jerusalem were upset at what they saw taking place among Jesus's followers. They tried shutting down the effect of that mighty blast from heaven.

But the Holy Spirit moved on Peter, anointing him to say, "You can threaten us and jail us. But you cannot stop the mighty wind that is blowing through the land. You can command us to shut up, but we cannot stop speaking. God has breathed upon us, anointing us, and we have to speak the word he has given us."[248]

The believers at Pentecost then gathered in a great praise meeting and prayed, "'Now, Lord, look on their threats, and grant to your servants that with all boldness they may speak your word, by stretching out your hand to heal, and that signs and wonders may be done through the name of your holy servant Jesus.' And when they had prayed, the place where they were assembled together was

---

247 Acts 2:2
248 Acts 5:29–32

shaken; and they were all filled with the Holy Spirit, and they spoke the Word of God with boldness."[249]

=== ==

What does the Bible say about the outpouring of the Holy Ghost on his church in these last days? When Peter and the disciples saw what took place at Pentecost, Peter stood up and declared, "This is that which was spoken by the prophet Joel... I will pour out in those days of my Spirit."[250]

Isaiah, Jeremiah, Ezekiel, and some minor prophets speak of a "former rain" and a "latter rain" outpouring of the Spirit. Malachi describes the latter rain as an earth-shaking event to come and offers proof that the greatest work of the Holy Ghost—this latter rain outpouring—is happening right now, in our generation.

I see evidence all around that we are living in the very time Malachi describes. Malachi's message is a two-part prophecy. First, he speaks to the ungodly, material-istic, secular, and pleasure-mad world. Second, he speaks to those who love and fear the Lord.

Malachi warns the godless nations, "For behold, the day is coming, burning like an oven, and all the proud, yes, all who do wickedly will be stubble."[251] If ever there was a day like a burning oven when everything is "hot" the world over—economi-cally, socially, and spiritually—it is today.

According to Malachi, a fiery holocaust is coming that will leave the ungodly nothing to protect themselves, "that will leave them neither root nor branch."[252] Every safe haven will be consumed, as will be all the proud and wicked.

The great wickedness Malachi speaks of here does not just refer to those who indulge in addictions and perversions. It suggests an arrogant fist-shaking at God. We see a modern example of this fist-shaking in the European Union. It proudly boasts itself to be a secular society. According to its constitution, God has no place in its society; he gets no recognition, and his name is wiped out completely.[253] As far as the leaders of the European Union are concerned, God is dead.

---

249 Acts 4:29–31
250 Acts 2:16, 18
251 Malachi 4:1
252 Malachi 4:1
253 This is also true of the U.S. Constitution, which does not make reference to God.

America seems to be headed in the same direction. We are slowly pushing God out of our courts, our schools, our society. We refuse to acknowledge his blessing on our nation, claiming instead that we have accomplished everything in our own strength. "We are the greatest, mightiest, wealthiest nation on earth," we boast, "and we have achieved it all on our own."

I shudder that this nation has stuck up its nose at God, shaking our fists at him and daring him to act. The Hebrew word for *wicked* as used in Malachi 4:1 means arrogant. It is the worst kind of arrogance to flaunt sin before heaven and say, "God does not see. He cannot do anything. He has nothing to do with us."

It is arrogant to trample his Holy Word, mocking everything that reflects his heart. Consider the mockery being made of marriage by the glorifying of sexual perversions. This wickedness unfolds before our eyes, and we seem helpless to stop it.

I wonder how long the wicked think God will wink at such arrogance and not judge it. America has out-sinned Noah's violent and wicked society, Sodom and Gomorrah and their perversions, even Israel of the days of the prophets.

Isaiah warns us, "For behold, the darkness shall cover the earth, and deep darkness the people..."[254] The Hebrew word for deep darkness here recalls the cosmic darkness in Genesis 1:2. Isaiah was saying, "A cosmic darkness is coming that will cover the whole earth."

Jeremiah speaks of such darkness when he cried out to backslidden Judah, "Give glory to the Lord your God before he causes darkness, and before your feet stumble on the dark mountains, and while you are looking for light, he turns it into the shadow of death and makes it dense darkness."[255]

Malachi also speaks of that time of darkness and gloom when God will humble the proud and arrogant. When that day comes, the prophet says, all roots and branches will be consumed, adding that God will dig up everything and leave them—meaning there will be nothing left to rebuild upon.[256]

---

254 Isaiah 60:2
255 Jeremiah 13:16
256 Malachi 4:1

But for those who fear God's name, there is an entirely different, glorious prophecy for the overcoming church. For God's people, it is not gloom. It is gladness! Malachi tells us that in the darkest hours "the Sun of righteousness shall arise with healing in his wings, and you will go forth leaping as calves released from the stall."[257]

In a world gone mad, Jesus Christ will rise up, and he will shine as a healing Sun, brighter than in all past generations. With that comes a fresh baptism of the Holy Ghost—a mightier sound from heaven. And once again, we will see signs, wonders, and miracles!

Christ himself will be preaching in all the homes of overcomers—laying hands on their sick. Elders will rise with a fresh faith in the power of the name of Jesus. Christians everywhere will be anointed to pray for the sick. Miracles, healings are made possible by and through the power of the Holy Ghost, just like Stephen who was a man "full of faith and power," who "did great wonders and signs among the people."[258]

$$==\equiv==$$

Perhaps you, like many, have lost your fight. You have not taken our authority over the devil and his evil empire, and the fire of the Holy Ghost is waning. Allow me to remind you today that it is written that you have the power to overcome the evil one. James reminds us, "Resist the devil and he will flee from you."[259]

But we let the devil run over our faith and provide no resistance. God does not answer prayers where there is no faith. And Satan will not flee where there is fear and unbelief.

And so I pray with you, declaring, "Oh Lord, I believe there is protection and healing under your wings. Give me a fresh baptism of the Holy Ghost. Put more fight in my faith. And may it be for me as Malachi prophesied, that I will go forth leaping as a calf released from its stall."

I have seen frisky calves locked up in stalls. They go round, kicking, making noise. In the same way, Satan has succeeded in locking up a multitude of believers in little stalls, keeping them locked out of green pastures and cool waters.

---

257 Malachi 4:2 *Spurrell's Translation of the Old Testament Scripture*
258 Acts 6:8
259 James 4:7

Some are confined in a stall of hopelessness. They are bored to death, going through the motions every day without a drop of joy. They have given up hope of ever being free. They look back at a time they rejoiced—once full of the Holy Ghost and fire. But now, they wonder where God is.

Others are trapped in a stall of bitterness. The Bible calls this bitterness a deadly poison.[260] If you have a single root of bitterness, you will be confined in your stall. You will live in fear, a stubborn calf. And little by little, you will spiritually die.

These stalls are ones we cannot open in our human strength. We need the Holy Spirit to set us free. And when he does, you will go forth leaping in joy and freedom.

In these days of uncertainty and gloom, however, the testimony of God's power will be seen in those being released from their stalls, living in true freedom. That is God's promise. **Whatever it takes, get along with God and pray for the Holy Ghost to bring back the fire so your faith can be renewed.**

Today, may the Sun of righteousness rise for you anew with healing in his wings.

---

260 Acts 8:23

18

Getting to Know the Holy Spirit

There is a song we sometimes sang at Times Square Church that said, "Send him down, Lord, let the Holy Ghost come down. We need him, Lord, let him come." **But the Holy Spirit came at Pentecost, and he has never left.**[261]

In my more than fifty-five years of preaching, I preached a lot about the Holy Spirit. **The truth is, you can know the theology and the doctrine of the Holy Spirit and not know him personally. You can live not knowing what the ministry of the Holy Spirit is.**

If I were to ask you if you have received the Holy Spirit, many would say, "Yes, I have. I have received the Holy Spirit because I have received Christ."

Now, that is true. But there is more to it. Your body is a temple of the Holy Ghost, but how well do you *know* the Holy Spirit? What can you tell me about his ministry?

Jesus said, "I will send to you a Comforter."[262] The Holy Spirit comforts you by bringing you into the knowledge of who you are. When the enemy comes in with a lie or a temptation, when he comes with discouragement, fear, or shame, ask the Holy Spirit to proclaim to you again who you are.

---

261 In John 14:17, Jesus said, "But you know him for he dwells with you and will be in you." The Holy Spirit took residence on earth within those who believe.
262 John 14:16, KJV, paraphrased

And because the Holy Spirit abides in you, you will hear him say, **"You are a child of the living God."**[263]

What strength, what power that is! You are not alone. You are not a victim. The enemy cannot bring you down, because you are a child of a living God. Whenever you are tempted, wherever you are, declare out loud, "I am a child of the living God!"

What's more, this God loves you. "God has loved you just as he has loved me …" Jesus said, "for you loved me before the foundation of the world. … And I have declared to them your name, and will declare it, that the love with which you loved me may be in them, and I in them."[264]

If that does not put some holy zeal in your heart nothing will.

===

Another source of comfort is to know and believe that the Holy Spirit has come to wage war against every lust and enticement of the flesh. He has been sent to take over the battle. "For the flesh lusts against the Spirit, and the Spirit against the flesh; and these are contrary to one another, so that you do not do the things that you wish."[265]

Now you see, you can say, "I love God. I can claim kinship, and I will walk in the truth of that kinship. I also know that I am justified and sanctified through the power of the Holy Spirit."

You can say all that, but there is a war raging within. There is a war going on between the flesh and the Spirit. The devil is after you. He comes at you because you invited the Holy Spirit to come in and take control. When you do that, it stirs all the powers of hell.

You and I are no match to our flesh. You may have made promise after promise and have failed on every one of them. But God has sent the Holy Spirit through his Son Jesus Christ to wage war against the flesh. And this battle will go on as long as you live.

Flesh is flesh; it will always be flesh. But the Holy Spirit has been given to wage war against the flesh, and it is a fierce battle. It demands faith. It demands confidence in the Word of God.

---

263 Hosea 1:10, paraphrased
264 John 17:20–26, paraphrased
265 Galatians 5:17

The Holy Spirit comes to remind you of the truth that he is there to do battle. He is your prayer warrior, your strength, and your might. He is the living power of the almighty God.

The devil will try to convince you that you are the most unclean and the most unworthy of all servants. That is a lie. Other than Jesus, there is no one who has not sinned.

When you are tempted, may you find courage in Paul's words to the church in Corinth, that God gives you a way out.[266] You can bear what you are facing because you know you have the Holy Spirit in you, and he will be faithful in this warfare! I can testify of his faithfulness. He has fought battles by my side, and he has forged strength within me.

The Holy Ghost will give you the power to fight the battle. But you have to acknowledge that power and in faith lay hold of it—receiving it into your being.

Yes, there is a power greater than the flesh.

== ==

Consider another aspect of the Holy Ghost. The Bible tells us, "Likewise the Spirit also helps in our weaknesses. For we do not know what we should pray for as we ought, but the Spirit himself makes intercession for us with groanings which cannot be uttered."[267]

So many people do not know what to pray for; they do not know how to pray. They wonder, "Am I praying according to the will of God? How do I determine the will of God?"

What Paul is saying is that we do not know how to pray, but there is a Holy Spirit in us who simply brings us to Jesus for communication and to just talk to him.

Even when I take walks in New York City and there's noise all around, I can shut out all the noise and the clamor by simply talking with God, telling him what I am going through.

Paul also says all of creation is groaning.[268] The reason for this groaning is the things that are happening in the world today. Never have we seen such turmoil. Never have we seen such levels of stress as we are seeing now.

---

266 1 Corinthians 10:13
267 Romans 8:26
268 Romans 8:22

The ecologists, for example, are saying that the ice caps are melting, that there will be floods, and New York will eventually be under water as will be most of the East Coast.

Sin is destroying the world, and we need to be aware of all of this. As you look at the world today and all the turmoil, everything seems to conspire to take away hope for a future.

I have ministered in countries in poverty all over the world—from South America to Africa to Europe and Asia. I have walked in the slums and I have seen the poverty. I have seen the terror in the eyes of the children.

Everywhere, you find people looking for hope. What can we do amid such hopelessness? **There is only one answer to the hopelessness of this world: the power of the Holy Spirit. That power flows through the prayer room. It comes through the intercessor. It comes through the Holy Spirit in you—if you would only allow him.**

The Bible says all of nature is groaning, and we too who are in the Spirit are groaning, wanting our redemption. In other words, there is something that is saying, "Lord, I have had enough. I want to see Jesus."

There is something in the Spirit that says, "Even so, the Spirit and the bride say come."[269] The Holy Spirit is groaning for a new world to come. And in these last days, the church will experience the same fire and moving of the Holy Spirit when thousands were saved on Pentecost. It is the same spirit that raised Christ from the dead.

Oh God, rise up. Rise up inside us, God, and give us faith and confidence that you will do in the last days what you promised.

Begin it in me, Lord. I have got a warrior that stands by my side. I will not give in to the lies of the devil. Glory be to the living God!

---

269 Revelation 22:17

19

The Indwelling Power of the Holy Spirit

The prophet Ezekiel was deeply grieved at what he saw in the house of God among the children of Israel, saying, "Repent, and turn from all your transgressions, so that iniquity will not be your ruin. Cast away from you all the transgressions which you have committed and get yourselves a new heart and a new spirit...turn and live!"[270]

Ezekiel was one of those many Old Testament prophets who had not only been touched by the Holy Spirit, but the Spirit lived in him.[271]

Those in whom the Spirit dwelled had the inner strength to fight sin and resist temptation. But not so with the congregation to which he preached. Several times in his message, he said to the sin-bound people of Israel, "Why don't you just stop what you are doing? What is your problem? Simply lay it down. Turn. Make yourself change. Get yourself a new heart. Just say no to your besetting sins."

Ezekiel was asking the people to do something that is humanly impossible. The people of Israel could no more create in themselves a new spirit or a new heart than they could raise the dead. No one could *will* themselves into a change of heart and turn away from their sins and their idols. Yet that is what the prophet told them to do.

===

270 Ezekiel 18:30–32
271 Ezekiel 2:2

Ezekiel's demand sounds much like the message I preached for years, pleading with the church, "Why are you going to let this sin ruin you? You know God hates it. Get mad at the devil. Get mad at hell. Get mad at your sin and say, 'That is enough.' Then walk away. It is not complicated."

Like Ezekiel, I was expecting the impossible—not only of others but also of myself. That is the problem with the old covenant. It demands total obedience yet does not provide a way to fulfill the command.

That is why God made a new covenant, a new agreement with mankind. Under the new covenant, God's demand for obedience is just as strong as it was under the old covenant. But through the cross, Jesus provides a way to conquer sin, and the Holy Spirit provides the power to walk in victory.

God still does not wink at sin. He still demands absolute, total, perfect obedience to his word. He still calls for a new heart and a new spirit.

One of my favorite passages is one the Lord gave me when he first called me to preach. This verse from Psalm 25 has been my heart cry ever since I was a young man: "The secret of the Lord is with those who fear him, and he will show them his covenant."[272]

Like David, Ezekiel was a man who feared God, and God had begun to open his eyes to show him the new covenant. I can imagine how the message God gave him to preach must have both thrilled and dumbfounded him.

Ezekiel had just been preaching up and down the land, "Quit your sinning. What is your problem? Turn around. Get a new heart. Get a new spirit." But then God comes upon him by his Spirit and his message changes to: "I will sprinkle clean water on you, and you shall be clean; I will cleanse you from all your filthiness and from all your idols."[273]

He had just been telling them to clean themselves up, and now he is telling them God will cleanse them. What's more, God says, "I will give you a new heart and put a new spirit within you; I will take the heart of stone out of your flesh and

272 Psalm 25:14
273 Ezekiel 36:25

give you a heart of flesh. I will put My Spirit within you and cause you to walk in my statutes, and you will keep my judgments and do them."[274]

Everything Ezekiel had been commanding them to do, God came and said, "By my Spirit, I will do these things in you. I will cause you to obey me." God would empower his people to obey him because he knew they could never do it. They did not have the power. They had come to the end of themselves, trying yet failing again and again.

I do not doubt that the prophet had to wonder if this message could be true. So, the Holy Spirit gave him a vision.

"The hand of the Lord came upon me and brought me out in the Spirit of the Lord," he said, "and set me down in the midst of the valley; and it was full of bones."[275] And the Lord spoke to him out in the middle of the valley of bones. There were bones everywhere.

Then God asked him, "Can these bones live?"[276] God was showing him the people he had been preaching to. This was Israel. So God told Ezekiel, "Go ahead and tell those bones to get up and walk. Go ahead and tell them to get out of their graves, get some skin on those bones, and walk."[277]

But even though the bones were transformed before Ezekiel's eyes, flesh and skin now covered the bones so they looked good, they could not move. There was no life in them. So God said, "You have been preaching to dry bones."[278] Then God told Ezekiel, "The only way these bones can walk is if my Spirit enters into them, if my Spirit does the work of restoration. That is the only way."[279]

With that, God told Ezekiel, "Prophesy to the breath, prophesy, son of man, and say to the breath, 'Thus says the Lord God: "Come from the four winds, O breath, and breathe on these slain, that they may live." ' " So, Ezekiel prophesied as God had commanded him, and breath came into the bones, and they lived, and stood upon their feet, an exceedingly great army.[280]

---

274 Ezekiel 36:26–27
275 Ezekiel 37:1–2
276 Ezekiel 37:3
277 Ezekiel 37:4–6, paraphrased
278 Ezekiel 37:11, paraphrased
279 Ezekiel 37:12–14, paraphrased
280 Ezekiel 37:9–10

The heart of God's message is this: The only way you will live, the only way you will have victory over the sin which killed you in the first place, is that God's Spirit comes in and takes dominion so that you can live and never die again.

That is the heart of the new covenant. The Spirit of God will do what the flesh has never been able to accomplish by taking up residence in you and me.

It is about more than just *looking* alive. When God pours out his Spirit on you, the Spirit will cause you to walk in the ways of the Lord. God will create in you a new spirit and a new heart. And God's Spirit living in you will lead you, guide you, and cause you to know the Father intimately and walk in his power.

===

Over the years, I have ministered to multitudes—including godly people who love the Lord with all of their heart. And they would tell me, "I know the Holy Ghost abides in me, but I have not been able to see the release of God's power. Why is that?"

If you intend to walk a holy and pure life, if you hate whatever sin has you trapped and you want victory, remember that God told Ezekiel—prophesy to the breath, tell it to come and breathe on the bones so they may live.

In other words, pray to the Holy Ghost to come and do what only he can do. This is more than meekly saying, "Holy Ghost, come and possess me." Instead, proclaim, "Spirit of the living God, an oath was made to me from the foundation of the world that you would come and enter my heart. A promise was made, a promise that you cannot break. Holy Ghost, you said you would cause me to walk in the Spirit. You would cause me to walk in holiness. Today, I hold you to the covenant!"

I had to come to that place in my life when I told God that I would take him at his Word. So can you. **With humility and love, you too can challenge the Holy Ghost to bring forth life where there was death, victory where there was defeat.**

Then, when the enemy comes to taunt you with an old sin, remind the Holy Ghost of his promise to put his Spirit in you and cause you to walk in the ways of the Lord. He will set you free, he will break the bonds of captivity to sin.

===

The apostle Paul said "...if you live according to the flesh you will die; but if by the Spirit you put to death the deeds of the body, you will live."[281] What Paul is saying is that you can look alive but not really live because of sin. **You can be dead while you still live because sin is death. But if you allow the Holy Ghost to put to death the grip sin has on you, then you will know what life is!**

Too often, you can focus so strongly on Christ's victory on the cross that you forget the other half of the gospel, that is, the ongoing work of the Holy Ghost in you. **The work and the ministry of the Holy Spirit make the victory of the cross a total victory.**

This is not just the gospel you preach, but a practical reality in life that is worked out every day by the indwelling of the Holy Ghost.

Invite the Holy Spirit to complete the work that Christ had started in you.[282] Like Ezekiel, you can do so with confidence. Then watch out. The Spirit is about to bring you back to life.

---

281 Romans 8:13
282 Philippians 1:6

20

The Church Is Not Ready for Revival

There are two kinds of churches in the world today. First, there is the kind of church that has a form of godliness but no power. And then there is the Holy Ghost church, a praying, God-fearing body of believers who pray, fast, and seek the face of God.

This message is concerned primarily with the latter as it is the only church in a position to receive a great outpouring of the Holy Spirit. Even so, I do not believe that the church is ready for revival, for the great, promised outpouring of his Spirit.[283]

Of course, God is sovereign and can pour out his Spirit on anyone he chooses. There are reports of the Holy Ghost falling on various peoples around the world, bringing resurrection life to those who neither expected it nor were prepared for it.

But God also gives us a biblical pattern showing that he works through a prepared people. He digs up fallow ground before he sets things in divine order.

I believe there are three reasons why the church is not ready for revival.

1. **We are not ready for revival if we are convinced this society has sinned away its day of grace.**

---

283 Joel 2:28–29, cited in Acts 2:17

America has so grieved God—its intensity of sin is so horrible—that many are convinced there is no hope left. In recent years, I have become convinced that in light of America's terrible moral landslide that God has no option left but judgment. So, I have preached his impending judgment intensely.

God may wait patiently for repentance, sending many prophets to warn of judgment. But a day will come when he will say, "Enough!" At that point, prayer is useless. There are several examples of this in the Bible.

It happened to Noah's generation. God strove with wicked mankind for 120 years with mercy and warnings. But finally he said, "No more!" With that, he wiped out all of humanity except for those who entered the ark.

It happened also in Sodom and Gomorrah. God counted the days of wickedness in that society. Finally, he said, "Your cup of iniquity is full. Your sins have ascended to heaven." Then God wiped them out.

It happened as well in Jerusalem. Christ walked the streets of that city and wept, warning of the coming judgment.[284] Seventy years later, God said, "Enough!" Then Jerusalem was razed to the ground and thousands were killed.

God put this message of judgment in the heart of Jeremiah. He sent the prophet to the gates of the temple with this solemn cry: "But go now to my place which was in Shiloh, where I set my name at the first, and see what I did to it because of the wickedness of my people Israel.... therefore I will do to the house which is called by my name, in which you trust, and to this place which I gave to you and your fathers, as I have done to Shiloh.... Therefore do not pray for this people, nor lift up a cry or prayer for them, nor make intercession to me; for I will not hear you."[285]

God was telling the righteous, "You can stop praying. My patience is gone, and I have determined judgment." Shiloh stands as a testimony to all generations that judgment begins in God's house. God's people had become so wicked that the Lord moved in with sudden and awesome judgments. The Lord removed all his glory, shut the doors, and departed—leaving it in ruin.

The Word of the Lord also came to Ezekiel with the same kind of warning: "'Son of man, when a land sins against me by persistent unfaithfulness, I will stretch out my hand against it; I will cut off its supply of bread, send famine on it, and cut off man and beast from it. Even if these three men, Noah, Daniel, and Job, were in

284 Matthew 23:37–39; Luke 23:28–31
285 Jeremiah 7:12, 14, 16

it, they would deliver only themselves by their righteousness,' says the Lord God....
'they would deliver neither sons nor daughters; only they would be delivered, and
the land would be desolate.' "[286]

God was saying, "Even Noah, Daniel, and Job could not pray down a revival.
Even their righteous prayers could not buy more time. I determine judgment, and
all the praying people in the world cannot change my mind."

**When I see what God did to Noah's generation, Sodom, and Jerusalem, I
cannot help but deduct that America is ripe for destruction.** We are a million
times worse than those generations—and God judged and destroyed them all. I
often pray, "Oh, God, if you destroyed them, how can you spare us?"

Experts say the economy is booming.[287] Our gross national product is increas-
ing. Inflation is holding steadily. Indeed, everything looks good ahead. Yet, why does
all this good news not bring any sense of security to people? All across the country,
people feel that something is hanging in the air, about to happen.

Why? I believe it is because, deep down, this nation knows it deserves judgment. We know we are living on borrowed time. How can we be ready for revival
if we believe that hope is gone? We cannot have faith for a revival until we are convinced God still wants to pour out his Spirit on us.

Why has America not yet been judged? It is because there is still a great harvest
ahead, and God is "not willing that any should perish, but that all should come to
repentance."[288]

I believe God is saying to America, "Show me I have walked away from you.
I have not yet removed my Holy Spirit. Rather, I am still at work all over this
nation—still calling for you!" The Lord is calling America back to repentance, back
to his own heart.

$$=\!=\!=$$

2. **We are not ready for revival when we are overwhelmed by the darkness
that has settled over the nation and by the fury of the enemy.**

---

286 Ezekiel 14:13–14, 20
287 This message was preached in 1995.
288 2 Peter 3:9

I see a fury and an intensity in sinners today as in no other generation. The spiritual darkness hovering over America is almost tangible. Isaiah says, "For behold, the darkness shall cover the earth, and thick darkness the people..."[289] Such a thick darkness is a darkness you can feel. And the darkness over America is intense, widespread, and thickening every moment.

But the Bible says God has a part in that darkness, he can cause it. "Give glory to the Lord your God before he causes darkness, and before your feet stumble on the dark mountains, and while you are looking for light, he turns it into the shadow of death and makes it dense darkness."[290]

When people are so set on their sin that they reject the Lord, they are driven to darkness. Likewise, David said of the wicked that the Spirit of God allows a darkness to fall over their hearts and minds.[291]

Sinners are driven to their dark acts.[292] And the fury and intensity of this present vileness is a thousand times darker than when I first came to New York a generation ago. Today, I look at people's eyes as they are on their way to make a drug connection, stumbling out of a bar, running to and fro looking for pleasure. They are driven to their dark acts.

When I first began this ministry, I spoke in churches all over America, warning of the moral landslide to come. I told people that drugs would strike even the smallest hamlets. I warned of blatant homosexuality. And I prophesied that nudity and sexual acts would air on prime-time television.

People ridiculed me, but all of that has come to pass.

As you see the darkness thickening, do you believe it will exceed the light of the gospel? Never! God's people must never be intimidated by the darkness and fury of the enemy. It does not matter how dark the world becomes. The Bible says Jesus will rise and shine in the darkness,[293] and God says that in such times he will shine his light the brightest.[294]

We are not to be overwhelmed by any darkness. When gross darkness covers the earth, we must expect the Lord to shine in all his glory and to deliver multitudes.[295]

---

289 Isaiah 60:2 ESV
290 Jeremiah 13:16
291 Psalm 69:23
292 Isaiah 8:22
293 Isaiah 51:12–13; Psalm 139:12; Daniel 2:22; Isaiah 9:2
294 Isaiah 42:16
295 Isaiah 60:1–3

No darkness will ever stop God's light. So, take your eyes off the darkness, off the sin, off the fury of violent people. And believe the Lord for the bursting forth of his light.

---

3. **The church is not ready for revival because of its weak faith in God's willingness and power to save hardened sinners.**

God put his finger on Judah's problem: They had given up hope, thinking they had gone too far and there was no going back. Judah doubted God's willingness and power to redeem a people entrenched in apostasy and idolatry.[296]

But the Lord asked Judah, "Is my hand shortened at all that it cannot redeem?"[297] In other words, "Have I lost my power to save? No! My mighty hand dried up the Red Sea. It opened blind eyes. Why do you think I have lost my power to redeem you?"

Would God then somehow decide not to save your family members for whom you have fasted and prayed faithfully? Absolutely not! Cry out to him in faith. Believe him for the impossible.

Jesus prophesied of a great harvest, and I believe we will see that as God's Spirit falls on vast multitudes—even entire nations. When the Spirit was poured out the first time in Jerusalem, thousands were saved at once.[298]

Yet God is asking his remnant church to begin with our own families. We are to pray and be patient, and he will gather in our loved ones, one at a time.[299]

God is waiting and anxious to pour out his Holy Ghost. Are you ready to pray down his rain? **We are to pray not for the fire of judgment, but for God's latter rain.**[300]

Yes, God's judgment is coming. But while we still have time, we are to believe for God to pour out his Spirit. Lay hold of his divine promises, and you will see a revival all around you.

---

296 Jeremiah 18:12
297 Isaiah 50:2
298 Acts 2:40–47
299 Jeremiah 3:14
300 Zechariah 10:1

21

A Passion for Christ

llow me to give you what I believe is the spiritual definition of a passion for Christ. **A true passion for Christ is an ever-increasing desire to obey God's Word.** This is more than a personal pursuit, though. As part of the body of Christ, there has to be a fervent desire to see the church engage in that same pursuit.

In the Old Testament, this used to be largely a personal pursuit through individuals such as Abraham, Noah, Enoch, Jacob, Isaac, David, the prophets, and many more. Individually, they desired to obey God and to compel others to do so.[301]

Then came Jesus. Because of Jesus and through the Holy Ghost, *all* believers—not just Jews but people from all nations[302]—we all become "the body of Christ, and members individually."[303]

As individual members of the body of Christ, this ever-increasing desire to obey the Word of God is no longer just a personal pursuit. Under the new covenant,

---

301 The word *church* does not appear in English translations of the Old Testament. In the New Testament, the Greek word that is translated as church is *ekklēsia*. It is used to describe a specific gathering of Christians. That same word is used in the Septuagint, the Greek translation of the Old Testament, to translate the Hebrew term *qāhāl* which means assembly. The word is used to describe when Israel gathered together to appear before God and as a general reference to all of Israel. So, technically, there was an Old Testament church, but only in the New Testament is it called "the body of Christ."

302 1 Corinthians 12:13

303 1 Corinthians 12:27

when one member suffers, all the members suffer along with the one. And if one member is honored, all the members are honored.

It is admirable—even scriptural—for you to pursue God with fervor, to want to serve him all your days, to resist sin in your life, to have an ever-increasing faith, to want to be more like Jesus, and in the words of John, to desire for Jesus to increases while you decrease.[304]

But your pursuit of Christ can no longer be for your spiritual edification only. What you do as an individual—both good and bad—affects the whole body.[305] If you fall into sin, you disgrace the whole body. Your sin is no longer a personal matter. How you live and what you pursue matter to every member of the body. Likewise, so is your passionate pursuit of Christ.

Some might want to go it alone, to say they are a believer but not part of the body of Christ. That is not an option, Paul tells us, as "the eye cannot say to the hand, 'I have no need of you,' nor again the head to the feet, 'I have no need of you.' "[306] In the same way, **you cannot separate your personal pursuit of Christ from having a genuine burning passion for the whole body to come into the same experience.**

As you passionately pursue Christ, the Holy Spirit sets your heart on fire and plants in you a desire to pray as you have never prayed, and the Word becomes a delight to you. **But a passion for Christ is not about emotion or intensity, and you are not the only one who benefits.** The Holy Ghost does this work within you to edify and build up the body of Christ.

===

It is impossible to have a passion for Christ without a walk of obedience to his Word. And **unless you are prepared to obey what God reveals to you through his Word, your zeal, the tears you have shed in God's presence, and all the time you have spent in prayer, none of it will produce one iota of passion for Jesus.**

You and I may think that we can achieve having a passion for Christ if we could just get as sincere and dedicated as possible. I have tried that. It does not work. Trying to be dedicated, sincere, and humble only wore me out.

---

304 John 3:30
305 1 Corinthians 5:6, 6:15, 10:16–17, 11:27–29, 12:26
306 1 Corinthians 12:21

Matthew tells about a time when Jesus was addressing a large crowd and had some tough words about leadership and humility. Jesus essentially said that these leaders were not capable of a true passion for Christ because they had set themselves above the law by not practicing what they preached.[307]

These were self-exalted men who thought they were so special that they could preach one thing but live another. They did not live in obedience to the very Word they were teaching. The same goes for us as leaders—whether we are teaching about turning away from lust and fornication, or about giving more to the work of the Lord while all we do is line our pockets.

"Whoever exalts himself will be humbled," Jesus told those gathered, "and whoever humbles himself will be exalted."[308] Those who exalt themselves love recognition and honor. They love the spotlight, the highest seats in public meetings, and they love to be recognized in public.

Jesus was not only addressing the religious leaders. We all have that desire to be noticed. But pastors can be especially guilty, talking about the size of their church, how much it has grown, how many programs they have.

What is this all about? Jesus reminds the crowd, "You are all brethren."[309] What he is saying is, **"You are one of many. Period. Nothing more. You do not have to be somebody important."** And in calling them brethren, Jesus also alludes to the fact that when one of the brethren sins, they all suffer. As such, self-exaltation is not a personal sin. It affects the entire body.

=== ==

Are you willing to open up your heart to his Word, to repent of any dishonesty or hypocrisy, to ask the Holy Spirit to convict you and deliver you of any self-exaltation? **Once you grow in humility, you can grow in your passion for Christ.**

Does it mean that you are to go through life quietly with no one knowing who you are? Does that make you humble? Far from it. Humility is not meekness. It is not quietness, self-abasement, or self-denial. Humility is not about ignoring praise,

---

307 Matthew 23:2–3
308 Matthew 23:12 ESV
309 Matthew 23:8

deprecating oneself, or walking around with a long face. **Humility is living in total dependence on the Lord**, to trust Jesus for all things and in everything.

In living in total dependence on the Lord, you have no agenda, no rights. It does not mean you are helpless, though. It is a matter of admitting that God's power is made perfect in weakness, so when you are weak, you are strong,[310] and holding on to that truth with confidence and faith, remembering if you humble yourself under the mighty hand of God, he will exalt you in due time.[311]

But how do you do that? How do you humble yourself before the Lord? By "casting all your care upon him, for he cares for you."[312] It is as plain as it can be. In humility, cast all your cares upon him.

Christ set the example of that. He "made himself of no reputation, taking the form of a bondservant, and coming in the likeness of men. And being found in appearance as a man, he humbled himself and became obedient to the point of death, even the death of the cross."[313]

Jesus humbled himself and became wholly dependent upon his Father, saying, "I do not do anything, I say nothing, I do nothing, I am totally dependent on my Father."[314] *That* is passion.

In living in such complete obedience to God the Father, Jesus's life, death, and resurrection were far more than a personal victory. He came to build a body—the church—here on earth as his body. Everything he did, every victory he won, everything had to do with building that body.

Christ's victory over sin provided your and my victory over sin. His death became your death. He paid the penalty for your debt. His resurrection was your resurrection. He brought you to Christ and set you in heavenly places.[315]

≡≡

If you were to pray, "Oh God, renew my passion for Christ," be prepared that God will show you areas of disobedience. He will change your heart to *want* to obey.

---

310 2 Corinthians 12:9–10
311 1 Peter 5:6
312 1 Peter 5:7
313 Philippians 2:7–8
314 John 5:19, 30; 8:28–29, paraphrased
315 Romans 5:12–19; Ephesians 2:4–6

God will also give you the faith to obey and the power to overcome obstacles. You will preach the truth. You will weep not just for yourself but also for those who are not yet pursuing the heart of Christ. You will want others to share your pursuit.

Those closest to you will see this pursuit produce in you an obedience to the Lord. They will see you being kinder to your spouse. They will see changes in your life, and they will see the likeness of Christ in you and experience God's presence through you. All of this will cause them to desire to pursue Christ just like you are.

That is why I want a passion for Christ—so others will be drawn to Christ.

═ ═

If you pursue a passion for Christ, be prepared to be shaken. God will allow you to experience things that have nothing to do with your own life or your own walk. Some of what you will go through will be for the edification of the body.

Some of you wonder why you are going through trials even now. It is simply because you are pursuing God. God has put it in you to pursue a passion for Christ, a deep desire to obey, a desire to love God with all your heart, soul, and strength.[316]

Jesus said, "If you love me, you will keep my commandments."[317]

Here is how you know you love God and are pursuing a passion for Christ— if you are obeying his commandments. It is not complicated.

316 Deuteronomy 6:5, cited as the most important command by Jesus in Mark 12:30 and Luke 10:27
317 John 14:15 ESV

22

How to Overcome Sin

I have an unusual kind of respect for the word *sin*—the same kind of respect I have for a rattlesnake coiled for an attack. In my years of ministry, I have wept my way through human graveyards of depravity and hopelessness due to sin.

I can tell you story after story of lives wrecked by Satan. There was Skinny Carlos, for example, a kid whose mom had left him to his own defenses when he was just fourteen. The boy lived in a rat-infested basement in Harlem where his rent payment was to stoke the furnace.

Carlos had a dirty mattress and a few rags that he used for blankets. He had not bathed in months, nor had he changed his clothes. But he shot narcotics into his veins day after day, and he ate only what he could steal.

I brought Carlos to the center where we cleaned him up, gave him good clothes, and talked to him about the Lord. But that very night, Carlos ran away uttering blood-curdling screams. He ran back to what he knew and died two months later of hepatitis.

Then there was Daisy, a prostitute addict who came to live at the center. Her veins had collapsed, so she started shooting up in the leg, and then the jugular. She left the center against our advice and went back to prostituting until someone pushed her off a roof for not paying a couple of dollars for drugs. She died instantly. The guy went down and took the little money she had from the corpse.

As for sixteen-year-old Fernandez, his friends left him on a rooftop after he died from an overdose. The next day, they went and stripped him of his clothes so they could pawn it for drug money. They left him naked, getting just $6 for his clothes.

Satan enslaved Carlos, Daisy, Fernandez, and countless others with appetites and habits that broke down their morals, their health, and their integrity.

— ═ ═ —

For some time, I studied the lives of the great missionaries, and I found that they fought the same battle that I was fighting, and that God used them once they had a revelation that you could live in complete victory over sin.

Take Hudson Taylor, for example. He was one of the greatest missionaries in the world, yet Taylor confessed having felt "the ingratitude, the danger, the sin of not living nearer to God. I prayed, I fasted, I strove," he said. "I made resolutions. I read the Word more diligently. I sought more time for meditation, all without avail. I knew that if I could only abide in Christ, all would be well. But I could not."

Taylor would begin the day determined never to take his eyes off Jesus. But at the end of the day, his sin had increased. So, he made up his mind to imitate Christ. He was still buffeted by temptations, though. Finally, Taylor asked friends to pray that the Lord would sanctify him.

We who have walked with the Lord fight that same battle. We can think we are too far along the road to be tempted, but you can walk with God for years and out of the blue face a battle you thought you would never have to face and do things that you hate.

You could feel like it is an inevitable force that pushes you into moods, actions, and indulgences of the mind and the body. And then you wind up perplexed, your soul in turmoil, and you end up with indescribable wretchedness and despair.

The apostle Paul knew something about this kind of wretchedness. He declared, "For what I am doing, I do not understand. For what I will to do, that I do not practice; but what I hate, that I do. If, then, I do what I will not to do, I agree with the law that it is good. But now, it is no longer I who do it, but sin that dwells in me. For I know that in me (that is, in my flesh) nothing good dwells; for to will is present with me, but how to perform what is good I do not find. For the good that I will to do, I do not do; but the evil I will not to do, that

I practice. Now if I do what I will not to do, it is no longer I who do it, but sin that dwells in me."[318]

Paul was a wretched man until God gave him the same spirit of revelation of power over sin in his life. "Who will deliver me from this body of death?"[319] Paul is speaking about his personal battle, his quest for deliverance and power over sin, but any mature Christian can relate.

This is the battle of prophets. It is the battle of those who seek the deeper things of God.

$$\equiv\equiv\equiv$$

I thank God that there is deliverance. Man does not have to be a slave to sin. You do not have to live your life in bondage to the habits of a sinful urge. There is power over *all* sin. But no definition of this power will work in your life and mine until we learn how to get this power.

Hudson Taylor said, "I felt assured that there was in Jesus Christ all I needed. All power over sin. All victory in him was the richness and fatness of heaven." The practical question, though, was how to obtain that power, that "abundant fatness."

Do you pray more, fast more often, make resolutions, try to be better? Do you work up feelings of righteousness and seek something of an outward holiness? That is what Hudson Taylor did at first. "I prayed, fasted, and strove," he said. "I made resolutions. I read the Bible more diligently. But without avail, every day, almost every hour, the consciousness of sin oppressed me."

Absolute power over all sin belongs only to Jesus Christ our Lord. It is he who came to destroy the works of the devil. **Victory over sin comes as Jesus,** and our power over sin depends entirely on our faith in his promise to live his life through us.

Paul never tried to strive for faith. He said, "I have been crucified with Christ." This dying is something Paul did daily. You and I have to die to our sins a thousand times a day so Jesus can live his resurrected life through us. "It is no longer I who live," Paul continued, "but Christ lives in me; and the life which I now live in the flesh I live by faith in the Son of God, who loved me and gave himself for me."[320]

---

318 Romans 7:15–20
319 Romans 7:24
320 Galatians 2:20

Paul found that this power over sin came by total faith that the life he lived was Jesus living *through* him and fighting off the enemy. The question remains how you and I get our faith that strong.

― ≡ ≡ ―

Hudson Taylor looked at a tree and its branches, realizing that no branch can grow by striving. They grow by staying attached to the tree, by resting in it. In the same way, you and I can strive in vain, or we can rest in God. **Faith that conquers sin comes not by *striving* but by *resting* in the Faithful One. But when we toy with unbelief, we lack power over sin.**

God promised to quicken us in the moment of temptation, to make a way to escape—that is, through the Holy Ghost, you can see temptation coming; you can sense it. You and I are not ignorant of the enemy's devices.

Paul prays for the church in Ephesus, "that the God of our Lord Jesus Christ, the Father of glory, may give to you the spirit of wisdom and revelation in the knowledge of him, the eyes of your understanding being enlightened; that you may know what is the hope of his calling, what are the riches of the glory of his inheritance in the saints, and what is the exceeding greatness of his power toward us who believe, according to the working of his mighty power which he worked in Christ when he raised him from the dead and seated him at his right hand in the heavenly places."[321]

Envision with me Jesus's body lying in the tomb, and the almighty Spirit of God coming down, picking up that body, and breathing life into him. He rose, and a new dimension walked out of that tomb.

Now, picture the same Spirit coming to you in your moment of temptation, picking you up right up, breathing into you a new dimension. Satan can no longer touch you.

All power over sin belongs to Christ, and as you allow Christ to live through you, you do not fight the battle against sin. Allow Jesus to quicken you with the same Spirit that raised him from the dead. Commit the battle to the Lord.

---

321 Ephesians 1:17–20

In doing so, you can declare, **"Christ's power over sin is Christ who lives in me. Christ in me will deliver me. Christ in me will set me free. I cannot fight it; it is too big for me. But Jesus has the power, so I will rest in him."**

Stay close to Jesus. Love him, trust him, believe in him, commune with him. "Draw near to him, and he will draw near to you."[322]

The answer to all power over sin is to become possessed with Jesus. Lovers of Jesus, learn and believe God's Word. Take hold of his promises. Stand on them.

Exercise the power of Jesus within you, and you too will find your definition of power over sin. In a moment of temptation, step aside and rest in God's glory.

---

322 James 4:8

23

Hell-Shaking Prayer

D aniel was both preacher and prophet—a great man of God. He started his ministry in Babylon as a very young man, and he started in prayer.

Daniel's prayers enraged the devil. He had been promoted under King Darius. There were 120 princes over the 120 provinces, and along with three presidents, they were all equals. But because of Daniel's talents and wisdom, King Darius set him above the whole realm.

Daniel was a busy man. But nothing could take away his time for prayer. Three times a day this man stole away from all his obligations, from all his burdens and leadership needs, and he spent time with the Lord. His time alone with God took precedence over everything else.

Daniel got his direction on his knees. He prayed, and God spoke, answering his prayers.

When Nebuchadnezzar had a dream, for example, none of his wise men could interpret the dream. When Daniel got news of the king's decree to kill all the wise men, he called a meeting with his three praying friends—Shadrach, Meshach, and Abednego—and they went to their knees to hear from God.[323]

After praying, Daniel declared, "I thank you and praise you, O God of my fathers; you have given me wisdom and might, and have now made known to me what we asked of you, for you have made known to us the king's demand."[324]

Where did Daniel get his wisdom? From the secret closet of prayer. He got it seeking the face of God.

The people of God were at their lowest point, in captivity. The praises of God had been silenced; they had lost their song, the Scriptures say.[325] They had hung up their harps. They were not singing, they were not praising God, they were not worshipping. They had drifted away and embraced the prosperity of Babylon.

Satan was set on destroying Israel because out of Israel was going to come the Messiah. Knowing about Nebuchadnezzar's decree, I believe all Israel was watching what Daniel and his friends would do, wondering, "Does God still speak to anybody anymore?" **Their faith depended upon somebody being in touch with God.**

Nebuchadnezzar had a dream, and he could not remember what it was. No one could interpret it. But because God revealed the king's dream to Daniel, he could interpret it. This happened twice, and both times Nebuchadnezzar repented, but then turned his back on the God of Israel again.[326]

Once Belshazzar became king, he held a feast where he and his guests used vessels taken from the temple in Jerusalem. During that feast, a finger appeared and wrote a message on the wall.[327] Daniel interpreted the message on the wall, and Belshazzar was slain that very night,[328] at which time Darius became king.

Daniel was appointed over the three presidents and the 120 princes. These leaders saw in Daniel's life something that made them very jealous. They saw wisdom they did not have. They saw the blessing and favor of God on this man. They saw the respect that he had, and there is no question in my mind that they

---

323 Daniel 2:17–18; Daniel's friends were given these Persian names in Babylon, and these are the names commonly used to refer to them. Their Hebrew names, used in most translations, are Hananiah, Mishael, and Azariah.
324 Daniel 2:23
325 Psalms 137:1–4
326 Daniel 2, Daniel 4
327 Daniel 5
328 Daniel 5:30

attributed it all to the prayers that he had been praying three times a day out his window toward Jerusalem.[329]

In their jealousy, the leaders initiated a decree to try to stop Daniel.[330] They made a decree that no one is to pray to any god. They could only worship King Darius. And because of the decree, Daniel was thrown into the lion's den. But King Darius had heard of Daniel's God and encouraged Daniel with these words, "Your God, whom you serve continually, He will deliver you."[331] And God did.

Daniel came not to flatter. He did not come to tell the people what he thought they wanted. Because he had been on his knees, he knew what they needed.

$$\equiv\equiv$$

Let me talk to you about the perils of a praying man or woman. Satan will do everything in his power to shut them down. In Daniel's case, the devil was so incensed at Daniel's hell-shaking prayers that he organized the entire government structure of an empire against one man!

The presidents sought to find occasion against Daniel, and they could not. It would not surprise me if they tried to involve Daniel in *so* much state business that he would have no time to pray. I call it a conspiracy of interruptions. "Let us just pile it on him," they may have said. "Let us make him so busy he will have no time to pray."

Ask preachers today why they do not pray, and they will say they have no time. By the time they fulfill all the demands of their work, they cannot do it all. And when it comes to the Bible, many turn to it simply to get a sermon.

In the same way, if you ask businesspeople who are no longer praying why that is so, they will say that they simply do not have time. This is a conspiracy of interruptions right out of hell. It is one of the most dangerous things that can happen to any Christian.

The philosopher Søren Kierkegaard referred to the busyness of Christians as a narcotic. I do not agree with everything Kierkegaard writes, but he had some powerful warnings to busy Christians. **"Busyness leads to double-mindedness,"**

---

329 Daniel 6:11
330 Daniel 6:12–16
331 Daniel 6:16

Kierkegaard said, "and as you fall deeper and deeper into busyness, your love for the truth slips more and more into oblivion."

The mirror of God's Word is there, but you have to stand still to see a reflection. Busy people move so fast that they have no time to reflect. And so, they become less prayerful, less conscious of the things of God until their convictions begin to wane. Eventually, their actions prove that they have lost the heat of their convictions.

How do you become a man or woman of prayer? What was it that motivated Daniel to pray so powerfully and shake hell that the devil had to organize a whole empire to try to shut him down? What was it that caused a man of more than eighty years to be praying with more intensity than when he was young?

All through the Bible, God is looking for those who seek after him.[332] But, says Ezekiel, God found no one. God found this type of man in Daniel, though, a man with the Word of God in his hand and his heart, a man interceding for his people.[333]

<hr />

God's eyes are going to and fro throughout the land.[334] He searches every church in every nation, looking for those who are in the Word of God because of the conviction of their hearts.

Those are the ones who see what is happening in the land, who understand the times by being close to God and being steeped in his Word.[335] This is how a person of prayer is made by the hand of God, by being shut in with God.

That is where Daniel got his knowledge, his wisdom. He was a man just like you and me, a man of like passions. He was not a saint any more than you and I are. But Daniel said, "I set my face toward the Lord God to make request by prayer and supplications, with fasting, sackcloth, and ashes."[336]

The praying person who shakes hell is the one to whom God has revealed the conditions of his church. That person humbles themself and identifies with that condition.

---

332 Jeremiah 5:1, Ezekiel 22:30
333 Daniel 9:3–19
334 2 Chronicles 16:9
335 Romans 10:17
336 Daniel 9:3

I have preached sometimes under such an anointing I knew that the Spirit of the Lord was on me. I stood between heaven and hell as a man standing in the gap. Yet I have seen some Christians sit with their hands folded, bored.

How can that happen when hardened sinners are getting up and walking down the aisle, some shaking at the knees, trembling while others are totally untouched? For many, it is because their minds have been satiated with pornography, and they cannot get those visions out of their minds!

You may even be watching that filth, and it is saturating your mind, and *that* is why you do not pray. You do not read your Bible because your mind is polluted.

Here is the prayer that shakes hell. It is when a man or woman has been in the Word of God and they see the condition of the church and the nation. Through the Spirit rising up in them, they declare, "Oh God, I do not want to be caught up in this cesspool of iniquity. I do not want my eyes polluted. I do not care who does not pray; I will pray. I do not care who does not read the Bible; I will read my Bible!" They cry from their hearts night and day because of men and women—even preachers—all over the world being ensnared in pornography.

Oh God, where are these voices? Where are the people who cry out against this? Where are the praying people? Whatever it takes, God, keep me on my knees!

Daniel was not standing there yelling at his crowd because of what they were doing. Instead, he identified with the sins of the people. "We have sinned," Daniel said. "We have been disobedient. We have rejected his voice."

As for you and me, may we say the same thing. God, open our hearts to what is happening in our own lives. Show us where we have been drifting. Show us where we lack, and deal with us, Lord.

Part 3

"Can These Bones Live?"

A Collection of Messages on the Church

"And [God] said to me, 'Son of man, can these bones live?' So I answered, 'O Lord God, you know.' "

Ezekiel 34:3

24

The Tender Mercies of God

David, in Psalm 145, describes the Lord as "gracious and full of compassion, slow to anger and great in mercy. The Lord is good to all, and his tender mercies are over all his works."[337]

Can those words be used to describe you? Are you a merciful person, someone who cares about the hurts and the needs of others? And if I were to ask your spouse or your coworkers, would they agree with your assessment?

Thinking about your day so far, would you say you are growing toward tenderness, or are you becoming a little grouchier? Getting frustrated with others is more than just irritability. It shows what is truly in your heart.

The truth is, we all often talk about the tender mercies of God, yet we neglect to extend mercy to others. Sadly, that is even true for the global church. We see a church around the world divided on doctrine, race, and their take on certain sins, deciding that some people are not worthy of God's mercy.

I do believe that there are values that are being embraced today that are contrary to God's Word. Still, I cannot believe that the Lord who is full of mercy would turn down the cry of a prostitute, a drug addict, an alcoholic, a homosexual, even a murderer.

---

337 Psalm 145:8–9

I do not believe the church has the right to decide who is not worthy of God's mercy. I do not believe the tender mercies of Christ shut out anybody from Jesus's work on the cross, from faith, or from salvation.

There is no limit to the mercy of God.

———

The world has come to the perfect storm. We do not know how to handle the news anymore. We cannot keep up with the fears, the fires, the floods, the hurricanes, the tornadoes, the terrorism, the genocides, the diseases, the wars and rumors of wars, the reality of nation rising against nation. People are living in constant fear, waiting for some nuclear explosion or something that will put an end to it all.

Many say they no longer turn on the news; they simply cannot handle how, every day, there seems to be something new breaking out. So, we numb out.

In the midst of it all, we find a powerless church that cannot withstand the tides of sin and iniquity that are coming. "We should be more tolerant," many say. But **tolerance is not the tender mercy of God. Tolerance can be blindness. Yes, we need to be tolerant, but only under the banner of the tender love of Christ.**

God has a plan, though. I believe God has something in mind amid this perfect storm that we are living in now. **I see God preparing a people by breaking their will, by bringing people to a place where they need a miracle to survive.**

Never in history has there been such intense testing and trials all over the world. You may be going through things that are overwhelming, things that only God can bring you through. **And as God brings you through the fire, you come to know the consoling power of the Holy Spirit.**

Having been tested, you know that the more intense the battle becomes, the more others will need consolation. They will need hope. They will need to look at somebody who has been to hell in the battle.

In these battles, the weapons God bestows upon us are mighty at pulling down strongholds—not with bombs, not with swords, but by the love of Jesus Christ and the tender mercies of the cross and the blood of Jesus. *That* is the battle plan.

———

What are the headlines and the news reports doing to your heart as you listen for hours and hours to talking heads? **The constant arguing gets into your system; it gets into your heart, plants seeds of bitterness, and robs you of a sense of mercy. Turn it off!** Do not get into some political mud bath that has no place in the church.

When it comes to having a lack of mercy toward others, the Bible has a story of a man who was brutally honest in admitting that he was biased concerning the mercy of God toward a city that he would sooner see God destroy than deliver.

But God tasked this man with a message to go and warn the wicked city—a city that wanted Israel to be destroyed—and warn the enemy to repent. So, the man takes a boat in the opposite direction. He revealed his heart as having a bias, a prejudice concerning the mercy of God. He believed in the mercy of God for Israel, yet he could not extend the loving mercy of God against the enemy.

While trying to get far away from the city to which God had commissioned him to go, there was a tremendous storm, and the other passengers were desperate to find out what they could do. Knowing that he was the reason for the storm, the man told them to throw him overboard. (Why he simply did not jump, I do not know.)

You know the story. The man is Jonah, and after he was tossed overboard, a big fish swallowed him. He writes of his time in the belly of the fish, "Out of the belly of hell I cried…" He said this was God's doing, that God had brought the waves. "The suffering that I am going through is God at work in me," Jonah said.[338]

Perhaps you can relate insofar as the trials you are facing. But unlike Jonah, it may be that you are *not* running from God. The Bible says that many are the afflictions of the righteous.[339] Be assured that what you are going through is rooted in love, for whom the Lord loves, he chastens.[340] **There is a divine purpose to what-**

---

338 Jonah 2:1–9
339 Psalm 34:19
340 Hebrews 12:6; see also Revelation 3:19

ever you are going through. Though it might not feel that way in the moment, what you are facing is served with the tender mercies of the Lord.

The older I get and the longer I walk with God, the clearer I see that God has a purpose with everything in our lives. As for Jonah, I believe God was trying to soften him and bring forth a tender spirit.

Jonah argued with the Lord, saying, "I know you. You are gracious and tender-hearted. I know that at the first impulse of repentance in Nineveh, you are going to lift your hand."[341]

So, God took Jonah down into the pit, stripping him of all hope. And then, God ministered to Jonah.[342] Having had a manifestation of God's tender loving mercy, one would expect Jonah to come forth not only warning the people of Nineveh but asking God to have mercy on that city just like he had on Jonah. But that is not what happened.

After warning Nineveh, a wave of repentance swept through the city. The king is sitting on an ash heap. Even the animals were covered with sackcloth in repentance.

So, what does Jonah do? He was exceedingly angry at God for letting the Ninevites get away with their sins. So, Jonah argues that if God will let their sinfulness, then God should take his life.

It is easy to judge Jonah, but perhaps you can relate. Perhaps someone has hurt you or grieved you. Is there something in your heart that wants to see God get them? I tremble in my heart to think of the times I was in such a place. And time and again, God reminded me of how many mercies he has extended to me, how many sins he has forgiven, how many times he has protected me.

---

341 Jonah 4:1–3; By Nineveh surviving, it would seal Israel's fate, since (as the reader of Jonah is expected to know), less than one generation later, the Assyrians ravaged the kingdom of Israel, massacring the people of the very region where Jonah was from. He wanted to see the Assyrians die so that Israel could live. His reputation was of no consequence, and it wasn't going to suffer either way because his prophecy was worded in such a way that it would be correct either way.
But Jonah's people were all going to die horrible deaths, the women raped, and those who did survive would be deported and made to serve Assyria. That is why Jonah said that if Nineveh was spared, he would rather die than live. If that was what was going to happen to his family and friends, there was nothing left for him to live for.
342 Jonah 2

But if you are like me, your heart still grows hard and you take out your anger on others. That is what happened with Jonah: He despised the mercy that God showed him. He did not allow it to register in his heart. He did not take it seriously.

The tender mercies of God that have been shown to you should break your hardened heart. It should strip you of any unforgiveness you might nurture. It should soften you and make you more patient regarding the sufferings of others. And when you see people trapped in sin, it should cause you to say, "But for the grace of God, that could have been me."

God, forgive us!

———

That is what we all are. God is not done with you; he is not done with me. He is showing you and me mercy and kindness so that it can flow out of you and me to people who do not yet know him, to sinners of all kinds. The Lord does not fight with the weapons with which the enemy fights. Our God is a God of love who combats the hatred and bitterness of the world with love and tender mercy.[343]

And he is shaping us so that we too may have a tender, gentle spirit.

Would you soften our hearts, oh God?

343 2 Corinthians 1:3

25

Are You Mad at God?

There is nothing more dangerous to a Christian than to carry around resentment against God. Yet I am shocked by the growing number of believers—even ministers in many denominations—who hold some kind of grudge against God.

Why? Based on the fact that God has not answered a particular prayer or has not acted on their behalf, they are convinced God does not care.

They become disillusioned, burned out, and angry with God. They walk away from their calling saying, "I did everything right, but nothing turned out the way I had hoped. I was faithful, but God failed me."

≡ ≡

I once read a memoir called *One Witness*.[344] The story illustrates the destructive power of holding a grudge against God. It is the story of two Swedish couples—David and Svea Flood and Joel and Bertha Erickson—who in 1921 answered God's call to missions in the Belgian Congo.[345]

---

344 Aggie Hurst (1986). *One Witness*. FH Revell Co.
345 The Belgian Congo later became known as Zaire and finally as the Democratic Republic of the Congo, the DRC.

Once they arrived in the Congo, they hiked a hundred miles into the heart of the Congo, using machetes to hack their way to the village where they had planned to work.

David and Svea had a two-year-old son, David Jr., whom they had to carry on their backs. Along the way, both families caught malaria, but they kept going.

When they finally reached the village, the local people would not let them enter. "We can't allow any white people here," they protested. "Our gods will be offended."

The Swedes went to a second village where they were once again rejected. With no other villages nearby, they hacked out a clearing in the jungle and built mud huts. This would be their home.

As the months went by, they had almost no interaction with any of the locals. The Swedes suffered from loneliness, various diseases, and malnutrition. After six months, the Ericksons decided to return to the main mission station. They urged the Floods to do the same, but Svea was pregnant and her malaria was flaring up, so they opted to stay.

During that time, a little boy from a nearby village would often stop by. He would bring the family fruit, and Svea faithfully shared the gospel with him.

Svea eventually gave birth to a healthy baby girl, Aina, but days later, the young mother passed away.

David was badly shaken. "Why did you allow this, God?" he cried out in rage. "After more than a year in this jungle, all we have to show for it is one little village boy who probably does not even understand what we have told him. You have failed us, God. What a waste!"

With that, David took his children and made the journey back to the mission station where he announced that only he and his son would return to Sweden. He left Aina for the Ericksons to raise.

On the ship back to Stockholm, David seethed at God. He had come to Africa to win people to Christ, no matter what the cost. And now he was returning a broken man. David believed he had been faithful but that God had rewarded him with total neglect.

In Stockholm, if anyone mentioned God, David flew into a rage. He began drinking heavily and eventually married Svea's younger sister, who also had no heart for God.

Back in the Congo, the Ericksons got sick and died, and Aina was left in the care of Arthur and Anna Berg, American missionaries. They called her Aggie. Years later, the Bergs returned to America, taking Aggie with them. She grew up to marry a man named Dewey Hurst who later became president of a Bible college in Minneapolis.

Knowing that Aggie had tried to locate her father for forty years, the college gifted Dewey and Aggie with a trip to Sweden. Aggie had learned that her father had four sons and a daughter in Sweden, and they agreed to meet her.

On their way to Stockholm, the couple spent a day in London. Strolling through the city, they passed by the Royal Albert Hall where they discovered a missions convention was being held. They went inside and heard an African preacher testifying of the great works God was doing in the DRC—the former Belgian Congo. After the meeting, Aggie asked the preacher whether he ever met the missionaries David and Svea Flood.

"Svea Flood led me to the Lord when I was just a boy," he told Aggie. "They had a baby girl, but I don't know what happened to her."

"I am the girl!" Aggie exclaimed. "I am Aina!"

The preacher hugged Aggie, weeping with joy. The little boy Svea had ministered to had grown up to be a powerful evangelist in the Congo.

The next day, Aggie and Dewey left for Stockholm. Her siblings greeted Aggie at a hotel. Her brother David was also there, but he was an embittered man who had destroyed his life with alcohol.

When Aggie asked about their father, her brothers admitted that none of them had talked to him in years. They all hated him. Still, Aggie's sister agreed to take her to see their father. Liquor bottles were strewn about the apartment where Aggie found her father lying on a cot.

"Dad," Aggie said, "I'm your little girl, the one you left in Africa."

With tears in his eyes, the old man confessed, "I never meant to give you away."

"That's okay," Aggie assured him. "God took care of me."

"God betrayed us!" David spewed. "Nothing came of our time in Africa. It was a waste of our lives!"

When Aggie told her father about the Congolese preacher and how the country had been evangelized through him, the Holy Spirit fell on David. Tears of sorrow and repentance flowed down his face, and God restored him.

Shortly after their meeting, David Flood died. Sadly, other than Aggie, his children were all embittered unbelievers.

Like David Flood, the prophet Jonah received a missionary call from God. He went to Nineveh to preach the message of judgment God had given him: The city would be destroyed.

After delivering the message, Jonah sat on a hillside, waiting for God to begin the destruction. But nothing happened. Nineveh had repented, so God changed his mind about destroying the city.

This enraged Jonah. "Ah, Lord, was not this what I said when I was still in my country? Therefore I fled previously to Tarshish; for I know that you are a gracious and merciful God, slow to anger and abundant in lovingkindness, One who relents from doing harm. Therefore now, O Lord, please take my life from me, for it is better for me to die than to live!"[346]

Peeved, Jonah sat under the hot sun, pouting. Yet, in his mercy, God caused a plant to spring up to shelter Jonah from the heat to be a shadow over his head, to deliver him from his grief.[347]

Jonah was grieved because things had not gone as planned. Jonah's pride had been wounded. This is where most rage against God begins—with disappointment.

God may call you, burden you, and send you. But he may also change the plans. And when things do not go as *you* had planned, you can feel misled or betrayed.

If you continue nursing an angry spirit, it will grow into a rage. And God will ask you the same question he asked Jonah: "Do you think you have a right to be so angry?"[348]

Vexed, irritated, and full of rage at God, Jonah told God, "I do not care whether I live or die. My ministry is a failure. And all my suffering has been in vain. I have every right to be angry!"[349]

Many Christians are like Jonah. "I pray, I read my Bible, and I obey God's Word," they claim. "So, why has all this trouble fallen on my life? Why do I not see the blessings God promised me? He has failed me!"

---

346 Jonah 4:2–3
347 Jonah 4:6
348 Jonah 4:4, 9
349 Jonah 4:8–9, paraphrased

It is possible to reach a point where nothing and no one can console you. Jeremiah wrote, "A voice was heard in Ramah, lamentation, and bitter weeping, Rachel weeping for her children, refusing to be comforted for her children, because they are no more."[350]

Israel was being led away into captivity. Their homes had been burned and destroyed and all their vineyards laid to waste. Jerusalem was reduced to a pile of rubble. So Jeremiah used Rachel as a weeping figure who was so distraught at seeing her children taken from her that nothing can comfort her.

Jeremiah was saying that the mourning Israelites had settled into their grief, and they were beyond all consolation. Jeremiah could not comfort them; there was no use even trying to talk to them. In their minds, God had allowed captivity to overtake them—and they had a right to be bitter toward him.

Here is the danger: **When you harbor questions and complaints for too long, they turn into irritation. The irritation turns into bitterness. And, finally, bitterness turns into rage. At that point, you no longer listen to reproof.**

Once you reach a point of rage against God, no one can reach you. You shut out the wooing of the Spirit.

God's Word says there is hope, though. Jeremiah said, "Stop crying. Stop complaining. I will reward you for your faithfulness!"[351]

Similarly, the apostle Paul reminds you that your labor is not in vain in the Lord.[352]

Your pain and tears have been for a purpose. You may see only ruin in your life, but God sees restoration. God says, "You think it is over. You see only your failures. So, you say, 'This is the end.' But I say it is the beginning! I see the reward that I am about to pour out on you."

As the rewarder of them who diligently seek him,[353] God has wonderful things in mind for you. Allow God's Spirit to heal you of all bitterness, anger, and rage before it destroys you. Let him restore you now from the desolation surrounding you.

---

350 Jeremiah 31:15
351 Jeremiah 31:16, paraphrased
352 1 Corinthians 15:58
353 Hebrews 11:6

26

God Has Not Forgotten You

Have you ever experienced what they call the blues? It starts not just with one issue; it comes from so many things hitting from all sides all at once, and you cannot explain it. Out of nowhere, despair befalls you, leaving you so concerned about things that are happening around you that you cannot sleep at night.

I believe that was what Asaph was talking about when he said, "God you are keeping my eyes open, I cannot even close my eyes. Because of what happened to me, I cannot even be comforted."[354]

Asaph was a musician. He was a singer and David's choir director. A man of prayer, Asaph wrote twelve Psalms.[355] And as a choir director, Asaph would also have been familiar with the songs composed by David, including David's declarations of God's faithfulness when he said, "I waited patiently for the Lord; and he inclined to me, and heard my cry. He also brought me up out of a horrible pit, out of the miry clay, and set my feet upon a rock, and established my steps,"[356] and "I sought the Lord and he heard me and he delivered me from all my fears.... The eyes of the Lord are upon the righteous. His ears are open to their cry."[357]

---

354 Psalm 77:1–11, paraphrased
355 Asaph wrote Psalm 50, 73–83.
356 Psalm 40:1–2
357 Psalm 34:4, 15

Nevertheless, Asaph faced a trial that brought him down to the depths of despair. He wrote, "I cried out to God with my voice—to God with my voice; and he gave ear to me. In the day of my trouble I sought the Lord; my hand was stretched out in the night without ceasing; my soul refused to be comforted. I remembered God, and was troubled; I complained, and my spirit was overwhelmed."[358]

We all face challenges, as have all godly men and women over the years. Even the apostle Paul experienced despair. In his letter to the Corinthians, Paul wrote, "For we do not want you to be ignorant, brethren, of our trouble which came to us in Asia: that we were burdened beyond measure, above strength, so that we despaired even of life."[359] In other words, Paul and his companions desired to die because they could not understand why God allowed their suffering.

Perhaps you can relate to what Asaph and Paul were saying. Perhaps you are being pressed beyond comprehension and you are despairing of life—and not just for a day or two. Paul was pressed beyond endurance, as was Jesus. When Jesus was facing the cross, he said, "My soul is exceedingly sorrowful."[360]

These were the very words of Jesus Christ who, before the world was created, had made a covenant with the Father regarding a plan of salvation for mankind. Jesus knew full well this plan included dying on the cross so mankind could be reconciled with God.

Still, Jesus said, "I am troubled," and on the cross, he cried out, "My God, my God, why have you forsaken me?"[361]

Jesus was being tested. He was in pain. And despite having known for all time that his suffering was God's plan,[362] in the moment of pain Jesus asked, "Why?" This was not an inquiry into God's purposes but a cry of anguish for feeling like the Father had forsaken him.

Had Job lived *after* Jesus's time on earth, he may have been able to find hope in Jesus's suffering. God allowed the enemy to test Job, and amid his trials, Job asked,

358 Psalm 77:1–3
359 2 Corinthians 1:8
360 Mark 14:34
361 Matthew 27:46
362 Mark 8:31

"Your hands shaped me and made me. Will you now turn and destroy me?... Why did you bring me out of the womb?"[363]

===

When you experience a time of despair and someone asks you why you are down, you may find that you have no words, no explanation. Like Asaph, you might not understand what you are going through. This may lead to sleeplessness.

"I cry to the Lord. I pray into the night and I know he hears me," Asaph said, "But I see no answer to my prayer."[364] Asaph knew that God answered the prayers of Job, David, Israel, and others, but for some reason, God was not answering his cry for help.

There is nothing that adds to despair than to believe God hears you but will not answer you. Asaph went on to say, "I keep remembering my walk with the Lord. I keep remembering the songs that I have sung and I remember all the times I have spent with the Lord and I remember all the good things he has done for me in the past."[365]

Still, Asaph could not pull himself out of despair because he believed that what he was up against was worse than anything he had gone through. So, he cried out, "Will the Lord cast off forever? And will he be favorable no more? Has his mercy ceased forever? Has his promise failed forevermore? Has God forgotten to be gracious? Has he in anger shut up his tender mercies?"[366]

Asaph was saying, in essence, "I was so close to God, I walked with him, and I knew such communion with him—but now I wonder, God where are you? Why are you distant?"

After pouring his heart out in desperation, **Asaph seemed to have a change of heart by choosing to remember the greatness of God.** "But I will remember the years of the right hand of the Most High," he declared. "I will remember the works of the Lord...Who is so great a God as our God?"[367] Like-

363 Job 10:8, 18
364 Psalm 77:1, 7–10a, paraphrased
365 Psalm 77:10–20, paraphrased
366 Psalm 77:7–9
367 Psalm 77:10–11, 13

wise, Job's life was restored when he declared that God's purposes were beyond man's understanding.[368]

For Job, Asaph, and David, **God allowed them to go through hard times as a path to total deliverance so the enemy could not shake their faith again.** They had seen God bring them through the valley of the shadow of death in the past. They knew that they could trust God again.

So can you and I. There is no denying that there is darkness in this world, but you and I can find solace in the fact that Jesus knows our despair. Despite facing death on a cross, Jesus chose to go through the darkest hour so that he might conquer death. **In the middle of despair, we may not understand why we are facing what we are, but we can look back and remember God's faithfulness in the past. And we can choose to trust him again.**

I believe we can also find encouragement in the life and words of Paul who told the church in Rome, "we glory in tribulations, knowing that tribulation produces perseverance; and perseverance, character; and character, hope. Now hope does not disappoint, because the love of God has been poured out in our hearts by the Holy Spirit who was given to us."[369]

To the church in Corinth, Paul said that "no one knows the things of God except the Spirit of God."[370] **I believe Paul is saying that when you are going through despair, as you hunger and thirst after God, he will produce in you perseverance, character, and hope.** And when others ask the reason for the hope you have, you can point them to Christ, your reason for hope.[371]

Paul suggests that when the Holy Spirit opens your eyes, you would be able to testify that God had not forgotten you, that he "comforts us in all our tribulation, that we may be able to comfort those who are in any trouble, with the comfort with which we ourselves are comforted by God. For as the sufferings of Christ abound in us, so our consolation also abounds through Christ."[372]

---

368 Job 42:2, 10
369 Romans 5:3–4
370 1 Corinthians 2:11
371 1 Peter 3:14–16
372 2 Corinthians 1:4–5

Did you get that? **Paul is saying that the more you suffer, the more you can offer comfort to those in need. People's eternal future hangs on your seeing and understanding that God has allowed your suffering so you can console another.**

═ ═ ═

My daughter, Debbie, and her husband, Roger, lost their twelve-year-old to brain cancer. Some time later, Debbie was in a mall, and there was a woman with tears streaming down her face. Debbie went up to her and asked if she could help her.

"I lost my child to cancer," the woman said through her tears. And there in the middle of a mall, Debbie was able to share her own loss of a child and bring comfort to a perfect stranger.

The incident reminds me of Paul's words, "Blessed be the God and Father of our Lord Jesus Christ, the Father of mercies and God of all comfort, who comforts us in all our tribulation, that we may be able to comfort those who are in any trouble, with the comfort with which we ourselves are comforted by God."[373]

Because of what Debbie had gone through, because she had experienced God's comfort, she could encourage someone else. Since then, she has ministered to countless parents around the world who have lost a child. Debbie can talk to them, she can comfort them. I cannot, but Debbie can.

And because of what you are going through, you may be able to minister to and encourage folks that no preacher could talk to. I believe the Lord is saying to you, "I am teaching you how to comfort others."

═ ═ ═

Remember how Paul told the Corinthians how he had despaired even of life? That was not the end. He went on to say to them, "Yes, we had the sentence of death in ourselves, that we should not trust in ourselves but in God who raises the dead, who delivered us from so great a death, and does deliver us; in whom we trust that he will still deliver us."[374]

---

373 1 Corinthians 1:3–4
374 2 Corinthians 1:9–10

And there you have it. **We all go through hard times so we may be reminded not to trust in ourselves but instead to trust in the God who can overcome all suffering, even death—in the past, in our present, and whatever the future may hold.**

That is what your suffering is all about. God has not forgotten you, nor has he forgotten those who will turn to you to comfort them.

27

The Ministry of Refreshing Others

Some think of the apostle Paul as superhuman because of his powerful writings and marvelous ministry. If Paul were not subject to the same temptations and trials as we are, though, he would have nothing to say to the church. His letters would have been written in vain.

In fact, Paul wrote many of his epistles during the most difficult times of his life. He confessed to the church in Corinth that he experienced times of deep trouble and mental anguish. "Outside were conflicts, inside were fears," Paul wrote when he was in Macedonia.[375]

He had gone there feeling downcast, ineffective, and rejected by the church having just written his first letter to the Corinthians. His letter contained a difficult message—addressing fornication—and for a season afterward, Paul regretted sending it. He worried how the Corinthians might respond.

Paul had also learned that false prophets were creeping into the Corinthian church. Wanting to chip away at his spiritual authority, they must have said of him, "If God is truly with this man, then why is he being thrown into prison?"

Yet Paul did not repent of sending the letter to the Corinthians. Instead, he instructed Titus to go to Corinth and explain the purpose behind his message. "Tell

---

375 2 Corinthians 7:5

the people I love them and meant them no harm, but that this situation has to be dealt with. Then meet me in Troas."[376]

After sending Titus on his mission, Paul set out for Troas, stopping along the way in Ephesus. God moved powerfully through Paul there, and his preaching moved multitudes. Many who heard his message rushed home to fetch their occult books, then gathered in the city center to burn them in a huge bonfire.[377]

This stirred up the silversmiths of Ephesus, who made most of their income from fashioning idols of the goddess Diana. With their trade being threatened, they rose up in wrath against Paul, sparking a massive riot. Paul narrowly escaped with his life.[378]

Paul's experience in Ephesus caused him to be "burdened beyond measure, above strength, so that we despaired even of life."[379] As he headed to Troas, persecuted, perplexed, cast down in spirit, he longed to see Titus so he could unburden his heart and learn the impact his letter had on the Corinthians.

Yet when Paul arrived in Troas, Titus was not there. Doors of ministry opened up for Paul in Troas, but by this time his heart had grown weary, so Paul did something he had never done—he walked away, wandering to Macedonia.[380]

That is what Satan does. He attacks us when we are weary from battle and vulnerable to his lies. I imagine the devil whispering, "God is no longer with you, Paul. You have been rejected in Asia. There is not one person left who stands with you. Even Titus has been infested with doubts by your opponents in Corinth. You are not loved, and you are no longer needed."

Here was a man so deeply weary that he was no longer himself. Paul was at the darkest time of his ministry, yet within a few short hours, he was completely out of that dark pit and reveling in joy and gladness.

How did this happen? First, when Titus arrived in Corinth to meet with the church leaders, he was refreshed learning of the awakening that was taking place in the church. Because they had heeded Paul's instruction, God was blessing them mightily.

If the Lord would have pulled back the curtain and shown Paul what was really happening, if he could have witnessed the revival taking place because of his mes-

---

376 2 Corinthians 2:1–13, paraphrased
377 Acts 19:11–20
378 Acts 19:23–41
379 2 Corinthians 1:8
380 2 Corinthians 2:12–13

sage, he would have seen Satan's lies exposed. He would have been reminded that God's thoughts toward him were good thoughts, that it was all a part of his plan.

However, after sinking into even deeper despair, waiting in Macedonia, God comforted Paul through Titus coming with encouraging news: "Paul, the brethren in Corinth send you their love. They have removed the sin that was in their midst and dealt with the false prophets. They no longer despise your sufferings, but instead, rejoice in your testimony."[381]

This refreshing word, brought by a dear brother in the Lord, lifted Paul out of his pit: "Nevertheless God, who comforts the downcast," Paul declared, "comforted us by the coming of Titus."[382] As the two friends had fellowship, joy flooded through Paul's body, mind, and spirit. Though he still faced problems, the Lord had given him what he needed for the battle.

God uses people to refresh people. Titus, having been refreshed by the news he received, in turn, refreshed Paul's spirit. This illustrates a glorious pattern that appears throughout Scripture.

In Acts 27, Paul was on a ship headed for Rome when the vessel came to a stop at Sidon. Paul asked the centurion in charge for permission to visit some friends in the city, and "Julius ... gave *him* liberty to go to his friends and receive care."[383] Here is yet another instance of God using believers to refresh other believers.

We see this also in 2 Timothy, where Paul writes of a certain believer: "The Lord grant mercy to the household of Onesiphorus, for he often refreshed me, and was not ashamed of my chain; but when he arrived in Rome, he sought me out very zealously and found me ... and you know very well how many ways he ministered to me at Ephesus."[384]

Onesiphorus was also one of Paul's spiritual sons, and he loved Paul so deeply and unconditionally that he sought him out in his sufferings. Once, when Paul was jailed, Onesiphorus went through the city looking for him until he found him. His motivation was simply that his brother was hurting. "He has suffered the terrors of shipwreck, and now he is being buffeted by Satan. I have to find him to encourage him."[385]

---

381 2 Corinthians 7:8–16, paraphrased
382 2 Corinthians 7:6
383 Acts 27:3
384 2 Timothy 1:16–18
385 2 Timothy 1:16–18

The ministry of refreshing includes seeking out those who are hurting. These days, we hear a lot of talk about power in the church. The power to heal the sick, the power to win the lost, the power to overcome sin. But I say **there is a great, healing power that flows out of a refreshed and renewed person.** Depression, mental anguish, or a troubled spirit can cause all kinds of physical sickness, but a spirit that is refreshed and encouraged—one that is made to feel accepted, loved, and needed—is the healing balm needed most.

We find this ministry of refreshing in the Old Testament as well. When David was being hunted down by King Saul, he was exhausted and hurting, forced to run day and night. During that time, he felt rejected by God's leaders and God's people.

At a crucial moment, though, David's friend Jonathan came to him: "Jonathan … strengthened his hand in God. And he said to him, 'Do not fear, for the hand of Saul my father shall not find you. You shall be king over Israel, and I shall be next to you.' "[386]

This word of refreshing could not have been timelier for David. He had just endured a horrendous rejection after performing a selfless act of kindness. David and his men had risked their lives to save the village of Keilah, and for a while, they found refuge there.[387] Yet later, when Saul was on the move, David prayed, "Lord, will these people turn me over to Saul?" God answered him, "Yes, they will reject you. Leave the town now."[388]

In a psalm David wrote during that time, he revealed just how downcast his soul was. He cried out continually, "God, where are you?"[389]

Consider also Jonathan's painful trial over his evil, possessed father. Yet this godly friend "strengthened David's hand in the Lord," telling him, "The Lord is with you, David, and you are still loved in Israel. You may not feel like it now, but you will be king. Your work has just begun."[390]

That was all David needed to hear. His spirit was immediately refreshed to go on.

---

386 1 Samuel 23:16–17
387 1 Samuel 23:5
388 1 Samuel 23:12
389 Psalm 22:1
390 1 Samuel 23:17, paraphrased

——— ═ ═ ———

Make no mistake: God uses people to refresh other people. He so loves this kind of ministry that he moved the prophet Malachi to point to it as a most-needed work in the last days. God's people had grown weary. They started to doubt that walking with the Lord was worth it.

But the Spirit of God began to move in Israel, and soon, the fear of the Lord came upon a God-hungry people. By the Spirit's prompting, people opened up to one another, edifying each other, and building up and comforting those around them.[391]

Malachi's word about this ministry is a mirror image of the present day. He has given us a picture of an outpouring of the Holy Spirit in the last days, as God's people stop gossiping and complaining and, instead, minister refreshment to those who are weary.

——— ═ ═ ———

Get your eyes off your situation. Stop trying to please God by planning something great. Instead, **get up and seek out whom you can encourage today.**

There are people who need you. Call someone today and encourage them by praying for them. Be a Titus to someone who is downcast in spirit. Pray to have the spirit of an Onesiphorus, who sought out the hurting to bring them healing.

---

391 Malachi 3:16

28

Beware of Dogs

"**B**eware of dogs, beware of evil workers, beware of the mutilation!" the apostle Paul warned Christians in Philippi in an otherwise tender letter.[392] Paul did not usually practice senseless name-calling, but when it came to defending the truth of the gospel of Christ, he had no qualms with facing down anyone who twisted the message of the cross. Hence, Paul stood up to the teachers who were saying that followers of Jesus had to act according to the law of Moses and be circumcised.

These teachers were former Pharisees, teachers of the law. Paul himself was a Pharisee, something of which he reminds the readers.[393]

He knew very well that in the early church, these converts among the religious leaders played a crucial role in teaching young followers of the Way of Jesus about the significance of the ways in which Christ fulfilled the Scriptures' prophecies, proving he was the long-awaited Messiah.[394]

On the subject of justification, these Jewish Christians taught that you had to come to Christ by faith. But then they added, "You are also to observe the law to mortify your flesh. This is the only way to please God."[395]

---

392 Philippians 3:2
393 Philippians 3:5; Paul continued to call himself a Pharisee after coming to Christ (Acts 23:6)
394 Acts 15:5
395 When these teachers referred to the law, they meant the ceremonial laws of Moses, which included some 400 rules and regulations. They were telling young converts they had to observe

Paul refuted this. He told them, "You are trying to beat down your lusts with rules and regulations. But you are only mutilating your flesh! You are practicing a gospel of *debt*, not of grace. If you could justify yourself through good works, why would you need grace, the cross, the sacrifice of Christ? Salvation is by grace alone, through faith, lest anyone should boast."[396]

$$=\!\!=\ =\!\!=$$

Paul similarly took on the apostle Peter about some discrepancies in his actions when it came to the subject of circumcision. Paul pointed out that when the visiting Jews were not around, Peter freely ate and worshipped with the gentile converts. But whenever the Jews were present, Peter dined with the Jews at a separate table, refusing to associate with the gentiles on account of them not being circumcised.

The Spirit of God stirred Paul to stand up for the truth of the gospel. He told Peter, Barnabas, and the other Jewish believers who despised gentiles, "You are not walking according to the truth of the gospel that you know. You have turned away from our Lord's gospel of grace to practice justification by works. You are frustrating the grace of God—and you are wrong!"[397]

In fact, these men were practicing an anti-grace gospel that resulted in the fracturing of the church.[398] Earlier in that letter, Paul lamented how quickly these Christians were turning from the grace of Christ and turning to a perverted gospel,[399] one that promoted confidence in human efforts.

"Do not listen to those who try to tell you that you can mortify your sins by your efforts," Paul wrote at the conclusion of his letter. "Such people always urge you to work harder at perfecting holiness. But the truth is, they have never once succeeded at living by their own rules and regulations. Their flesh is circumcised, but their hearts never have been!"[400]

---

all of Israel's dos and don'ts to please God.
396 Ephesians 2:9, paraphrased
397 After the council in Jerusalem (Acts 15), Peter went to Antioch. In Galatians 2:11–13, Paul confronts him to his face for his hypocrisy that had caused division among believers.
398 Galatians 2:11–21
399 Galatians 1:6–7
400 Galatians 6:12–13, paraphrased

Paul knew that there is *nothing* we can do to win God's favor.[401] On more than one occasion, he wrote about trying to please God, concluding, "When it came to relying on the flesh to gain God's favor, I outdid everybody. Today, I can say that being blameless concerning the law never did me any good. With all of my fleshly self-confidence and human effort, I missed Christ!"[402]

Paul gives us his secret to knowing and winning Christ. "What things were gain to me, these I have counted loss for Christ," he tells us. "Yet indeed I also count all things loss for the excellence of the knowledge of Christ Jesus my Lord, for whom I have suffered the loss of all things, and count them as rubbish, that I may gain Christ."[403]

Paul is not talking about the loss of material things. Rather, he is saying, "I have given up all confidence in my own efforts. I have quit all hope of pleasing God on my own!"

Paul recognized that to know Christ, he had to submit to God's righteousness.[404] He explained that any efforts to *produce* righteousness were futile without the Spirit. But once a person has the Spirit, that person had to "work out your own salvation with fear and trembling."[405] He also added that the believer had to place all of his faith in Christ's work for him so he could be "found in him, not having my own righteousness, which is from the law, but that which is through faith in Christ, the righteousness which is from God by faith."[406]

Where are you on this matter? Have you suffered the loss of all confidence in your flesh? Have you come to the point that Paul did, repudiating all hope of pleasing God through striving? Have you given up trying to conquer your sin and lust by self-will and determination?

Until you give up all hope of improving your flesh, you will be doomed to a million broken vows. You will be plagued by failure after failure, a river of tears, continual guilt, and condemnation.

---

401 Philippians 3:3
402 Philippians 3:4–13; Romans 7:15–20; 1 Timothy 1:15; 1 Corinthians 2:2, paraphrased
403 Philippians 3:7–8
404 Romans 10:3
405 Philippians 2:12
406 Philippians 3:9

Any victory you win by your strength or willpower will only turn you into a proud, judgmental hypocrite. Sin will still be at your door, and before long you will fall again.

Perhaps you are tired of constantly being on the merry-go-round of sin and confess, sin and confess, weary of summoning all your willpower, trying your hardest—even promising God you will not go down the same path of sin again—and thinking you have finally conquered sin... only to fall flat on your face again.

I have heard from countless Christians who struggle with a besetting sin in their life, desperate for help. Letter after letter, these individuals would pour out their hearts, sharing how hard they have tried to break their sin patterns.

To them, I say: **You must abandon the gospel of works and accept the gospel of grace.**

If you could reach deep into your soul and find the inner strength to overcome every wicked thought, and if you could summon the willpower and fortitude to free *yourself* from every habit and bondage so no past sin could hold you, you would boast, "I made it. I am free! There is nothing evil or unclean in me."

And if you could fulfill all the demands of the law by your own ability, you would come to God as a proud boaster, saying, "Who needs grace? I have justified myself. Christ died in vain!"

To this, Paul answers, "Righteousness is a gift, and it cannot be gained any way other than through faith."[407]

While you may agree, it may be your experience that despite trying to live out this truth, you keep falling back into your old ways.

I get it. I have been down that road at various times in my life, finding that the very act of trying to live by faith became a work of the flesh.

== ==

How is it, then, that God requires only faith and not works? God the Father and Christ the Son made an agreement—a covenant. God agreed that if Christ offered himself as a sacrifice for all sin, God would show mercy, love, and kindness, not only to his Son but also to humankind. The prophet Isaiah described it as fol-

---

407 Romans 3:21–22, 28

lows: "I, the Lord, have called you in righteousness, and will hold your hand; I will keep you and give you as a covenant to the people, as a light to the gentiles..."[408]

God was saying to his Son, "If you will take on human nature and become humankind's mediator, I promise to hold you and keep you every day. I will be responsible to keep you while you are on earth and bring you back to glory. No power in hell will be able to hold you. I will carry you through it all."

What's more, God added, "Not only will I hold you and keep you from the enemy as long as you are in human flesh. I will also make the same promise to everyone who trusts in you. Because they are all gathered up in you, I will count them as one party with you in this covenant. And no matter how badly they sin or fall, they can return to my mercy and grace."[409]

And so it was that Christ agreed to come to earth. He was obedient and fulfilled every command of the law. In doing so, the covenant was ratified by his blood. As a result of this covenant, Jesus tells us, "If you will trust in me, you will share in my obedience. And **when I present my obedience to the Father, he will recognize it as *your* obedience too.**"[410]

——

Just as Jesus kept the covenant with his Father, obeying him alone, he asks you to do the same with him. "Abide in me, and I in you...for without me you can do nothing,"[411] Jesus declared, inviting you to lay all our guilt, strivings, and burdens on him.[412]

God is reaching out his hand to you, saying, "Lay hold of this covenant. It is meant for you!" Once you lay hold of the covenant, your obedience to God is not for the purpose of being accepted by him; it is your gift of grateful love to him.[413]

Instead of striving in your weak flesh, through faith in Christ, you receive mercy, grace, and blessing.

---

408 Isaiah 42:6–7
409 Psalm 89:27–34, paraphrased
410 Romans 3:21–26; Galatians 3:20; Paul does not state that God will recognize Jesus' obedience as our obedience (without *us* actually obeying) but that we will obey the way Jesus did because the Spirit will guide us.
411 John 15:4–5
412 Jude 24
413 John 14:15

Beware of those trying to convince you to *do more* or *try harder.*

Do not turn to a perverted gospel. Instead, hold on to God's covenant.

29

Overcoming Wild Donkeys

There are thousands of Christians who are waging a losing battle against overpowering lust and lingering habits they cannot seem to get victory over. Their lust and habits are constantly driving them.

Over the years, I have heard from countless men and women who were struggling. Men have even come forward confessing their addiction to pornography, weeping, saying, "Brother David, I do not know why I do it. I sit there hating it but something picks me up and drives me right to it."

There was one drug addict who came to Teen Challenge. He had reached the point of despair. One day, he was lying there, dying, and still, he pulled a syringe of blood from his veins and sprayed it on the ceiling, writing, "HELP!"

"Where is God in all of this?" you may wonder.

"If there cannot be absolute victory over sin, then this Bible is a lie, and everything we have been doing is a hoax. We might as well shut down the church and never believe again."

Not so fast. There are countless people who have been delivered from drugs, alcohol, sexual habits, and lust of all kinds—men and women who are no longer fighting their problems. They are completely free!

How did they get free? Did God love them any more than he loves you who are struggling with sin patterns? No.

If you were to ask those who have been delivered from bondage to tell you how they got free, they would tell you it was through repentance. They would also talk to you about reading their Bibles, becoming lost in the Word of God. They would talk to you about their renewed prayer life. They would talk about studying the Bible and witnessing to others about the freedom they found.

$$= = =$$

To walk in freedom, you have to be delivered from the spirit of a wild donkey. Through the prophet Jeremiah, God talks about this in no uncertain terms, saying, "You are a wild donkey accustomed to the wilderness, that sniffs the wind in her passion. Who can turn her away in her mating season? None who seek her will grow weary; in her month they will find her."[414]

The passage goes on, with God essentially saying, "Look, I see you. You started out right. I planted you as a pure vine. Everything was right when you gave your heart to me. You began right. How did you become degenerate? How did you give yourself over to your lust?"[415]

Earlier in that same chapter, God reminds his people of the devotion of their youth, how they followed him in the wilderness as the first fruits of his harvest.[416] But then they turned to doing tragic things to themselves, changing gods. "My people have changed their glory for what does not profit.... For my people have committed two evils: They have forsaken me, the fountain of living waters, and hewn themselves cisterns—broken cisterns that can hold no water."[417]

God even says they should be appalled at what they have been doing.[418] "My bride to be is cheating on me," God laments, "prostituting herself."[419]

$$= = =$$

---

414 Jeremiah 2:24 NASB
415 Jeremiah 2:21–25, paraphrased
416 Jeremiah 2:2–3
417 Jeremiah 2:11, 13
418 Jeremiah 2:12
419 Jeremiah 2:20 NASB, paraphrased

People are preaching a gospel in America about so-called freedom. Christians all over the country are doing whatever their hearts desire, doing things that just a few years ago would have made him blush. And they call it freedom.

I say to you, that is not freedom. That is the spirit of the wild donkey. What a vivid picture of a Christian who is still ruled by a secret passion, having affairs and all manner of sexual entanglement, driven by this lust for, what, ten minutes of pleasure? And then comes the shame and the hopelessness.

"We lie down in our shame, and our reproach covers us," Jeremiah says.[420] "For we have sinned against the Lord our God, we and our fathers, from our youth even to this day, and have not obeyed the voice of the Lord our God."

Hear this: When you have given into your sin and the spirit of the wild donkey has driven you back to your lust, you will do one of two things. **You will either harden your heart and give yourself over to this hardness, having no fear of God in you,**[421] **or you will repent.**

If you choose to harden your heart, God will take his hand from you. Jeremiah warns us, "Hear this now, O foolish people, without understanding, who have eyes and see not, and who have ears and hear not: 'Do you not fear me?' says the Lord. 'Will you not tremble at my presence?'… But this people has a defiant and rebellious heart, they have revolted and departed. They do not say in their heart, 'Let us now fear the Lord our God, who gives rain, both the former and the latter, in its season. He reserves for us the appointed weeks of the harvest.' Your iniquities have turned these things away, and your sins have withheld good from you."[422]

Later in the same book, Jeremiah says, "And I will make an everlasting covenant with them, that I will not turn away from doing them good; but **I will put my fear in their hearts so that they will not depart from me.**"[423]

Fear the Lord your God. Let him be your fear.[424]

420 Jeremiah 3:25
421 Jeremiah 2:19
422 Jeremiah 5:21–25
423 Jeremiah 32:40
424 Isaiah 8:13–15

I have these two fears in me, and I do not ever want these two fears to ever leave me—the fear of not spending eternity with Jesus, and the fear of eternal hell.

Let me be clear: I do not serve God only out of fear. **I love Jesus with all the love in my heart, and I obey him. But I have a deep fear of a holy God who means every word he says.**

Jesus talked about hell. He talked about the weeping and wailing and gnashing of teeth.[425] Why would there be weeping and wailing and gnashing of teeth? I believe it is because in hell there will be an ever-increasing knowledge that you are in the damnation of lostness.

"I am lost, and it will never end. I am lost. It will never change."

Jesus told the parable of the rich man who died and went to hell. The man prayed. All he wanted was for Lazarus to dip his finger in cool water and put it on the tip of his tongue. He was in such torment.[426]

This seems much like drinking the wine of the wrath of God, tormented with fire and brimstone in the presence of the holy angels and in the presence of the Lamb, as depicted in Revelation 14.[427]

Did you catch that? This is happening *in the presence of the Lord and the angels of heaven!*

There are people living right now on the face of this earth who are already in this kind of hell. Giving in to their lust, they are tormented. They need more and more, never being satisfied.

For the person living with the spirit of the wild donkey, having no fear of God, living under the bondage of lust, may the majesty of God grip your heart! **May you realize anew that you serve a God who is holy and worthy of being feared.** And when you stand before the throne of God, may he not cast you out of his presence.[428]

In prayer, you can come before the throne of God *today* with your hands raised to heaven, crying, "God, have mercy on me, a sinner."

That is the second option. The first was to harden your heart. The second is to fall face down at the feet of Jesus, crying for mercy, repenting.

425 Matthew 8:12; 13:42, 50; 22:13; 24:51; 25:30; Luke 13:28
426 Luke 16:19–31
427 Revelation 14:10
428 Jeremiah 23:39

Like David did after he had given in to the lust in his heart for Bathsheba, you can cry out, "Have mercy upon me, O God, according to your lovingkindness; according to the multitude of your tender mercies, blot out my transgressions. Wash me from my iniquity, and cleanse me from my sin."

David goes on to confess, "For I acknowledge my transgressions, and my sin is always before me. Against you, you only, have I sinned, and done this evil in your sight."[429]

Playing with God and playing with sin is no joke! It is a matter of life and death, and the consequence of sin is death—eternal death.[430]

Cry out to God with David,

> Create in me a clean heart, O God, and renew a steadfast spirit within me. Do not cast me away from your presence, and do not take your Holy Spirit from me. Restore to me the joy of your salvation.... Deliver me from the guilt of bloodshed, O God, the God of my salvation, and my tongue shall sing aloud of your righteousness. O Lord, open my lips, and my mouth shall show forth your praise. For you do not desire sacrifice, or else I would give it; you do not delight in burnt offering. The sacrifices of God are a broken spirit, a broken and contrite heart—these, O God, you will not despise.[431]

The prophet Isaiah tells us about a highway of holiness. No impure shall walk on it, and the Lord himself shall walk with us on that way.[432]

You can give in to your desires, or you can walk daily with God on the highway of holiness. You have a choice.

---

429 Psalm 51:1–4
430 Romans 6:23
431 Psalm 51:10–12, 14–17
432 Isaiah 35:8

30

Walking in the Power of the New Covenant

I n the Old Testament, it was the practice of godly men to lay hold of the covenant to find relief and strength in times of trouble. Take David for example. Even in his final days, he said, "Although my house is not so with God, yet he has made with me an everlasting covenant, ordered in all things and secure."[433]

What David was saying is that God had given him a promise that someday, his descendants will rule and reign on this earth. David was not thinking about his own name, but holding on to the words of the prophets, he was referring to the coming Messiah.[434]

And then there was Jacob whose father, Isaac, sent him away to find a wife. It was a long and dangerous journey, and Jacob had nothing but his walking stick when he crossed the Jordan.[435]

While it might seem like Isaac had sent Jacob away in poverty, in reality, he sent him with something far more valuable than any riches—a covenant blessing passed down from Jacob's grandfather, Abraham.

I picture Isaac laying his hands on Jacob's head saying, "You know how God had revealed himself to your grandfather as his shield. I now bless you with the knowl-

---

433 2 Samuel 23:5
434 Isaiah 11:1; Jeremiah 23:5
435 Genesis 28:1–3; 32:10

edge of whom God had shown himself to be to Abraham—not only his protector, but the very one who made a covenant with him."[436]

With that, Isaac laid his hand on Jacob's head, saying, "Cursed be everyone who curses you, and blessed be those who bless you."[437]

The knowledge of the covenant was passed down from Abraham to Isaac and now to Jacob. One of the nights along Jacob's journey, though, he had an encounter with God through a dream that made the covenant a reality to him. In the dream, he saw a ladder reaching all the way to heaven, with God standing at the top of the ladder.

"I am the Lord God of Abraham your father and the God of Isaac; the land on which you lie I will give to you and your descendants," God said to Jacob. "Also your descendants shall be as the dust of the earth; you shall spread abroad to the west and the east, to the north and the south; and in you and in your seed all the families of the earth shall be blessed. Behold, I am with you and will keep you wherever you go, and will bring you back to this land; for I will not leave you until I have done what I have spoken to you."[438]

No longer was knowledge of the covenant just hearsay. Jacob encountered the covenant-keeping God of his father and grandfather.

When mankind was just a thought in the heart of God—long before the creation of the world—the Father, Son, and the Holy Ghost made a covenant with each other regarding the salvation of mankind. Christ would be at the center of that plan.

Matthew says that the parables Jesus told were so that the prophecy would be fulfilled, that Jesus would "utter things kept secret from the foundation of the world."[439]

I believe Jesus would say, **"Everything I tell you was devised at a triune council before the world was created. I speak to you words that have come to me before the foundation of the world."**

But before Jesus would be incarnate in man to live out that which had been planned, the Holy Spirit would move upon certain men and they would reveal what

---

436 Genesis 15:1, 12–21
437 Genesis 27:29
438 Genesis 28:13–15
439 Matthew 13:35, referring to Psalm 78:2

was devised. John the Baptist would be sent to prepare the hearts of the people. And then Jesus would come to atone for the sins of the world.

So it came that after the birth of John the Baptist, his father, Zacharias, prophesied that the God who made a covenant with Abraham would save us so we can serve God without fear all the days of our life.[440]

No matter what comes, we need not fear. God is in control! That does not mean that the new covenant walk is one without suffering and trouble. **But if you are living with fear and dread, having no power to resist the enemy, then you are not walking in the new covenant.**

═ ═

The book of Hebrews says, "For this is the covenant that I will make with the house of Israel after those days, says the Lord: I will put my laws in their mind and write them on their hearts; and I will be their God, and they shall be my people."[441]

In other words, the God of Abraham is also your God and mine. **But the covenant he made with Abraham was connected to works. It had to do with striving to please God through human actions. Under the new covenant, we can rely on the work of Christ to bring us into right standing with God.**

How can you lay hold of the covenant? There are conditions.

First, you have to renounce your confidence to please God in the flesh.[442] You will not understand the new covenant until you come to the place where you realize that you cannot please God through striving, by working harder to live in right standing with God.

Instead of working harder, you are to respond in love. You and I have been created as an expression of God's love. And that is what the new covenant is all about—love. Christ came to prove the love of God.

By living a perfect life, Jesus would fulfill the old covenant, he would fulfill the law.[443] And when you stand before God, there will be no good works that will

---

440 Luke 1:68–75
441 Hebrews 8:10
442 Philippians 3:3–11
443 Galatians 3:10–13

bring any merit. I can imagine God saying to Jesus, "The only merit man can bring to my throne is *your* merit."

But what if you stray? I can imagine Jesus offering during the heavenly counsel, "I will go and find the lamb who has strayed. I will not rebuke him—I will neither chastise him nor beat him. Tenderly I will restore him to the fold."[444]

What if you fall into sin and are in despair? What if you are bound by habits and chains? Jesus would have said, "I will go and release them from their prisons by breaking every chain."[445]

I believe these were the kind of conversations held between the Father, Son, and Holy Spirit before the beginning of time. The covenant was planned in the heavenly counsel eons before God spoke creation into being. There is nothing in your life that God the Father, the Son, and the Holy Ghost did not take into consideration.

As for the Holy Ghost's role in the new covenant, he would have agreed that his mission would be to be poured out as power upon those who believe. He would be the power man needs to overcome sin and temptation.

The Holy Ghost in you is the very power of the living God. He has power over all sin, over human power, over the devil's power.

That is why Peter and John prayed for new believers to receive the Holy Ghost.[446] He comes in and sets up his power base in his temple—your body.[447] The Holy Ghost cannot do the work of strengthening you until you surrender your efforts of strengthening yourself.

I believe that is why many believers do not walk in the power of the new covenant—they are trying to do the work the Holy Ghost is meant to do. If that is you, tell the Lord, "Holy Spirit, I believe you can dwell in me, becoming the strength I need to overcome sin's grip on me. I have not yet experienced the fullness of your power, but you have made a covenant that includes me, so I will hold onto your promises!"

Do so, and the Holy Ghost will incline you toward obedience. He will prompt you, remind you, and invite you to surrender to God's love.

---

444 Alluding to Luke 15:4–6
445 Alluding to Isaiah 61:1–3, which was quoted by Jesus in Luke 4:18
446 Acts 8:14–17
447 1 Corinthians 6:19

How much more does our heavenly Father love you? No matter whether you are beaten up by sin, he says, "I am coming after you. I will never let you go."

God is not willing to let anyone perish.

The second condition to coming into the new covenant is that you have to have an affectionate response to the wooing of Christ. The prophet Hosea tells of God having just discovered the terrible lewdness of his people.

He begins to judge them. First, he takes all their joy away, then he dries up all their fields. But then, the heart of God is moved, and he says, "... I am now going to allure her; I will lead her into the wilderness and speak tenderly to her."[448]

That word *allure* means that she may not want to come, but God will entice her so he can restore her. I believe that is an invitation for us to respond to God in the same way he responds to us while we are still in sin. He comes to you with love. The only way to respond is in love.

Do you love God? Do you want to walk in the power of the new covenant? Then you have got to move out of the old covenant mindset. The old covenant has done its work if you can say, "I cannot do it in my strength. Lord, I come to you. I cast myself into your loving arms. Holy Spirit, be my strength."

It is about leaping out of a works mindset and trusting Jesus's promises, including his love for you. Then, when you sin again, you run to him. Run to his promise of forgiveness, allowing him to restore you.

---

448 Hosea 2:14 NIV

31

Taking Hold of the New Covenant

Throughout the Bible, there are references to God's covenant. Through the pen of the psalmist, God declares, "My covenant I will not break, nor alter the word that has gone out of my lips."[449]

A covenant is an agreement or pledge between two or more parties—a contract. And like any contract, a covenant contains terms or duties that each party has to perform to fulfill the agreement.

In the Old Testament (or old covenant), God makes one covenant after another with humankind. The New Testament (or new covenant) is marked by the coming of Christ as the new covenant.

Jeremiah tells us, "Behold, the days are coming, says the Lord, when I will make a new covenant with the house of Israel and with the house of Judah. ... I will put my laws in their mind and write them on their hearts; and I will be their God, and they shall be my people. ... For I will be merciful to their unrighteousness, and their sins and their lawless deeds I will remember no more."[450]

If you have faith in Jesus, you are considered the spiritual seed of Abraham. God, through Christ, made his new covenant with *spiritual* Israel—anyone born

---

449 Psalm 89:34
450 Jeremiah 31:31–34; also quoted in Hebrews 8:8–13; 10:16–17

again in Jesus. As a repentant believer in Christ, all of the promises of the new covenant are yours.[451]

——==——

God formed this covenant with his Son, Jesus, and they agreed to the terms before the very foundation of the world.[452] We are brought into it by faith.[453] Amazingly, this heavenly contract was not forged in secret. The Bible openly records the terms of the covenant so that we can be encouraged.

In the Psalms, we find an example of the discourse between Father and Son, with the Father saying, "This is a mysterious word I am about to give you. Because of their sin, mankind will become overwhelmed, helpless to find their way back to me. So, I am appointing you as my Holy One to help them. I am sending you to them as one mightier than they to bring them back into my favor."[454]

The Father was not willing to lose his beloved creation to the powers of hell. **The purpose of God's making of the new covenant was to recover a lost humanity from the devil's power.** He formed a rescue plan—one forged from love.

The Son responds, saying, "You have shown me that your help to humanity will be laid upon my shoulders. You are sending me to rescue the imprisoned, heal the hurting, break satanic strongholds and reconcile the creation back to you. I accept this charge to take on the redemption of the lost. And I accept the might and power you give me to accomplish the task."[455]

Everything Christ did on earth was in fulfillment of the covenant. He testified, "My food is to do the will of him who sent me, and to finish his work."[456] His every word and deed reflected what they had agreed upon before the world came into being. Therefore, Jesus said, "For I have not spoken on my own authority; but the Father who sent me

---

451 It is true that in many Bible passages, the word *Israel* refers to Jacob's natural descendants. Yet in others, it clearly points to God's spiritual seed.
The apostle Paul distinguishes between two kinds of Israel, one natural and one spiritual. Paul says it is not the natural Jew but the person who puts his faith in Jesus Christ who becomes Abraham's spiritual seed. Hebrews 8:8–13, 10:16–17; Romans 2:28–29; 9:6, 8; Galatians 3:7; 4:25–26

452 Titus 1:2; 2 Timothy 1:9

453 Hebrews 8:8–13, 10:16–17; Romans 2:28–29, 9:6; Galatians 3:7, 4:25–26; Romans 9:8

454 Psalm 89:19, paraphrased

455 Psalm 40:7–8, paraphrased

456 John 4:34

gave me a command, what I should say and what I should speak."[457] And, "For I have come down from heaven, not to do my own will, but the will of Him who sent me."[458] According to the terms of the covenant the Father had cut with his Son:

- Jesus was to divest himself of all his glory—to strip himself of all attributes of the Godhead.[459]
- He was to take on the form of a servant—one who was holy, blameless, and undefiled.[460]
- He was to endure sufferings, reproaches, and injustices. He would be called "a man of sorrows," someone acquainted with much grief.[461]
- He was to grow up in the presence of his heavenly Father "with no beauty or majesty," meaning he would be undesirable to the world.[462]

After all this, Christ was to humble himself, be placed in the hands of wicked men, and in great agony lay down his life as an offering for man's sin. In making atonement for all of humankind, he would have to endure God's wrath for a season.[463]

God had laid out before his Son the type of ministry he would have to undertake in order to redeem humankind. He told Jesus, "Your ministry will be that of a priest. I have known all of my children from the foundation of the world—forming their very members in their mothers' wombs, numbering the very hairs on their heads. And now I am giving all of them to you. They will be your flock, and you will be a shepherd to them. You will lead them beside still waters and into green pastures. You will walk with them through every shadow of death. And if any one of them ever goes astray, you will take him in your arms and bring him back to my love. You will restore his soul and bring him great comfort!"[464]

The Father also gave his Son these instructions: "You must preach good tidings to the meek, bind up the broken-hearted, proclaim liberty to the captives, open

---

457 John 12:49
458 John 6:38
459 Hebrews 10:5–7; Galatians 4:4
460 Philippians 2:7; Hebrews 4:15
461 Isaiah 53:3
462 Isaiah 53:2
463 Galatians 3:13–14; Matthew 17:22–23; 20:19; Luke 18:32–33, paraphrased
464 Jeremiah 1:5; Matthew 10:30–31; Luke 12:7; Ezekiel 34:12; Psalm 23:1–4; John 10:27–30; Luke 15:4–7, paraphrased

prison doors to all who are bound, bear with the weaknesses of the frail, not break a bruised reed, nor quench a smoking flame, bear tenderly with the ignorant, supply their shortcomings with your strength, feed the flock, gather all the lambs in your arms and carry them in your bosom, gently lead the young, lend your strength to the weak, guide them with your counsel, promise to send them the Holy Spirit to carry on the work of freedom, cherish them, perfect them—and bring them home to glory with you."[465]

In return, the Father gave his Son these everlasting promises: that the Holy Spirit would be upon him without measure; he would always have God's help available to him; that he would lift Jesus up in all times of opposition and discouragement; he will highly exalt Jesus and give him a name above all other names; and once Jesus's work is finished, the Father would bring him back to glory.[466]

Jesus gladly accepted and kept the terms of the covenant. Not that it was easy. He would be beaten, scourged, and spat upon. Yet he knew this was one of the terms of the covenant. And he was willing to fulfill it because he knew the Father had a plan. He knew God's love for his children—and Jesus shared that love because he shared the Spirit of the Almighty God.[467]

What does this have to do with you and me? **God gives his Son, the Son gives his life, and we get all the benefits.** This includes the Father's promise, "My hand will always be holding yours. You will never be away from my keeping power. I pledge to keep you safe."[468]

What a picture of God's love for his beloved creation. He cut this covenant because of his undying love for humankind. He was unwilling to lose even a single child to destruction. **The Son's sacrifice on the cross brought us into their covenant agreement, and faith in Christ brings us into all the blessings of the covenant.**

---

465 Isaiah 61:1–3; 42:3; 11:2; John 14:6, paraphrased
466 Isaiah 61:1, John 3:34; Hebrews 1:5; Isaiah 42:4; Philippians 2:9–10; Luke 24:26, paraphrased
467 Isaiah 50:5–6
468 Isaiah 42:6, paraphrased

When Jesus utters his final prayer, we see once more the covenant dealings between Father and Son: "And now, O Father, glorify me together with yourself, with the glory which I had with you before the world was."[469]

At that point, Jesus had fulfilled all the terms of the covenant. But before returning to glory, he reminds the Father, saying, "I have fulfilled my part of the covenant—I have brought about the redemption of humankind. Let us talk now about what will happen to those who believe in me."[470]

Before his ascension to heaven, Jesus prayed for us, saying, "Now, Lord, sanctify them through your truth. Make them holy and pure. And keep them from the wicked one. Let all the promises you gave me be 'yes and amen' to them as well. Cause them to endure as you caused me to endure."[471]

———————

The Bible tells us that in the last days, Satan will pour out his wrath on the earth because he knows his time is short. When that happens, we will need the full assurance of his new covenant. This unbreakable pledge has the power to release in us all the strength we need to be more than conquerors—no matter the situation.

In the perilous times to come, Satan may try to convince you that you have sinned too often, that you are unclean, unholy, no good, a disgrace to the gospel, that God will cast you from his presence.

The next time you are struggling with a besetting sin and you hear Satan's accusatory voice, declare, "I am one in covenant with the Father and Son. Jesus signed the covenant with his blood. He promised to keep me through all my temptations. He will hold my hand, no matter what. He will never remove his love from me. He will lead me to victory!"

Indeed, you have been given a covenant promise that you are headed for glory. Christ made this pledge with the Father, saying, "Father, I know that just as you will bring me to glory, you will bring my seed to glory too!"[472]

---

469 John 17:5
470 John 17:1, 4, 11, paraphrased
471 2 Corinthians 1:20–22, paraphrased
472 John 17:24, paraphrased

Abide in Christ, trust him, depend on him. He made an everlasting covenant with the Father to ensure that if you put your faith in him, you *will* see his glory—no matter what.

32

Another Jesus, Another Gospel

There is something I believe Jesus wants to say to his church. It is just six words, but they are very important: **That is *not* who I am.**

Some of us have a wrong conception of who Jesus is. We have constructed an image of Jesus that is not at all who he is.

There are many books these days claiming that Jesus was merely a mystical, wandering teacher who shared some important truths or some information. Books like those by Deepak Chopra are filed in the bookstores under the banner of Christianity. Books like those portray *nothing* about the real Jesus.

This is nothing new. We often hold on to an image of Jesus that fits what *we* want him to be like. We build our image of Jesus in our own image.

The Jesus I want to talk to you about is the resurrected Christ, the historical, the biblical, the God-sent, God incarnate Savior. The one who lived a sinless life, who died on the cross for you and me. The one whom God raised from the dead on the third day. The Jesus who is alive, sitting at the right hand of the Father, yet who is with you today. That is the Jesus I want to talk to you about.

Even the apostle Paul warned about being confused about who Jesus is. "But I fear, lest somehow, as the serpent deceived Eve by his craftiness, so your minds may be corrupted from the simplicity that is in Christ," he wrote. "For if he who comes preaches another Jesus whom we have not preached … you may well put up with it!"[473]

Another Jesus?

The Jesus we know from God's Word is holy, forgiving, merciful, present, alive. But due to life's disappointments—maybe you trusted God for something that did not come to fruition or that failed—**your reality of who Jesus is does not seem to match what you believe to be true about him.**

Instead of being present, Jesus may feel distant. Instead of being compassionate, Jesus may feel hard to please. Jesus could even feel untrustworthy. After all, he said, "If you ask anything in my name, I will do it."[474] But you still do not have what you have been asking for.

If your image of Jesus is one who feels distant, hard to please, and unreliable, how sincerely are you really worshipping him? You would say, "I love you, Lord, even though you are distant and terrible to get along with, even though you disappoint me all the time. But I love you…"

In the earlier passage where he referred to "another Jesus," Paul goes on to say, "And no wonder! For Satan himself transforms himself into an angel of light."[475]

So this false image of Jesus you have could be Satan pretending to be Jesus, saying to you, "I do not like you. You are not doing good enough. You are a failure."

If those are the types of words you believe Jesus is telling you, it is the angel of light disguising himself as another Jesus, trying to deceive You. It is *not* Jesus. Do not be deceived.

Dead religion is this angel of light trying to disguise himself as something good, loving, and pure. But when you follow that, you become miserable, messed up, and depressed. You do not enjoy worship. You have to force yourself to go to church. And giving, surrendering, loving, and witnessing? Those things are horrific! You have to grin and bear it so you can someday get into heaven.

That is *not* who Jesus is. That is not the Savior who died on the cross for you.[476] That is not the God in heaven who hears every cry.[477] That is not the Jesus

---

473 2 Corinthians 11:3–4
474 John 14:14
475 2 Corinthians 11:14
476 1 Peter 2:24
477 Psalm 34:17

at the right hand of the Father who has the Holy Spirit bottle up every tear you have ever cried.[478]

The Jesus worthy of our worship is a man who came from heaven and lived in a bodily, earthly, human form. After living a sinless, perfect life, this Jesus was crucified for humankind's sins. He was buried in a tomb and on the third day rose again, living forevermore, the resurrected Christ, a friend of sinners, the Savior of our souls.[479]

That is the Jesus we have come to know and to love. And *that* Jesus can tear down every spiritual stronghold, because he has crushed Satan under his feet. Allow *that* Jesus today to destroy this false image the enemy has sold you on so you can once again be passionately in love with Jesus.

The most powerful influence to shift your thinking, your construct, of this false Jesus—another gospel—into the real one is found in Paul's letter to Timothy where he says, "But evil men and impostors will grow worse and worse, deceiving and being deceived."[480]

Impostors come to you and whisper in your ear time and time again you have messed up and rejected God too many times. You have failed him. You keep making the same promise that you will never commit whatever sin it is again that has you bound up, yet you turn around and commit that very sin again. So, impostors come and convince you that God is done with you.

That angel of light comes as an impostor, convincing you that the words he is whispering in your ears are from the heart of God. Please hear me: They are not!

Paul goes on to write, "But you…" Some translations say, "But *as for you…*"

Do you see the shift? Here is the key that the gospels are unleashing to you to bring you to a place of freedom from this fake Jesus. Paul tells Timothy, "But you must continue in the things which you have learned and been assured of, knowing from whom you have learned them, and that from childhood you have known the Holy Scriptures, which are able to make you wise for salvation through faith which is in Christ Jesus."[481]

---

478 Psalm 56:8
479 1 Corinthians 15:3–4; Matthew 11:19; Luke 7:34
480 2 Timothy 3:13
481 2 Timothy 3:14–15

Knowing Jesus and worshipping him with your heart, loving him deeply, and having a true view of Jesus comes from what you have learned and been assured through God's Word.

The Word of God directs your life. It sets your course. It causes the church to grow and move in the direction of God's prompting. The Spirit of God moving through his Word is what sustains marriages, what helps you to raise godly children, what keeps you pure, what makes you holy. It is what causes God's people to see Jesus as he is, rejecting any other version of Jesus.

You cannot know what is a counterfeit unless you know the real thing. And when it comes to Jesus, you cannot know the real thing unless you know the Word of God—the whole counsel of the Word of God found in the pages from Genesis to Revelation—even Leviticus.

You may laugh, but I love the book of Leviticus. It is powerful and talks about the Lamb of God. It reveals to us the true Jesus. Study the book of Leviticus and you will no longer see Jesus as distant; you will see the blood sacrifice and what he has done for you.

Every book of the Bible is there for you to learn about Jesus. But sadly, so many Christians only look for what is exciting.

$$\equiv\equiv$$

Back to Paul's letter to Timothy. He concludes, "All Scripture is given by inspiration of God, and is profitable for doctrine, for reproof, for correction, for instruction in righteousness, that the man of God may be complete, thoroughly equipped for every good work."[482]

All Scripture is Spirit-breathed, breathing life into you so that you can walk intimately with the true Jesus—the forgiving, tender, merciful Christ who loves you so very much.

No matter your life experience, whether you grew up with an abusive, distant, or difficult man as a father, whether you have dabbled in things you know you should not have, leaving you so unclean that you believed Jesus is angry at you, that he is against you, Jesus is telling you today, "*That* is not who I am."

---

482 2 Timothy 3:16–17

Or if you grew up in a home where your father never showed affection and he never poured out love, never told you how proud he is of you and how much he loves you, so you are always trying to do more to earn God's favor, working hard every day trying to please God, Jesus is telling you today, "*That* is not who I am."

You have the Holy Spirit and God's Word telling you what is true and what is not true. And what is true is that Jesus is your friend[483] **and the lover of your soul.** He is closer to you than a brother.[484] He loves you whether you are hurt, lonely, broken, or messed up.[485] He loves you even if you feel filthy, if you feel distant from God, if you feel like you have to earn God's favor.

Jesus wants to remind you today, "I am the Jesus who fights for you. I am the Jesus with thunder in my voice, with lightning in my eyes, and I will destroy this false image of another gospel—of another Jesus—so that you can walk filled with confidence, authority, and the anointing to say, '**I know whom I have believed, and he is able to keep me.**' "[486]

---

483 John 15:15
484 Proverbs 18:24
485 Ephesians 2:4–5
486 2 Timothy 1:12, paraphrased

33

God's People Will Never Be Ashamed in the Time of Calamity

K ing David records a prophecy that is so very applicable to the times we live in. "A little that a righteous man has is better than the riches of many wicked," he declares. "For the arms[487] of the wicked shall be broken, but the Lord upholds the righteous. The Lord knows the days of the upright, and their inheritance shall be forever. They shall not be ashamed in the evil time, and in the days of famine they shall be satisfied."[488]

Isaiah heeds a similar warning. "I have stretched out my hands all day long to a rebellious people, who walk in a way that is not good ... A people who provoke me to anger continually to my face ... I will not keep silence, but will repay..."[489]

But at the same time, God assures us through David that God's people shall not be ashamed in the time of calamity. God will never put his people to shame.[490] We will face impossibilities like they did in the Old Testament. Things will get so bad that it will take a miracle to get through it. Still, God will be exalted.

---

487 *Arms* refer to wealth.
488 Psalm 37:16–19
489 Isaiah 65:2, 3, 6
490 Psalm 25:3; 37:19

God allows us to come into impossible situations that demand faith for the miraculous. We *say* we believe. We testify to the whole world that our God has made promises that see us through.

Take Moses at the Red Sea, for example. Moses and the children of Israel were in a hopeless situation. They were in this valley with mountains on each side. The Egyptians were coming, and the Red Sea was in front of them. The Israelites were trapped.

With that, God's honor was at stake and his promises on trial. What if God did not show up? The Israelites would be finished. They would never again believe God.

So here came Moses. He stood before the people in a hopeless situation, and he said, "Move on."

Moses simply declared that he believed God's promises were true. He believed the word he had received, and he would act on it. What kind of faith is that? Moses spoke into the face of the impossible, saying, "God will do a miracle. We are going through."

===

There are times in life when it looks like God has not shown up and that there is shame and despair. But the whole story has not been told. Once the story has been told, there will be those who will say, "God's honor—not mine—is at stake."

As for Moses, he did not want to be looked at as a prophet. He was not building his own reputation. Moses was committing God to keep his word.

How about you? If you are facing a difficult situation today, have you taken your faith out into the distant unknown? If so, you can say, "God, only a miracle will solve this."

Hold on for that miracle. When you get a word from God, commit God to his word. That is how it was with Joshua. The army had marched around Jericho every day for six days. Imagine Joshua telling them on the seventh day, "I have a word from the Lord. He says that we should march around the city seven times today, and the seventh time we will shout for God has given us the victory."[491]

What kind of faith is this? What kind of a committing of God to his word? Imagine how the people of Jericho were laughing at them, thinking they were fools. Joshua may have even thought, "If God does not show up, I will look like the biggest fool."

---

491 Joshua 6:3–5, paraphrased

But Joshua did not say that. He said, "I know God is able, and I know what I heard, so I will speak it. No matter the consequences, I will speak it. I believe those walls will come down because God will never put his people to shame."

And those walls came crashing down.

It is also how it was with Daniel's friends. King Nebuchadnezzar had built this ninety-foot golden idol, and all were commanded to bow. The Babylonians must have shuddered when they saw these young men standing up to the king, declaring that they would not bow.

Even when they were told they would be thrown into a furnace, Shadrach, Meshach, and Abednego committed the Lord at his word. "We know our God," they insisted. "We know he is able to protect us. But even if he does not, we will not bow to you."[492]

Can you imagine the crowd watching as those young men committed themselves into the hands of God for a miracle? The king watched as the three men were thrown into the furnace. But instead of seeing three men in the fire, the king saw four.[493]

God had shown up on the scene. He would not let his children be put to shame. God would not be put to shame. God did not appear in that furnace to impress the king, nor did he show up for the sake of the crowd. He showed up to comfort, bless, and commune with his children.

≡≡

To be able to commit God to his promises, you have to know them. You have to know his Word and his voice to know which promises are for *you*. The promises God gives you may not be for me. But those God had given me, I hold on to, I stand on them when my family and I face challenges.

When you are facing the impossible, inquire of the Lord. Ask God for a word. Listen for what God says. **If what you hear is from the Holy Spirit, it will woo you to the Word of God.**

Commit to going further in your faith than you have ever gone. Ask the Holy Ghost to give you the kind of faith that can look at any issue and every impossibility

---

492 Daniel 3:16–18, paraphrased
493 Daniel 3:24–25

and say, "God, I stand on your Word. You promised to deliver me, and your honor is at stake."

$$= =$$

God's honor was at stake when, during the reign of King Hezekiah, Jerusalem was surrounded by the Assyrian army, the greatest army of that time. The army was about to invade Jerusalem. Multitudes would be devastated and decimated.

When it looked like there was no hope, a word came from God to Isaiah. Isaiah committed God to this word, saying, "Tell the commander he is not going to shoot a single arrow into the city. He is not going to set foot into this city. And God will turn him around and send him home the way he came."[494]

Then God sent an angel—just one angel—and 185,000 soldiers died mysteriously. They just dropped dead.[495] How? I do not know. But God showed up. He never puts to shame those who trust in him.

$$= =$$

When facing the impossible, I do what David did at Ziklag.[496] I step aside and inquire of the Lord. I wait until God speaks. I take God at his word and reach for the impossible.

You and I will never be able to figure out how God will deliver us from whatever problems we face. God's plans are beyond our comprehension.

Think of when Peter and John went to the temple and saw a lame beggar. Peter and John stopped, obstructing traffic at the entrance. "Silver and gold I do not have," Peter said, "but what I do have I give you: In the name of Jesus Christ of Nazareth, rise up and walk."[497]

Peter put God on trial, committing God to a miracle.

"Walk? This man has never walked," the crowd must have objected. "We have been coming here for years, and that man has always been there. He has never taken

---

494 2 Kings 19:32–33, paraphrased
495 2 Kings 19:35
496 1 Samuel 30: 6–8
497 Acts 3:6

a step." Imagine the look on these people's faces as the beggar started wiggling his toes and ankles, getting energy into his limbs until he pushed himself up.

That the beggar could walk was God's handiwork, just as it was when the waters parted before Moses and the people of Israel. In the same way, God protected Daniel's friends in the fiery furnace, tore down the walls of Jericho, and wiped out the Assyrian army.

None of this was humanly possible. In the very same way, we all face situations where we have to believe God for the impossible.

When you pray, believe God to answer your prayer in miraculous ways. The answer does not always come immediately, but God starts the miracle the moment you trust him for it. Just wait. Commit to believing God. Then, expect the impossible.

Sometimes it may take years before you see the answer. Wait patiently. Other times, you may not have time to wait. You may be facing a crisis that requires a miracle. Will you believe Jehovah Jireh? Will you commit to believing? God's honor is at stake in keeping his promises.

Through the prophet Ezekiel, God declared, "But I acted for my name's sake, that it should not be profaned before the gentiles, in whose sight I had brought them out."[498]

God acts not just to answer you or me, but because his honor is at stake. And when he acts, God does not do so in secret. God saves you before others, and those around you—even your enemies—can see the evidence of God being at work.

But those who rely not on God but only on themselves to find a way through life's challenges? Isaiah says that God will bring down the pride and the glory of this world and bring it into contempt. "The loftiness of man shall be bowed down, and the haughtiness of men shall be brought low; the Lord alone will be exalted in that day."[499]

Those who are preaching the gospel of wealth and prosperity should be trembling. God says, "I do not have to send a storm; I am just going to breathe and cut off the money supply."[500]

God will purge pride from his church. From this will come a people who will teach about miracles, but not for whatever offering you give. Not for that at all. It will be for the glory of God alone.

---

498 Ezekiel 20:14
499 Isaiah 2:17
500 Isaiah 2:20–21, paraphrased

34

Jesus, the Lamb of God

J esus Christ is the Lamb of God. He is the sacrifice for sin for all mankind. When John the Baptist saw Jesus, he declared, "Behold! The Lamb of God who takes away the sin of the world!"[501]

"Look," John is saying while thinking of all the people lining up at the temple to buy goats and lambs—or pigeons, if you are poor—to atone for their sins. "*This is the sacrifice for sin. This is the Lamb of God.*"

Peter the apostle likewise points out, "We are redeemed not with silver and gold but the precious blood of Christ as a Lamb without spot or blemish."[502]

In the book of Revelation, John mentions Jesus eighteen times, referring to him as the Lamb of God. Jesus had been crucified and buried, and he had been raised from the dead and ascended to the Father. Writing from the island of Patmos to which he had been exiled, John says, "I see him seated on the throne, the Lamb of God. The overcomer."[503]

In the vision, John saw nations and multitudes from all tongues and tribes bowing before the Lamb. Then he saw an angel bind the devil and all the principalities and powers of darkness, he saw him cast them into the pit of hell.[504]

---

501 John 1:29
502 1 Peter 1:18–19, paraphrased
503 Revelation 5:6, paraphrased
504 Revelation 20:1–2

Before his death and resurrection, Jesus had told his disciples, "I am going to prepare you a place. I will come back."[505] Jesus went to prepare this place John is seeing in his vision from Patmos. In the vision, Jesus had built the new Jerusalem and he had established a new paradise.

———— ≡≡ ————

Weather permitting, I take walks daily. I often walk around the Times Square area, looking at the crowds of tourists. Tourists come to our city from all over the world, from places with more gods than you can imagine. They come to New York City from India, for example, where they have more than a million Hindu gods.

As I walk the streets of New York, looking at all the tourists, I often wonder what they are looking for. I also wonder what they are thinking of, what is going on in their minds. On such a walk, the Holy Spirit spoke to me, telling me that these men and women were looking for peace. They were looking for hope.

But this is not only true of tourists from abroad. Day and night, you see people all over this city going here, there, and everywhere, to bars and clubs, and the cry of their heart is for peace. People are living in guilt and trying to find at least one ray of hope. They are trying to pay God back for the transgressions of their heart. They are looking for someone to help pay for their sins so they can have peace. They are looking for atonement.

While I was in Florida once, there was a story in the newspaper that there were seven people who had passed out in restaurants and bars. They had been taking drugs and then went and drank alcohol so they passed out. There seemed to be such a sense of emptiness and hopelessness.

The same happens in New York. You see people searching for something. They keep trying to make atonement for their sins, trying to find some way they can pay God back for their transgressions.

But you and I can never make atonement for our sins. Jesus came as the Lamb whose blood would atone for our sins. The blood of this Lamb has power—the power to cleanse and power to heal.

---

505 John 14:2–3, paraphrased

Millions of men and women around the world have experienced the glory and the power of this cleansing blood of Jesus Christ.

Before Jesus was crucified, he rode into Jerusalem on a colt. As he looked over the city, Jesus wept.[506] The Bible also tells of Jesus weeping at Lazarus's tomb,[507] but the Greek used in that case means silent tears. As for when Jesus approached the city of Jerusalem and wept, the Greek means to wail loudly, to give a cry that could be heard everywhere.

What did Jesus see that made him wail? I believe he was seeing a constant stream of people who were going to the temple to offer sacrifices to try and make peace with God. They were looking for a way to pay for their transgressions.

I believe Jesus saw the whole world and all the gods and religions that people would turn to in a desperate effort to find peace and hope.

So, Jesus wailed, and afterward, he went to the temple and drove out the money changers. As for those who were coming to bring sacrifices, Jesus knew they were sincere. He did not chase them out of the temple.

The multitudes in this city, I believe, are sincerely looking for hope. There are people who would do anything to please God, to appease his wrath, to find favor with God.

Perhaps you too are looking for peace. Truth is, if you do *not* know Jesus, if you are not walking with Christ, if you are living for yourself and living in sin, you will find yourself lying in bed, your mind racing as you are searching, looking for hope.

As I watch people searching for peace, searching for love in all the wrong places, I hear Jesus saying, "Come to me all you who hunger and thirst, and I will give you peace."[508]

---

506 Luke 19:41
507 John 11:35
508 Matthew 11:28, paraphrased

I first came to New York City to establish Teen Challenge. When the Lord called me here the second time, I was standing on 42nd Street and Broadway watching the masses go by. There were drug pushers using death as an advertisement to sell crack cocaine. They were yelling, "I've got the stuff that will kill you."

While I was standing there, the Lord said, "I want you to come to this city, and I want a church in the middle of all this." That is when Times Square Church was born.

All around there was open sinfulness. I cried that day in a way I could not cry again. And still, I did not reach the depth of Christ wailing for Jerusalem. Jesus was wailing for a nation to whom he had proclaimed, "I am your peace."[509]

The prophet Zachariah had foretold Jesus's entrance to Jerusalem on a colt. "Behold, your King is coming to you; he is just and having salvation, lowly and riding on a donkey, a colt, the foal of a donkey."[510]

And Isaiah prophesied about the Messiah being "a man of sorrows acquainted with grief."[511] As Jesus wept over Jerusalem, he gave the cause of his weeping, saying, "If you had known, even you, especially in this your day, the things that make for your peace! But now they are hidden from your eyes."[512]

If only you had known… **This is what broke Jesus's heart—if only they knew the peace that was right there, about to be sacrificed once and for all.**

This Messiah that we are talking about, this Lamb of God, you or I cannot raise him from the dead.[513] He has already done that. Our Messiah is alive, and he is with us—with *you*. If only you had known and believed that while you were looking for peace in other places.

It is difficult to tell a man that all his charity, all his good works, all this trying to do what is right is of no merit. It is commendable. What he is doing is wonderful, but it will not save his soul.

509 John 14:27, paraphrased
510 Zachariah 9:9
511 Isaiah 53:3
512 Luke 19:42
513 Romans 10:7

You are not saved by works but by faith in what Jesus did on the cross.[514] All you have to do is believe. **Confess that he is Lord and that the blood of the Lamb has the power to cleanse you, heal you, and change your life. It can even give you the power to live right.**

Let it not be said of you, "If only she had known the peace. If only he had known the joy."

But as Jesus wept over Jerusalem, he said blindness had come over the people of that city.[515] God forbid that you should become blind by hardening yourself to his merciful call of God the Father offering you an atonement for your sin.

═ ═ ─

We as the Church of God worship and serve the Lamb of God, the resurrected Lord. John describes it as follows:

Then I looked, and I heard the voice of many angels around the throne, the living creatures, and the elders; and the number of them was ten thousand times ten thousand, and thousands of thousands, saying with a loud voice:

"Worthy is the Lamb who was slain to receive power and riches and wisdom, and strength and honor and glory and blessing!"

And every creature which is in heaven and on the earth and under the earth and such as are in the sea, and all that are in them, I heard saying:

"Blessing and honor and glory and power be to him who sits on the throne, and to the Lamb, forever and ever!"[516]

Glory be to God for his sacrifice. Jesus Christ is our Lord and Savior, ruling in glory and power and majesty.

---

514 Galatians 2:16
515 "But now they are hidden from your eyes." Luke 19:42
516 Revelation 5:11–13

35

Man's Hour of Darkness
Is God's Hour of Power

In the gospel of John, we read about Jesus and his disciples attending a wedding in a town called Cana.[517] Such weddings could last for as many as seven days. We do not know how long that wedding has been going on, but there comes a time when the hosts run out of wine.

Jesus's mother, Mary, comes to Jesus and tells him that the hosts had run out of wine. And Jesus responds, "Woman, my hour has not yet come."[518]

I can imagine Jesus standing there watching what is happening. Over in a corner, there are six clay pots for water.[519] Jesus waits until there is no other answer, when the only thing that can solve the situation is a miracle. Then Jesus says, "Fill them up." His hour had come.

The hour of God's power manifests at the end of man's resources. Man's darkest hour is the hour of God's greatest power.

517 John 2:1–7
518 Addressing Mary as "woman" was not a put-down. It was culturally appropriate at the time.
519 It is estimated that these pots could hold up to a total of 180 gallons of water.

This principle occurs many a time in the Bible. Think of Gideon.[520] Israel is facing extreme poverty, one of the darkest times in their history. The Midianites would come in with their camels, their cattle, their families, and they would move right into the land, stripping the land and the crops.

Meanwhile, the people of Israel are at the end of their hope, hiding in caves, saying, "God has forsaken us!"

That is when God begins to move, manifesting his power. **He comes to the poorest tribe, to the poorest family, and to the poorest man in that tribe, Gideon. And God says, "I will change things."** God tells Gideon how to scare away the Midianite army with a meager 300 men using nothing but trumpets and torches.

Another time, Israel lives under the rule of the Canaanites, facing extreme poverty and judgment, living without hope. The captains of the armies have given up and fled. **God waits until they come to a place of absolute hopelessness until he sends Deborah, a prophetess.** God sends a woman who is living under the palm trees in the hills to deliver Israel. People are coming up to this hillside to Deborah's open-air meetings. While all of Israel is in darkness and groaning, "God has forsaken us," Deborah sees through the darkness, and she preaches a different message—a message of hope.[521]

$$=\!\!=\;=\!\!=$$

There are dark days in life, but God is never surprised by those times. God always has somebody he has prepared for the darkest hours. He prepared Deborah and Gideon just like God prepared Moses and Abraham.

There comes a time in your life and mine when we reach a point that we feel we cannot carry on. You may be at that point where you have prayed and you sought the face of God, yet you see no evidence of change or an answer to your prayers.

The Holy Spirit is standing by. He knows the hour. He knows the time when your friends have failed you, when your cup is dry and you have run out of wine—when you need new wine from heaven.

God knows the day and the hour, so, pray on. Seek the face of God!

$$=\!\!=\;=\!\!=$$

---

520 Judges 6
521 Judges 4:14, 24

Consider the time when King Jehoshaphat receives a frightening message of a huge army coming against him. The messenger comes and says, "A great multitude is coming against you from beyond the sea, from Syria… And Jehoshaphat feared, and set himself to seek the Lord, and proclaimed a fast throughout all Judah. So, Judah gathered together to ask help from the Lord; and from all the cities of Judah they came to seek the Lord."[522]

This is a dark hour for Israel. So, they begin to praise the Lord. Something happens when you begin to praise the Lord, when you abandon yourself to praise, believing that God is still on the throne.

Praising the Lord in a mighty fashion, the Spirit of the Lord falls upon them. While they are praising the Lord, the Lord ambushes the enemy.[523] **Their dark hour becomes God's hour of power and deliverance.**

The prophet Isaiah also speaks about there being a light that rises amid a gross darkness.[524] I believe Isaiah is speaking about the last days. He is prophesying that in the midst of this gross darkness, there will be a light that rises, and gentiles will come to the light by multitudes.

That prophecy has not yet been fulfilled. Gross darkness began when at the crucifixion, gross darkness covered the earth.[525] The Roman Empire was being ruined. There were sexual perversions of all kinds, evil corruption, deception, greed, apostasies of all kinds. Even among God's people, there was hypocrisy. The teachers of the Law were robbing widow's houses.[526]

Even today, there is a gross darkness in the world, a darkness that can be felt. Do not let your heart be burdened by this darkness—the sins of mankind, the perversions that we see and hear today. Jesus is still the light of the world.[527] He has come to break through the darkness.

The greater the darkness, the greater the light of Jesus Christ.

---

522 2 Chronicles 20:2–4
523 2 Chronicles 20:22
524 Isaiah 60:2–3
525 Mark 15:33
526 Mark 12:39–40; Luke 20:46–47
527 John 8:12

I believe that we are facing a significant ingathering of lost souls such as what Isaiah talks about. I believe with all my heart that what is coming will be an amazing ingathering of many thousands of lost souls.

In prayer, I recently asked God, "Lord, how can we know this to be true?" God began to speak to my heart of the simple things of the inner knowing. God took me to the Scriptures, showing me that almost every time the Spirit moved, God prepared people for what he was about to do.

"The Spirit himself bears witness with our spirit that we are the children of God."[528] There is an inner witness.[529] But there are also signs and wonders and gifts of the Holy Ghost.[530]

You and I have a witness in our hearts. It is the same witness that tells you that you are a child of God. It is the same witness that has borne witness down through the ages for all who walk with Christ.

And at the same time, we live at a time where there is bad news almost every day. Still, there is a witness in your heart and mine that we have to do something. God has made it clear that the church is not going to be vanquished,[531] that the church of Jesus Christ will prevail, that God will do a work right to the very last moment. And then, there will be an ingathering of souls.

The Holy Spirit is leaving entire denominations. But at the same time, he is stirring the hearts of his people, stirring a godly remnant. I have a stirring in my heart, something deep in my soul that declares, "God, this is who you are. This is how you work. You do not leave whole generations. You do not forsake generations because of the perversions, because the blood you shed on the cross endures to the very last breath and to the last of the last days."

I have been noticing how God has been laying hold of his people with a spirit of prayer. Who would have ever believed that there would be prayer meetings called in churches such as Times Square Church and Brooklyn Tabernacle?

---

528 Romans 8:16
529 Hebrews 10:15
530 Hebrews 2:4
531 Matthew 16:18

Who would have believed, even a few years ago, that over 50,000 people would meet in Times Square to pray, and that a holy hush could fall on such a large crowd as everyone is looking to the throne of God?

God is creating an atmosphere that even those who do not know Christ can walk through these doors and sense something supernatural.

Do you feel God drawing you to pray? For there to be a harvest, the ground has to be broken through prayer. You need to pray now more than ever before. This is the time to seek the face of God.

———

This generation has run out of wine. There are two kinds of wine—the wine of the world, and the wine of the Spirit which makes glad the heart of man.[532] Gladness and joy has been stolen from this present generation. It is gone. There is little joy, little gladness. The Bible says sin robs of mirth and gladness.[533]

Sunday nights at this church, there are testimonies of people who have been saved. Almost every testimony goes something like this, "I have tried everything. I came empty to the place where there is nothing left but tears."

The wine of the world has left them empty. I do not think any word more describes the mood of this generation than *emptiness*.

In light of this, what do we do? Mary turned to the disciples and said, "Just do what he tells you."[534]

When you seek the Lord, he will tell you what to do.

———

In Revelation 7, John describes multitudes worshipping God.[535] And one of the elders asked, "Who are these arrayed in white robes, and where did they come from?"[536]

---

532 Psalm 104:15
533 Jeremiah 7:34; 16:9; 25:10
534 John 2:5
535 Revelation 7:9–10
536 Revelation 7:13

The answer came that those who were worshipping were those who had come out of great tribulation.[537] They were washed white by the blood of the Lamb, "and he who sits on the throne will dwell among them. They shall neither hunger anymore nor thirst anymore ... for the Lamb who is in the midst of the throne will shepherd them and lead them to living fountains of waters. And God will wipe away every tear from their eyes."[538]

No matter how dark it gets, no matter how difficult, may you find comfort knowing that this is God's hour of deliverance, God's hour of power.

When you stand before the throne of God, know that this is not just an hour of judgment. This is the finest hour. There will be conviction and anointing. And there will be an outpouring of new wine.

537 Revelation 7:14
538 Revelation 7:15–17

36

Men of Another Sort

When I read the Old Testament, I am overwhelmed at the intensity of the men of God. I wonder where they get that spiritual authority and where they get the stamina to do what they did.

Take Ezekiel, for example, who lay on one side for 390 days and forty days on his other side to warn Jerusalem of coming judgment.[539] And then there is Elijah, who fasted forty days and forty nights while I cannot even fast for three.[540] Likewise, I am amazed at Daniel, who mourned for three weeks, barely eating and not even washing his face.[541]

As I read those stories, I can only say, "God, those are men of another sort!"

If there was ever a time that the world needed men of such intensity, it is now. Why then would God not raise up extraordinary men and women for our time?

God's Word says that in the last days, he will pour out his spirit upon all flesh.[542] In other words, **we have something those men did not have. We have been promised an anointing the prophets could only yearn for—an outpouring of the Holy Spirit.**

This obligates us to search the Word of God and find the patterns of how these men became men of another sort. Why did God anoint them and use them? Why

---

539 Ezekiel 4:4–6
540 1 Kings 19:8
541 Daniel 10:1–3
542 Acts 2:17

were they so marvelously changed by the power and the hand of God? Once you discern those patterns, you can follow that same path.

"Well, those were men of destiny," you might object.

That is true. But you can be a man of destiny and still thwart God's plans. Look at Saul, for example. God told him all about the plan he had for an everlasting kingdom from him, but he aborted the plan of God.[543]

It is your choice whether to abort the plan of God or to study the Word of God, find the patterns, and pursue God's path.

———

I want to be a man touched by the hand of God so even the enemies of the Lord know that I have spiritual authority that moves people toward the Lord. I searched the Word of God and found a pattern in the lives of three extraordinary men of faith, men of another sort.

First, there is Ezra, a scribe. The Bible describes him as a man who awakened his entire nation, a man who was strengthened when the hand of God came upon him.[544] Why among all the scribes does God choose Ezra? The Bible says, "For Ezra had prepared his heart to seek the law of the Lord, and to do it…"[545]

Ezra made a conscious decision to obey God. God saw a man who hungered for his Word, who loved the Word and was saturated in it. And God used this man who had prepared his heart.

Like Ezra prepared his heart, so can you. You can choose to saturate yourself in God's Word just like you do when you choose to watch television for hours.

God did not supernaturally baptize Ezra with a love for the Word. Instead, Ezra sought God's Word and then lived accordingly. In the process, God baptized him with a vision and a heart for the people.

Not only was Ezra a man of the Word, but he set his heart to fast and pray. When Ezra told King Artaxerxes he and others were going back to Jerusalem, the king offered to send an army to protect them along the treacherous way. But Ezra

---

543 1 Samuel 13:13–14
544 Ezra 7:6
545 Ezra 7:10

turned down the offer saying, "We serve a mighty God; he is able to protect us. Thank you, King, but no thanks. We have a God."[546]

Ezra did not only take God at his Word; he spoke it from the heart of God, and then he called for a fast.[547] Ezra comes to his people and essentially says, "I spoke what I believe to be from God. But now, we will fast and pray until it comes to fruition."

So, they fasted and kept seeking the Lord, and God protected them along their way.[548]

Once they were back in Jerusalem, Ezra learned how God's people had broken the law. Ezra was so distraught that he tore his garments, plucked out some of his hair and his beard, and fell facedown before the Lord.[549]

Realizing the many ways in which they had failed to keep God's ordinances, Ezra issued a decree that all the people had to come to Jerusalem.[550] Nehemiah, meanwhile, had been working on restoring the walls of Jerusalem.[551] And once the exiles had returned to the city, Ezra read the law to the people. Hearing the decrees, they fell to their faces before the Lord and they wept.[552] But Ezra declared, "Do not sorrow, for the joy of the Lord is your strength."[553]

The principle is this: **Once you get hungry for God's Word and you saturate yourself in the Word, God's Word will purge you. It will challenge you and compel you to fall on your face before God, broken by your sinfulness. Only** *then* **can you truly rejoice.**

The only brokenness I have known has come through being hammered—broken—by the Word of God.[554] I have been hammered by Matthew 25, standing before the throne of God, having to answer for taking care of the widows and fatherless and all of these things that the church is commanded to do.[555]

Would you allow God's Word to break you?

---

546 Ezra 8:21–22, paraphrased
547 Ezra 8:23
548 Ezra 8:31
549 Ezra 9:3
550 Ezra 10:7
551 Nehemiah 2–7
552 Nehemiah 8:1–9
553 Nehemiah 8:10
554 Jeremiah 23:29
555 Matthew 25:41–46

Let us consider Jeremiah, another man of a different sort. **Jeremiah spoke of engaging the heart to seek the Lord.**[556] Like Ezra, Jeremiah was a man who loved the Word. Again and again, the Bible says, "And the Word came to Jeremiah…"[557] Why did God's Word come to Jeremiah? Because he asked for it, he sought it.

This is the prophet who gave us the most praiseworthy gospel in all of the Old Testament. He is the one who said God will satiate the soul of the priests with fatness.[558] He is a man of the new covenant,[559] declaring that God would cleanse us from all our iniquity.[560]

That is good news indeed. But Jeremiah came to such insight through being broken before almighty God.[561]

This man was so broken before God that God shared with Jeremiah his own brokenness. You may say that God is not broken. God does not weep. But Jeremiah tells us how God wept after speaking judgment over his people.[562] **Sin wounds the heart of God.**

It is Jeremiah who said that God's Word "was in my heart like a burning fire shut up in my bones; I was weary of holding it back, and I could not."[563] Because God's Word was a fire in Jeremiah's bones, because he knew how to weep and get the heart of God, he understood the mind of God. "The Lord has pronounced evil against Israel," he said, "and the Lord has given me knowledge of it and I knew it and he showed me all their doings."[564]

Jeremiah essentially says, "I have been on my face, and God has pronounced evil against Israel. The Lord has given me knowledge of it, and I knew it."

---

556 Jeremiah 30:21
557 Jeremiah 1:4, 11, 13; 13:8; 18:1; 21:1; 24:4; 28:12; 33:19, 23; 34:12; 35:12; 36:27; 39:15; 40:1; 42:7; 44:1
558 Jeremiah 31:14
559 Jeremiah 32:40
560 Jeremiah 33:8
561 Jeremiah 4:19; 9:1
562 Jeremiah 9:9–10
563 Jeremiah 20:9
564 Jeremiah 11:17–18, paraphrased

Finally, there is Daniel. **Daniel also had a burning hunger for the Word of God, living in obedience to the Word of God.** Daniel fasted, prayed, and was broken by the things that broke God's heart. God had revealed to Daniel through studying the Word that the exile would last seventy years.[565]

This moved Daniel to intercede for God's people. "Then I set my face toward the Lord God to make request by prayer and supplications, with fasting, sackcloth, and ashes."[566]

What happens as a result of Daniel being moved by the Word of God? I believe **Christ himself appeared to Daniel in a vision.**[567] But those who were with Daniel were so afraid that they ran away. Daniel alone heard what God said.[568]

I believe there is only one thing that causes anybody to run from the presence of the almighty God, and that is sin. No other reason. These men did not see, they did not hear what God had to say.

Perhaps you can relate with many who sit in church and have never seen or heard God—you are still running. You have not allowed the Holy Spirit to come yet and break you through his Word.[569]

Every day, I am more and more aware of the hour that I will stand before the judgment seat, when there is the separation of sheep and goats.[570] We will all stand before God's throne. I wonder if God will show us what could have been and say to you and to me, "*This* is what I had in mind for you. This is what you missed."

I do not know about you, but I for one do not want to stand before God one day and have the Lord say to me, "Let me show you what could have been. If you had not turned the grace of God into lasciviousness, if you had not walked in pride, if you had just obeyed the Word of God."[571]

God will honor you if, like Daniel, you set your heart toward the Lord.

---

565 Daniel 9:2
566 Daniel 9:3
567 Daniel 10:5–8
568 Daniel 10:7
569 Jeremiah 23:29
570 Matthew 25:32–46
571 Galatians 5:19–21, paraphrased

He will touch you if, like Jeremiah, you engage your heart to seek the Lord.

He will work through you in powerful ways if, like Ezra, you make a conscious decision to do what God tells you.

These are conscious decisions, ones I make every day, as can you. Daily, choose to focus on God, on the high calling of God in Christ Jesus.[572]

Nothing else matters.

---

572 Philippians 3:14

37

Moving Your Mountain

Over the years, I have read this one story in the gospel of Mark many times. On the way into Jerusalem, Jesus and his disciples came upon a fig tree that was bearing no fruit, so he cursed it, saying, "Let no one eat fruit from you ever again."[573] From there, they went into the city.

Sandwiched between Jesus cursing the fig tree and the results of that curse, Jesus goes to the temple in Jerusalem and drives out the money changers from the temple, saying, "My house is not going to be a den of thieves anymore."[574]

The passage I have read over and over transpires on their way back out of the city. "Now in the morning, as they passed by, they saw the fig tree dried up from the roots. And Peter, remembering, said to him, 'Rabbi, look! The fig tree which you cursed has withered away.' So Jesus answered and said to them, 'Have faith in God. For assuredly, I say to you, whoever says to this mountain, "Be removed and be cast into the sea," and does not doubt in his heart, but believes that those things he says will be done, he will have whatever he says. Therefore I say to you, whatever things you ask when you pray, believe that you receive them, and you will have them.' "[575]

---

573 Mark 11:12–14
574 Mark 11:15–17, paraphrased
575 Mark 11:20–24

Keep in mind the timing of this event. This is shortly before Jesus is crucified. These are his final days. Jesus understands the bigger picture, that there is death and resurrection ahead for more than just him.

By cursing the fig tree, Jesus is saying, "I am finished with religion that does not produce good fruit; it is dead to the roots." What will be birthed instead is a church that lives in the power of the Spirit.

When Peter said, "Look at this. This tree has withered to the roots," Jesus's response was to have faith in God. He does not answer Peter's observation. Instead, Jesus puts his message in the context of having faith.

In that context, **the mountain Jesus is referring to is unbelief.** The disciples were to be the foundation stones of the church,[576] yet they had a mountain of unbelief in the way. This would keep them from making it through the hard times that lay ahead—the cross, the persecution, the bloodshed.

Whatever sin you are struggling with, you may think it is your mountain, the thing that stands in your way. But the root of your sin is unbelief—perhaps unbelief that God can break the hold your sin has on you. And **unbelief opens you up to every conceivable sin.**

Do you remember the story of Zacharias the priest? The angel Gabriel appeared to him and told Zacharias that he and Elizabeth were going to have a child, and they were to name him John. John would be a forerunner of the Messiah, among other things.[577]

This was an incredible promise, not only because of who the boy would be but because Zacharias and his wife were well past the time of being able to have a child. So, when Gabriel told Zacharias the news, Zachariah essentially responded with a declaration that it was impossible.

Zacharias' mountain was unbelief. So, God told him that he would be mute until the child was born.

576 Matthew 16:18; Ephesians 2:20; Revelation 21:14
577 Luke 1:5–25

God pressed on my heart that we will never understand this message until we know how much unbelief grieves him. "If you think unbelief is something that I can pass over lightly," God told me, "you will never know how to move your mountain."

God reminded me of the countless miracles I have seen. I could fill pages with stories of how God has answered my prayers when I have believed him and trusted him. Then a crisis comes and suddenly I wipe out that whole history of witnessing miracles and I say things that grieve God, things like Peter said. "Lord, if it is you, command me to come to you on the water."[578]

Despite Peter's unbelief, the Lord simply said, "Come."[579]

That is the whole gospel. In your trials, the Lord is saying, "Just come to me." But Peter looked at the storm around him and began to sink. Jesus took Peter by the hand and asked, "Why did you doubt me?"[580]

Jesus was not trying to comfort Peter. Instead, God was grieved by Peter's unbelief.

Perhaps, like me, you tell people that you believe God is the God of the impossible. You have countless testimonies of God answering your prayer, but then there comes a crisis, and you feel hopeless.

═══ ══

King Asa of Judah would be able to relate to our predicament.[581] He wiped out sodomy. He wiped out idolatry, tore down heathen temples, and brought revival to Judah. In the midst of a revival, a million-man army came out of Ethiopia.[582] They came against Judah to destroy Jerusalem and wipe out the nation.

The Bible says that Asa turned to the Lord and relied on him.[583] He humbled himself before God and called the people to pray. The Ethiopian army was far mightier than his army, yet he had a great victory. He came home singing the praises of God.

On the way home, a prophet stopped him and instead of congratulating the king, he said, "As long as you walk this way, as long as you rely on the Lord, as long

578 Matthew 14:28
579 Matthew 14:29
580 Matthew 14:30–31, paraphrased
581 1 Kings 15:9–24; 2 Chronicles 14:2–16:14
582 2 Chronicles 14:9
583 2 Chronicles 14:11

as you fully trust him and never give up your confidence in God, I will walk with you and you will have victories. But if you turn away from me you will have wars and disorder."[584]

King Asa took that message to heart, and for thirty-six years he walked in faith. He saw great victories. He built the house of God to splendor, and he turned the nation around.

But then, another crisis came. All the trade routes were cut off. This would bring economic collapse to Judah. It would bring famine. After thirty-six years of walking in faith, King Asa panicked. He gathered his counselors and asked what they were to do. A thought was planted in his mind to ask the Syrians to help them out.[585]

King Asa stripped the temple of its gold and silver. He sent emissaries to Syria, a nation that was their enemy. And in plain words, he said, "Here is everything I own. Now, deliver me and my people."[586]

What absolute unbelief!

A prophet came to Asa. "Because you did not believe, from now on you will have wars," he said. "Everything is going to be out of order. Everything will turn into flesh. You will get all your directions from the flesh now."[587]

$$= =$$

The hardest part of faith is the final half hour. Perhaps you are in that final half hour. While God is making plans to give you the most glorious deliverance, you find yourself before a mountain of unbelief, helpless, powerless, fearing, and in a panic.

Are you in panic, standing before the God who has answered you a thousand times? I say this with brokenness because I see it in my own heart. I see it, and I despise it.

I asked God how to get the mountain to move. How do I get this thing out of my life that hinders everything that God would do?

I do not know about you, but I have been in a place of getting out of God's will and out of a place of faith and trusting. I asked God, "Lord, how do I cast this thing out of me?"

---

584 2 Chronicles 15:2, paraphrased

585 2 Chronicles 16:2

586 2 Chronicles 16:2–3, paraphrased

587 2 Chronicles 16:7–9, paraphrased

God reminded me that he had made it our responsibility to speak to the mountain and say, "Be gone!"[588] **Once that mountain of unbelief is gone, then whatever you ask or whatever you say, everything you want and desire, you shall have it.**[589]

"Wait a minute!" you might object. "I have been there and done that, and it does not work."

If you really want to walk a life of faith, God showed me that it would cost you, just like it cost Jesus.

If you want authority over this mountain, there is a place you have to go, and there is a prayer you have to pray when you get there. That place is Gethsemane.

Jesus went to Gethsemane not to address a mountain of unbelief for he had no sin. The mountain before him was the cross. Jesus went to the garden and said, "My soul is exceedingly sorrowful, even to death."[590]

Have you ever prayed that prayer? What you are saying is, "This is too much. This is beyond my understanding, and if this goes on, it will kill me."

We cannot do away with this Gethsemane experience. Jesus wept. He prayed. He interceded. He called on God. "O my Father, if it is possible, let this cup pass from me..." he pled.[591]

Before coming to Gethsemane, Jesus had fasted, prayed, and wept. Then he prayed the ultimate prayer, "Nevertheless, not as I will, but as you will."[592]

You cannot move your mountain until you have prayed the ultimate prayer. And you cannot pray that prayer until you have unloaded everything that is weighing on your soul. You quit looking at your circumstances and believe instead that God loves you, that he will not allow anything in your life except what is good and what is his will. Then you give up trying to figure it out.

It is only then that you can cast yourself into the arms of the heavenly Father and say, "Lord, this is not what I want. I do not think I can handle much more, but I know you are God Almighty, and I place everything into your hands, declaring your will to be done."

---

588 Mark 11:23, paraphrased
589 Mark 11:22–24, paraphrased
590 Matthew 26:38
591 Matthew 26:39a
592 Matthew 26:39b

Once you do that, be prepared for God to allow afflictions in your life.[593] Jesus knows the path, and he knows the cost. God will shape you. And even in the time of being shaped, hold on to the faith that God loves you. Then, cast yourself fully into God's care.

---

593 Psalm 119:71

38

Reaching the Lost in Uncertain Times

J esus never added exemption clauses to his promises. He did not say, "Go out and reach the world except in hard economic times." He did not say, "The world is too hard, the world is too bitter, the world is too bound by lust to reach, so just hide away in a prayer closet and just ride out the storm."

Instead, God made provision for difficult times. The Holy Ghost is not bound by the economy. In fact, Jesus said, "Now when these things begin to happen, look up and lift up your heads, because your redemption draws near."[594]

In other words, do not stop during a recession. Carry on doing mission work. Keep feeding the poor. Keep sending missionaries around the world. The work of God goes on, no matter what—even if we are surrounded by darkness.

The Bible says that in the last days, there will be a gross darkness.[595] **How can we penetrate the darkness of the days ahead? We do what Jesus commanded us to do. We love.**

The Bible says the world hates Jesus because he came as a light. Those who are lost hate the light because it exposes the darkness which they love.[596] To many, our idea of heaven is far from appealing. They feel robbed of the pleasures of the sins they so love.

---

594 Luke 21:28
595 Isaiah 60:2
596 John 3:19–20

Why is it that the world hates Christ with such voracity? Why is it that society so despises those who use the Bible as their moral compass? Jesus said that light has come into the world and men love their darkness rather than the light because their deeds were evil.[597]

We are all commanded to cast off the works of darkness and turn to Jesus, the light of the world.[598] In him, there is freedom.

The world thinks that freedom comes from taking off every shackle of God's law. "Freedom?" they say, "I have freedom! I have a god of my own choosing, and I do what I want. This body is mine, and I can do with my body what I please. Freedom? Man, I have freedom."

This is what we are up against in trying to penetrate the darkness with the gospel.

If you were of the world, the world would love its own. But because you are not of this world, because God chose you, therefore the world will hate you.[599] And Jesus said if the world hates you, you know that it hated me before it hated you.[600]

If you expect to be loved, you know you should be nice because you are a Christian. You should be loving because you have Jesus in your heart. But it does not matter how sweet you are, because the light is in you, the darkness will hate you.

The way to eradicate hate is to love no matter what. Toward the end of Jesus's time on earth, he told his disciples, "A new commandment I give to you, that you love one another; as I have loved you, that you also love one another. By this all will know that you are my disciples, if you have love for one another."[601]

"I give you a new commandment," Jesus said, adding a warning, "And if you obey this commandment all men will know who you are, they will know where you stand. Know that they may hate you for that. They may throw you out of the synagogues and out of their presence. They may despise you."

597 John 3:20
598 John 8:12
599 John 15:19
600 John 15:18
601 John 13:34–35

Do you want to penetrate that darkness? Do you want to win the lost? Do you want to get through to those who will not listen to you talking about surrendering to Christ? Then love one another no matter what.

The enemy tries to destroy the church from within, bringing disunity, prejudice, and racial tension. Loving one another as Christ loves you? That is the only way you will be able to penetrate the darkness.

"By this all will know that you are my disciples, if you have love for one another," Jesus said.[602] And he prayed for his disciples "that they all may be one, as you, Father, are in me, and I in you; that they also may be one in us, that the world may believe that you sent me."[603]

———— ————

There is tension brewing not only among those who do not know Christ but even within the church. The devil is walking in our midst.

In all the years of ministry in New York City, Jesus made it clear to me that I have to be able to sit by someone, stand by them, and worship Jesus no matter who they are. And in doing so, I have to know that in my heart I have nothing but love them.

I have asked the Holy Spirit to show me if there is anything but love for others in my heart. I cannot allow politics or race or differences in theology to come between me and the person next to me.

Jesus prayed for his disciples "that they may be one in Christ that the world may know, that the world may see me."[604] How do we do that? **How do we live as one? By loving one another.** And we love by forgiving anyone who has sinned against us—not simply saying we forgive, but forgiving from the heart those who have hurt us.

You love by reaching out to seek restoration. If some brother or sister has fallen, do not isolate yourself from them. Do not back away. Instead, reach out to them, put your arms around them and say, "I am praying for you. God still loves you, and I still love you."

---

602 John 13:35
603 John 17:21
604 John 17:6–21, paraphrased

When the church reaches out in love to those who have fallen, when people experience this kind of love, something supernatural happens within them.

In the days ahead, you may not always feel safe. But here is my plea, that you **allow the Holy Spirit to do a deep work in your spirit, that he would transform you to love in such a way that the darkness will give way before the light.**

Years ago, before this church had been started, I was on my knees in my office in Texas. The Lord told me to go to New York and start a church on Broadway. And the Lord said I would find a remnant here who would love one another, and God would protect them.

I have lived to see that come to pass. I have lived to see God raise up pastors and elders from many races. If we lose the love we have for one another, when we lose the unity we have, we have lost our testimony.

I cannot stress enough how important this is. Loving one another is the only way to have the blessing of God. Walking in union with God in the days ahead is the only way to enjoy the protection of the Holy Spirit. If you want to know that God will hear you when you pray, you cannot sit in church with anything in your heart against any other person or any other race.

Ask God to set you free, to break the chains of prejudice, disunity, and a lack of love.

I do not want anything to hinder my heart and my voice when I approach the throne of God. Perhaps you can relate. You and I have to be vigilant and resist even the smallest seeds of prejudice, hatred, or division entering our minds, whether through news reports or pop culture.

We have it in our power to stop the intrusion of any seeds of hatred and discord that the devil would like to plant in our hearts, for Jesus said, "The gates of hell shall not prevail against my church."[605]

---

605 Matthew 16:18, paraphrased

When there is unity in the body, anybody who comes in and tries to disrupt that will be exposed by the Holy Spirit. How? By you speaking up. You can say, "That is not what this church is about. Here, we do not bring division. We love one another. You are welcome to talk about Jesus and about how we can love one another, for that is what we are all about."

It is true. We are about loving one another—and not just by hugging. You can hug and still put a knife in somebody's back. But loving your neighbor is something you can do, not only say. Such love comes from the Holy Spirit working in you.

The apostle Peter encouraged the church with these words: "But the end of all things is at hand; therefore be serious and watchful in your prayers. And above all things have fervent love for one another, for 'love will cover a multitude of sins.' Be hospitable to one another without grumbling. As each one has received a gift, minister it to one another, as good stewards of the manifold grace of God."[606]

Indeed, the end of all things is at hand, and God is establishing his kingdom. You and I are a part of that kingdom, and we can have that quiet confidence in the Lord that everything is right before the Lord. All malice, all bitterness has been dispelled.

And in these last days we can live without holding grudges, being hospitable, open, willing to listen, willing to be the hands of Jesus.

Do not ask the Holy Spirit to help you love unless you are willing to grow in love. And if you do allow the Spirit to change your heart toward those around you, get ready to see darkness shatter.

---

606 1 Peter 4:7–10

39

Right Song, Wrong Side

I f you grew up going to church, you will know this story well. After being in Egypt for 430 years, the children of Israel were finally allowed to return to the Promised Land. It took ten plagues to convince Pharaoh to release the Israel- ites—more than a million of them.[607]

God guided them using a cloud during the day and a pillar of fire at night.[608] No sooner had they left and Pharaoh regretted losing his workforce, so a chase ensued.[609]

The people of Israel found themselves in a terrible situation trapped between a sea and their enemies. Despite having seen God free them in a miraculous way, panic set into the camp. The people complained, essentially telling Moses, "We told you this would happen. Why did you drag us out here?"[610]

You can imagine the roar of that crowd. They rose up against Moses. But God had told Moses that he would protect them.[611] And yet, he was so overwhelmed by this situation, he fell on his knees and wept. Then God said, "Why do you cry to me? Tell the children of Israel to go forward. But lift up your rod, and stretch

---

607 Exodus 12:37
608 Exodus 13:21
609 Exodus 14:5–6
610 Exodus 14:11–12, paraphrased
611 Exodus 14:4

out your hand over the sea and divide it. And the children of Israel shall go on dry ground through the midst of the sea."[612]

That night, God sent a strong wind to open up the sea and let the Israelites pass through on dry land.[613] "So the Lord saved Israel that day out of the hand of the Egyptians," Moses tells us, "and Israel saw the Egyptians dead on the seashore. Thus Israel saw the great work which the Lord had done in Egypt; so the people feared the Lord, and believed the Lord and His servant Moses.."[614]

Once they had seen the miracle, out came the tambourines. Out came the dancers, and they sang a beautiful song. "The Lord is my strength and song, and he has become my salvation," they sang. "He is my God, and I will praise him; my father's God, and I will exalt him."[615]

Right song. Wrong side. **They sang a beautiful song, but I believe this was the song God yearned for on the other side of the waters, when their faith was being tested. Anybody can praise the Lord after the victory has come.**

What are you facing that you cannot understand, that looks dark and hopeless? I have argued with the Lord at times and said, "Lord, it is only natural to fear. If I were there that day facing mountains on two sides, a sea before me, and the enemy closing in from behind, I too would have trembled. My faith may have wavered or may have even failed—just like the children of Israel."

God is a tender, loving Father. We can tell him what we really think. So I continued, "They were human, Lord. We are human! Are you demanding that your children praise you when everything is bleak? When there is unemployment? When people are losing their homes? Because there have been times I have been there, when I have gone through similar situations and I did not feel like praying, I did not feel like singing, and I certainly did not want to dance."

God was asking his people to trust him, to march toward the water and even step into it without any evidence at that point that they would not drown.

---

612 Exodus 14:15–16
613 Exodus 14:19–22
614 Exodus 14:30–31
615 Exodus 15:2

Perhaps you have been sensing the Holy Spirit telling you—like God told Moses, "Why are you crying? Why are you mourning? Have I failed you in the past? Did you not see all these deliverances? Do they not count? Get up."

When will you come to a place where you say, "God, I am not going to let this get me down," where you can say with Job, "Though he slay me, yet I will trust him"?[616]

═══

The world demands a song in hard times. Years after crossing on dry land, Israel had been taken captive again and exiled to Babylon. In Psalm 137, we find them sitting by the river, weeping. "By the rivers of Babylon, there we sat down, yea, we wept when we remembered Zion. We hung our harps upon the willows in the midst of it. For there those who carried us away captive asked of us a song, and those who plundered us requested mirth,[617] saying, 'Sing us one of the songs of Zion!' "[618]

Can you imagine God's people sitting there, weeping? They had lost everything, but having heard that the Israelites could make beautiful music, the Babylonians came, asking them to sing some happy tunes.

The Babylonians, I believe, were without hope. But they had heard that the God of Israel can take you through hard times. They had heard that this God puts a song in your heart, even when you are facing incredible times. So they came and demanded a song.

There is a generation today that is demanding a song. They came looking for a song, demanding mirth. Yet they are empty. On weekends, you can often hear people wailing on the streets of New York City in the middle of the night. Whether it is because of drugs or alcohol, I do not know. But you can hear this cry of hopelessness.

Perhaps you feel like the people of Israel, declaring, "How can I sing? How can I have joy when my heart is asking, 'How will I make it through this?' "[619]

Still, people want hope. They want to see an ordinary person like you or me who has gone through hell on earth and walked out the other side. Looking for hope, they demand a song.

---

616 Job 13:15
617 *Mirth* means gladness.
618 Psalm 137: 1–3
619 Psalm 137:4–6, paraphrased

I am not talking about dancing around your home or singing out loud. **Some of the loudest songs you will ever sing cannot be heard. They are quiet.**

How do you sing such songs? You fix your mind on Christ, and God will give you peace. You have to **choose to fix your mind on Christ**—no matter how dark it gets, because you trust God, you keep your eyes on him.[620]

When you encounter trials, people are watching, saying, "You said that your God can take you through anything. Were you lying?" That is when you can hear the Spirit lovingly inviting you to trust him more.

Watching the people of Israel wailing, I believe the Babylonians walked away, saying, "Their God does not hear them. Look how hopeless they are."

Around 1990, when we first started Times Square Church, we had a small choir. One of the men in the choir came to see me, saying, "Pastor Dave, I had a high-paying job in media and they asked me to make a compromise I could not make, so I quit my job. It was months ago, and try as I may, I cannot find a job."

At that time, there was a lot of unemployment in America. The man told me, "I know about testing, I know about trials. But if God is saying something to me, I am not getting it yet. There is one thing I do know from having had such a good job, I have a testimony. Those around me who know what I am going through also know that I do not murmur, I do not complain. I want to be a testimony of trusting God."

This man's heart was right with God. It was several months before he got another job, but he lived that testimony.

Around 1990, when we first started Times Square Church, we had a small choir.

The Lord spoke clearly to my heart, telling me there are many who are bound by a spirit of fear. Hear what I say: **Fear is a spirit. It is a tormenting spirit. It can put you in a pit of despair.** But you can get out of that pit today.[621] You need not go another day going deeper and deeper into fear.

---

620 Isaiah 26:3
621 Psalm 40:1–2

The apostle Paul reminded Timothy, "God has not given us a spirit of fear, but of power and of love and of a sound mind."[622]

I believe the Holy Spirit is saying that God led you—just as sure as he led Israel—to whatever crisis that is before you. Until you understand that, you cannot get out of the pit. You cannot get out of that pit until you declare, "God you have led me all my life. I have testified to that, but right now, I do not understand what I am going through. From where I am standing today, the future looks bleak. But I trust you."

Even if you no longer feel like praying, you can stand up today and say, "No more!" You can take authority over the spirit of fear. Next, you can acknowledge that God has led you to this place. God has kept his hand on you in the past, and God still has his eye on you.[623] **Even though you cannot see through the storm, you know there is another side. No matter what the circumstances look like, you can choose to trust God through it all.**

$$\equiv \equiv$$

How long are you going to allow the devil to harass your mind and your thoughts, bringing fear, loneliness, and emptiness? How long will you put up with it knowing that Jesus said, "I give you power to cast down evil spirits."[624]

"You take a stand and resist the devil," the Bible says, "and he will flee from you."[625] That is God's Word!

It is time to rise up and take a stand. Then, even before you see the waters part, even before you see God's redemption, you can start singing a song of praise.

---

622 2 Timothy 1:7
623 Psalm 32:8
624 Matthew 10:1, paraphrased
625 James 4:7, paraphrased

40

The Healing of the Home

Something is happening in homes across the world—even Christian homes— that dismays me. It is the alarming rate of divorce. When you hear about someone getting a divorce, it often is somebody you never would have imagined it happening to. People say, "It could never happen in my home."

And yet it is happening.

At Teen Challenge, most—if not all—of the young men and women who end up at the center are ones who have come from broken homes. Children, even toddlers and babies, can sense when there is tension between their parents. From our experience at the center, divorce causes more teenagers to run to drugs, sex, and alcohol than all the drug pushers and bad influences combined.

God spoke to me about this, saying, "If you want to help the kids, talk to their parents about their marriages."

———————

A pastor told me once, "Young people these days say, 'Marriage is not working.' They simply want to live together if they love one another. Perhaps we should come up with some kind of a spousal ceremony, so we could take the guilt problem out," he told me. "But I agree that marriage isn't working." He assured me that there were many other pastors who thought the same.

That shocked me! Pastors might be changing their minds about marriage, but God has not. Malachi the prophet tells me that God hates divorce,[626] and Jesus stated that marriage is to be a permanent bond between one man and one woman. To break it off and marry another, according to Jesus, is adultery.[627]

If your marriage is a part of the divorce statistics, my goal is not to further hurt or alienate you. If you have been hurt by the church because you have been a victim of divorce, I am here to remind you of Jesus's response to the woman caught in adultery. He said to those who wanted to stone her, "He who is without sin among you, let him throw a stone at her first."[628]

I have heard the many reasons why people choose to give up on their marriage, but the number one excuse is that their spouse no longer understands them. It seems like people are running around looking for someone to understand them. If they do not get it from their mate, they go and look for understanding from a third party.

Truth be told, if you leave two people in love alone and they face a challenge, they could work it out, no matter the problem. But if you introduce a third party, then there's no hope for them to work it out.

Even in the church, there are men and women flirting with one another and before they know it, the third party drives a wedge into their homes and marriages! This third party is not always another man or woman, though. It can be overreliance on a parent's opinion rather than that of your spouse. It can also be a job that takes up all your time and energy. Or it can be the loss of a job leading to financial pressures. Or it can be a pornography addiction.

If you have been guilty of giving up on your marriage and seeking companionship or affirmation from something or someone outside of your holy union, may

626 Malachi 2:16
627 Mark 10:11–12
628 John 8:7

this be a warning. So far, you may have gotten away with it. But the Bible is clear that your sin will find you out.[629]

You may have gotten away so far with flirting with someone and see it as innocent fun. Watch out! If you do not take it to the cross, if you do not forsake this behavior and run from it for your life, you are headed for exposure. And then your whole life comes tumbling down.

God forbid you are someone nurturing an affair or indulging in pornography thinking nobody knows about it. Be careful. Be very, very careful. The devil is out to destroy you.[630] The Holy Spirit is warning you to pluck it out by the roots before you lose your home, your children—everything.

$$\equiv\equiv$$

I have had some couples tell me that they did not want to live a lie, that they would rather be honest and call it quits on their marriage.

In seeking wisdom on how to heal marriages, I have found five simple steps.

1. **Turn down the volume at your house.** The Bible says, "A soft answer turns away wrath, but a harsh word stirs up anger."[631] We have people who go to church having bickered and fought all the way to church, and they pick up the fight the moment they close the car door back behind them. And then they wonder why their kids grow up to have disrespect for the house of God.

   In their fighting, too many men and women think the louder they get, the more power they have. That is not the case. Stop the arguing and the bickering. Turn down the volume.

2. **Learn to say, "I am sorry."** The apostle Peter asked Jesus, "How many times do I forgive the person who wrongs me? Seven times?" to which Jesus said, "No, seventy times seven."[632]

   Be the first to apologize, and do it often. You might object, saying, "Me? Say I am sorry? I always have to say I am sorry."

---

629 Numbers 32:23
630 John 10:10a
631 Proverbs 15:1
632 Matthew 18:21–22, paraphrased

I know it does not make sense to apologize when you were not the one to have wronged your spouse. Apologize anyway. That is what Jesus said we should do. Be the first to say you are sorry, and do it as often as necessary.

It may also be helpful to recall what Jesus said about being aware of our shortcomings by taking the plank from our own eye before trying to find the speck from someone else's eye.[633]

3. **Quit your jealousy.** The Bible says that jealousy is crueler than anger.[634] How many marriages has this cancer destroyed? If you have jealousy in your heart toward your husband or your wife, pray for a miracle. Ask God to deliver you of jealousy, else it will destroy your marriage.

4. **Quit being so cranky.** The Bible says to be kind and tenderhearted to one another.[635] Tenderness too often is missing in our marriages. Buy your wife flowers. Write each other love poems. Take out the garbage without being asked and without complaining.

5. **Quit dancing to somebody else's tune.** Jesus said, "But to what shall I liken this generation? It is like children sitting in the marketplaces and calling to their companions, and saying 'We played the flute for you, and you did not dance.' "[636] Everybody hast a tune, wanting somebody to dance to it.

    Seek God's Word regarding who you are in God's eyes and what your role is in your marriage rather than subscribing to the cultural view of things.

If you were to tell me your marriage is hopeless, or that it used to be nice, allow me to remind you of the day you and your spouse stood before an altar or before a judge, all dressed up, and you said, "I will love you until death do us part." With that, you were married in the sight of God.

I do not know what may have happened in the meantime. I do not care if you are tired or feel misunderstood. I do not know if one of you has been looking for

---

633 Matthew 7:3–5
634 Proverbs 27:4
635 Ephesians 4:32
636 * **PLEASE NOTE: If you are experiencing abuse or harm at the hands of a spouse, please seek safety and help.**
Matthew 11:16–17

greener grass. Maybe you would tell me, "The magic is gone, David. I will never be able to sense what I had before."

Well, we do not live by feelings. We live by faith. And if by faith you will come to God and pray for him to do a miracle and heal your marriage, God can do that. God can heal your marriage.*

Jesus affirmed the permanence of the marriage bond,[637] but he also acknowledged that due to the depravity of the human heart, immorality is grounds for divorce.[638]

The Greek word Jesus used for *immorality* is *porneia*—from where we get the words *pornography*. *Pornos*—from the same Greek root and translated as *prostitute*—also pertains. Only in the case of such betrayal is divorce permissible, *yet not advisable*.[639]

If you are facing such heartbreaking betrayal, I urge you to follow the guidance of the apostle Paul in his letter to the Galatians: "If anyone is caught in any trespass, you who are spiritual, restore such a one in a spirit of gentleness."[640] It may be hard work, but I believe it is worth the work.

$$\equiv\equiv$$

If you are struggling, remember how things were at the beginning, repent, and go back. **Work on your marriage. And ask God to work on you, to show you what else you can do differently.**

Choosing to recommit to one another and work on your marriage is not about repeating your vows. It is about choosing to be kind, choosing to say you are sorry, choosing to extend forgiveness, and choosing to trust. It is about choosing to be tenderhearted.

---

637 Mark 10:2–9

638 Matthew 19:9

639 It is important to remember that Jesus' words here are specifically to men. In the ancient context, women pledged complete sexual exclusivity to their husbands, but many marriage contracts did not include the same pledge for husbands (who might take a second wife, for example, though that was a rare practice among Jews of Jesus' day). Men, however, vowed to provide food, shelter, and safety for their wives and their children.
In that context, a man's abuse of a woman is a violation of the terms of the marriage covenant analogous to the woman's violation of her vow of sexual exclusivity. This is why, historically, many interpreters have understood spousal abuse as breaking the covenantal terms and therefore as grounds for divorce, that is, the dissolution of the (broken) covenant. In either case, divorce is only permitted, as Jesus explains, because of a hardness of heart (Matthew 19:8)—the very thing corrected by walking in the Spirit.

640 Galatians 6:1

It is also about determining in your mind, "We will make this work. I believe in miracles. I believe in God. I believe God can keep my home. I am not going to give up, I am not going to let the devil destroy my home and ruin my kids. I will not allow it. Never."

Perhaps it is time for you to confess, "Lord, I needed this word. I acknowledge it. I admit that I need help."

That is where healing begins.

41

The Healing Power of Afflictions

A fflictions are the circumstances and the troubles that cause you to lose sleep as you try to figure out what is happening and how to make your way through it all. "Many are the afflictions of the righteous," the psalmist says, "But the Lord delivers him out of them all."[641]

I am convinced that God not only uses afflictions to heal the saved, he also uses them in the life of the sinner. Take Manasseh, for example, one of the worst kings in the history of Israel. He turned against God, established altars to Baal right in the temple court, and offered his children as sacrifices.[642]

But then God raised up the Assyrians to capture Jerusalem and take Manasseh and his people as prisoners. The Assyrians tortured them, marching them hundreds of miles through the desert with hardly any food or drink. This caused wicked King Manasseh to seek God.[643] Manasseh humbled himself and began to pray.

As a result, this once-evil king became a fighter for God, was restored to his throne, and tore down the very idols he had established.

≡ ≡

---

641 Psalm 34:19
642 2 Kings 21:2–7
643 2 Chronicles 33:11–13

You may know someone who has turned their back to God. Do not give up on them. **Sometimes, you have to watch them go through whatever it is they are facing. You cannot do anything about it but pray. God can use their afflictions to bring them back to Christ.**

But it is not only those who have turned their backs on God whom he allows to go through difficult times. King David said his affliction came from the hand of God. "In faithfulness, you have afflicted me," he said.[644]

How did that happen? "Before I was afflicted I went astray," David confessed, "It is good for me that I have been afflicted, that I may learn your statutes."[645]

This is from the psalm where David famously declared, "Your Word is a lamp to my feet and a light to my path."[646] How did the Word of God become a lamp to David's feet? God had worked in David's life through afflictions. "Unless your law had been my delight, I would then have perished in my affliction,"[647] he admitted.

———

Perhaps you have a hard time believing a loving God would allow you to face hardship. **But unless you see God in all your circumstances, it will not take much for your faith to be shipwrecked.**

Because I have committed my life to God, in *all* that comes my way—both good and bad—I hold fast to what the Bible teaches, which is that the angel of the Lord encamps around me and will deliver me, no matter what.[648]

Whether I face a fire or a flood, I believe that God is ordering my steps.[649] I know God is with me, even if I am facing a fiery furnace,[650] and that he has a reason for everything he is doing, including refining us. "For you, God, tested us; you refined us like silver," the psalmist said. "We went through fire and water, but you brought us to a place of abundance."[651]

---

644 Psalm 119:75
645 Psalm 119:67, 71
646 Psalm 119:105
647 Psalm 119:92
648 Psalm 34:7
649 Proverbs 16:9; Jeremiah 10:23
650 Daniel 3:6–27
651 Psalm 66:10–12 NIV

The Bible makes it clear that God does not take delight in mankind's suffering. Jeremiah said, "Though he causes grief, yet he will show compassion according to the multitude of his mercies. For he does not afflict willingly, nor grieve the children of men."[652]

Like a surgeon cutting into a patient's body to remove a malignant tumor, when God allows pain in your life, it is because he is working at removing that which will destroy you.

$$\equiv\equiv$$

I do not know about you, but when afflictions come my way, the first thing I do is to blame the devil. The devil can indeed attack us, but like with Job, he cannot touch us without God's permission, and even then, God will put limitations on the devil.[653]

You and I know when we experience attacks, but these have to be permitted by God. And just as God allowed the King of Assyria to attack Manasseh, it was simply for a time.

$$\equiv\equiv$$

Asaph, the music and choir director in the temple during the reign of David and Solomon, also knew about afflictions. Asaph was a praying man, a godly man. But there came a great affliction into his life, of which he said, "I am so troubled that I cannot speak."[654]

He gives no details, but said, "God is good to those with a clean heart."[655] This does not mean if you are good nothing bad happens to you, and if you are bad, nothing good happens. Asaph goes on to confess, "But as for me, my feet had almost stumbled; my steps had nearly slipped. For I was envious of the boastful, when I saw the prosperity of the wicked."[656]

Asaph was envious of those who were prospering, those who did not seem to have a problem in life. It was Asaph's jealousy that caused him to sin. His envy could

---

652 Lamentations 3:32–33
653 Job 1:12
654 Psalm 77:4b
655 Psalm 73:1, paraphrased
656 Psalm 73:2–3

have destroyed him. **There is nothing more dangerous, more serious, or crippling than envy and jealousy.** God allowed Asaph to go through hardship until he could admit his foolishness and his ignorance.[657]

Over the years, I have said many times that when you are in trouble, look at all the miracles God has done in the past. Go back to the Red Sea.[658] Go back to the manna.[659] Go back to the water out of the rock.[660] That is what Asaph did. He recalled what God had done.[661] But things only got worse for him. Asaph said, "I remembered God, and I was troubled."[662]

When you are being tried by God, it takes more than just looking back because in looking back, you might not see God doing the same miracles again. In that time, do not lose your faith as you try to figure it out.

Yes, go back and remember the good things God has done. But you hold on to your faith. God is with you in your trial.

God is not with you despite your failures. God is with you in it and through it. He is with you in your struggles, your pain, your failure. God will never leave you nor forsake you.[663]

That is the lesson Asaph finally learned.

= =

The apostle Paul also experienced afflictions. "I prayed three times that God would release me from this messenger of Satan that torments me,"[664] he said.

What did God say to him in response? "My grace is sufficient for you, for my strength is made perfect in weakness."

To this, Paul declared, "Therefore most gladly I will rather boast in my infirmities, that the power of Christ may rest upon me."[665] In other words, **God's grace will not only let you endure; it will make you strong.**

---

657 Psalm 73:22
658 Exodus 14–15
659 Exodus 16:13–36
660 Exodus 17:6
661 Psalm 77:11–20
662 Psalm 77:3
663 Deuteronomy 31:6
664 2 Corinthians 12:7–8, paraphrased
665 2 Corinthians 12:9

The Scriptures also remind us that Christ, who intercedes for us,[666] says he will no longer remember our lawless deeds.[667] And that "there is therefore now no condemnation to those who are in Christ Jesus, who do not walk according to the flesh, but according to the Spirit."[668]

In light of these truths, I believe the right response to afflictions is to ask God, **"Lord, are you trying to say something to me in this affliction? Do you have a message? Have I been blinded to something that you are trying to speak into my life?"**

God speaks through afflictions. We need only listen.

≡ ≡

Sometimes the worst afflictions come from friends, from people. They have a conflict with you, turn on you, and speak evil of you. Over my lifetime in ministry, many have wounded me deeply.

On one occasion, someone got in touch with me who I thought was a friend. I had mentored them and did much to help them financially and in many other ways. But then, the person attacked me, saying things that wounded me deeply. I went home that day, convinced that it was the devil trying to destroy me.

I went to the Lord in prayer, quoting verses, telling God how I felt. Then, I heard God's still, small voice. "I have allowed this because I have been talking to you about something," God told me, "and you have not been listening." The moment I heard it, I knew what issue God was putting his finger on.

Next, the Holy Spirit prompted me to get my concordance and study every passage on the tender lovingkindness of the Father. This was the first verse I found: "Let, I pray, your merciful kindness be for my comfort, according to your word to your servant."[669]

"Do you understand what I am saying?" I sensed the Lord asking me. "I will comfort you, and you will learn who I really am."

---

666 Romans 8:34
667 Hebrews 8:12
668 Romans 8:1
669 Psalm 119:76

God reminded me that when afflictions come, he "is gracious, and full of compassion; slow to anger, and of great mercy. The Lord is good to all, and his tender mercies are over all his works."[670]

Whatever you are going through, God's mercy is there. God's tender loving kindness is within reach.

"Why then do some of the godliest people suffer?" you may ask. I cannot explain that to you. But in my life and in the lives of godly men and women close to me who have suffered for years, I can tell you that if we have learned anything in life, we learned it in our darkest hours.

In times of pain and agony, I have held on, declaring, "God, I believe you are in this."

It takes the load off when you realize you do not need to figure everything out but you can know instead that God is with you, no matter what.

---

670 Psalm 145:8–9

42

The Lord Will Fight for You

In the book of Deuteronomy, you find Moses reminding the children of Israel why they had wandered in the wilderness for another thirty-eight years after they had been so close to the Promised Land that they could see it. But when the Lord commanded them to enter Canaan, they disobeyed.

Grieved by their unbelief, God had sent them back into the wilderness. **Their unbelief had caused less than one year of wilderness wandering to stretch to almost forty years.**[671]

So, Moses spoke to the children whose fathers had died in the wilderness, reminding them that their parents had been a people who were called and anointed, a people whom God loved and miraculously cared for. Still, doubt and murmuring entered their hearts time after time.

God used some strong language when referring to the unbelief of the Israelites—words like *wrath* and *abhorrence*. That was God's attitude toward their unbelief. God was wrought with anger.

Moses reminded Israel that God had led them to Kadesh Barnea where he tested them while affirming that **he would fight for them**. Instead, Moses and the elders sent spies into the land instead of acting on God's commands.

---

671 Deuteronomy 1:21–35

If they had gone right ahead and marched into the Promised Land, they would have had victory after victory, and God would have seen them through every one of their crises.

But instead, they sent spies into Canaan. Ten of those came back reporting there were giants and that the cities were walled up to heaven. **They had opened themselves to the lies of the enemy because they did not take God at his word. They did not move when God said to move.** Having opened themselves to lies, the people of Israel were weeping, shaking their fists at God, thinking he had deserted them.

God's words to them also pertain to us today, urging us to beware lest we, in the last days, fall into the same unbelief that caused the Israelites to be driven back into the wilderness.

Like with the children of Israel, God is reminding you he will lead you. No matter what you face, you can trust him. But you need faith. Instead, you believe lies. When did those creep in?

When did you start believing that you are not good enough, that God is mad at you and has not forgiven you, that you have to fight for yourself? When did you start doubting God's promises? He said, "I will never leave or forsake you. I will be merciful and will forgive you if you confess your sins."[672]

God told the Israelites at Kadesh Barnea, "Fear not, neither be discouraged."[673] Still, they dragged their feet. They questioned God's promises. **I believe God brings all his children to a Kadesh Barnea at some stage, a place of ultimate testing of our faith.**

This place-name means fugitive, vagabond, or wanderer for if you make the wrong choice at Kadesh Barnea, you will find yourself wandering until you finally choose to take God at his word.

If you look back on your life, you will notice many places where God has brought you through. He has never failed you. God made a way, whether financially, in your health, or otherwise. And when you face a time of testing, you can be assured

---

672 1 Kings 8:57; 1 John 1:9, paraphrased
673 Deuteronomy 1:29; Joshua 1:9, paraphrased

that God is trying to produce in you a kind of faith that is pure gold. For you see, without faith you cannot please God.[674]

===

The Lord brought the Israelites to Kadesh Barnea where they had to decide whether to move ahead in faith—trusting God even if there were giants and walls ahead—or to turn back in unbelief.

Earlier, God had spoken clearly through the lips of Moses, saying, **"I am the Lord your God, and I will fight for you."**[675] At Kadesh Barnea, God was repeating this promise.[676] Still, they asked, "Is God with us?"[677] I believe what they were really saying was, "If God were still with us, we would not be facing this hopeless situation."

Though God spoke, Israel's unbelief got in the way of them truly hearing God's promises.

The same can be true for you as you come to church each week or as you read the Word of God. **Unless you receive God's promises in faith and ask the Holy Ghost to imprint them on your mind, you will simply move on and when you face a crisis, you will have nothing of substance to hold on to,** so you ask God whether he is with you.

===

If only the Israelites would think back on when they were camping in Rephidim and they could find no water to drink. Even there, they were asking if God had deserted them, and they were ready to stone Moses. But then God told Moses to strike the rock and water poured forth.[678]

Instead of trembling because of their thirst, they were trembling before the Lord, in awe of his miraculous provision.

As for you and I, the way out of a crisis is *not* by the simple determination to do better, by making all kinds of promises to God, by gritting your teeth, and by

---

674 Hebrews 11:6
675 Exodus 14:14, paraphrased
676 Deuteronomy 3:22, paraphrased
677 Numbers 13:25–14:4, paraphrased
678 Exodus 17:1–7

pushing ahead. **What changes your circumstances is when you surrender to God, saying, "God, would you give me the mind of Christ?"** With that, the Holy Spirit will come and imprint God's promises on your mind.

You have something that the Old Testament saints could only dream of—the fact that your body is the temple of the Holy Spirit[679] and you can know his voice.[680] **Still, how often do you walk through life stone deaf to God's voice within?**

As for the generation of Israelites who had encountered God at Kadesh Barnea, because of their unbelief, they left that spot and wandered in the wilderness until an entire generation had passed away.[681]

Here is what I have found: If you have one area in your life where you doubt God, it spills over into other areas, becoming like a cancer that defiles every part of your being.

God has been telling me, "If you say you have faith, trust me with *everything* in your life. And if you want peace, you cannot hold a grudge against someone and expect peace in other areas. Trust me in *every* area of your life, not only to forgive you."

But you and I tend to put God on a timeline saying, "Well, Lord, you did not yet answer me, so I will have to do something myself." That is arrogance. You must come to a place where you trust God so much that you do not even fear death.

Instead, you get impatient with God and take matters into your own hands. When you do that, you end up back in the wilderness.

I went down to 42nd Street to the spot where God first spoke to me about planting Times Square Church. I went there in the early evening when it is the most crowded with people heading to different shows.

I went up the steps of the Ford Theater and prayed and wept as I watched the multitudes. It is said that during rush hour, about a quarter of a million people pass through the heart of New York City.

---

679 1 Corinthians 6:19
680 John 10:27
681 Deuteronomy 2:14–16

As I sat there, watching the crowds rushing by, I heard the Holy Spirit whisper, "They have no God. There are only a few believers. They have no God except sports and entertainment. They have the false gods of pleasure, success, and money. They have no joy."

As I sat there watching the crowds, I thought about what it had to be like among the Israelites in the wilderness. There would be more than half a million men who would pass me, all going into the desert full of unbelief.[682]

Then the Holy Spirit reminded me of this multitude of men who left Kadesh Barnea, only Joshua and Caleb would eventually enter the Promised Land.[683] The rest had died before their time—died because of unbelief.

Watching the crowds on 42nd Street, the Spirit asked me, "How do you reach the masses?" And he reminded me of when Jesus wept over Jerusalem.[684] He said, "O Jerusalem, Jerusalem, the one who kills the prophets and stones those who are sent to her! How often I wanted to gather your children together, as a hen gathers her chicks under *her* wings, but you were not willing!"[685]

The multitudes rushing by me on 42nd Street all had access to the gospel, but they rejected it. The Lord said to me, "It is about time." God is about to come and search the hearts of all men and women, looking for those who trust in him.

God would go all over the country—to football stadiums, hockey arenas, basketball courts, to Washington DC—searching for men and women of faith. And he could find none.

As I sat looking at the crowds, thinking of how it would grieve the heart of God, I heard him say, "This does not grieve me nearly as much as what I feel when I look at my body, the church, and there are only a few who believe and trust me with everything in their lives."

---

682 According to the census in Numbers 1:17–46, the men alone who left Egypt numbered more than 600,000.
683 Numbers 14:30
684 Luke 19:41–44
685 Matthew 23:37

Today, God comes to you and asks, "Do you trust me? When I come, will I find faith in you—the kind of faith that will not take matters into your own hands?"

May you have faith to wait on God, faith to stand still, faith to trust that the Lord will fight for you, no matter what your circumstances might look like.

43

The Making of a Man of God

I do not know about you, but more than anything else, I want to be known as a man of God. I want my life to bring glory to Jesus. That ought to be the desire of every believer.

What are the forces that go into the making of a man or a woman of God? What do these men and women have in common as far as inner battles and complexities?

In the Bible and in the lives of contemporary men and women of God, there are forces and patterns God uses to shape people. In the life of all great men and women of faith, there was suffering.

Job, in the middle of his cup of pain, cried out to God. He said, "I have bathed my soul in tears."[686]

David said he made his couch a bed of tears.[687] He said, "My bones are consumed with pain; my flesh is consumed with pain."[688]

Sweating blood, Jesus cried out to the Father in the Garden of Gethsemane, "If at all possible, let this cup depart from me."[689]

I do not know what your cup of pain may be, but there are some people who have prayed for years for deliverance. **Just because you are going through pain**

---

686 Job 16:16–20, paraphrased
687 Psalm 6:6
688 Psalm 32:3, paraphrased
689 Matthew 26:39 conflated with Luke 22:44

does not mean you are being attacked by the devil. The psalmist said, "If I had not been afflicted, I would not have sought the Lord."[690] To say that the devil was behind his pain would suggest that the devil was driving him to the Father.

There have been years in my life when I had to bear **physical pain**. I sought God and prayed for him to remove the pain and yet, through all that pain, I could feel God at work in my life. And after the pain passed, I could say that it had been good for me.

Do not think that a person used by God has all the answers. Do not think for one moment that he hears from God all the time. I experienced a **night of confusion** when for months, I went without hearing God's voice. I walked in a state of confusion with no guidance from God.

Or you may have to face your **hour of isolation** when you have no support from friends or family, and when it appears as though God has hidden his face from you. Is it at all possible that God would hide his face from a man or woman of God in the making? Could it be possible that there is a season when God lifts his hand, turns his face, and hides?

Job said, "God does not hear me; he has become cruel to me."[691]

Hezekiah had a reputation for excellence. But when ambassadors of the princes of Babylon came to inquire about his success, God withdrew from Hezekiah to test him.[692]

The psalmist said, "Has God forgotten to be gracious? Has he in anger shut up his tender mercies?"[693]

And Jesus famously cried out on the cross, "My God, my God, why have you forsaken me?"[694]

Jesus's cup of pain had never been more real to me than when I experienced the terror of getting on my knees and finding I could not pray. I could not reach God. There was nothing but blackness, emptiness, and fear.

Is that strange to you? Have you never faced that in your life? Then you have not yet been to Calvary.

---

690 Psalm 119:71, paraphrased
691 Job 30:20–21, paraphrased
692 2 Chronicles 32:31
693 Psalm 77:9
694 Matthew 27:46

God does not stay hidden forever, though. He said in just a moment of wrath I hid but I will turn to thee in tender, loving mercies.[695] When you drink your cup of pain, when you face a night of confusion and your hour of isolation, you can know that the Lord knows this path that you are on. And when he has tried you, you will come forth as gold because you trust in him.

The psalmist, amid his hour of confusion and isolation, drinking his cup of pain said, "I will sing of the mercies of the Lord forever."[696] His faith remained intact; nothing could touch it.

But what does that have to do with you and me? When I was preaching in San Francisco, a young man from Times Square Church who happened to be working in San Francisco came to see me. I had originally met him in New York and remember the night that he came to Christ, when he walked out of that prayer room with joy in his heart. But when he came to see me in San Francisco, he was a different man.

"God seems to be so far away from me, I am being tempted," he told me. "In fact, I feel like I am going to lose the touch of God. I feel like I am slipping back into the world. I walk the streets in fear and trembling, panicking. I have lost my joy."

I laid my hand on his shoulder and said, "Son, this is your hour of trial. God is testing you to see what is in your heart."

Tears began to stream down his cheeks. "So, you mean God isn't mad with me after all?" he asked, sharing that he had a "terrible habit." I assured him that God was not mad at him but that he would have to deal with the habit.

With that, the Spirit of the Lord fell on him, and he raised his hands and praised the Lord. When I left him in the prayer room, he was still thanking the Lord for bringing him through his time of testing.

"Weeping may endure for a night, but joy comes in the morning," the Bible says.[697]

---

695 Isaiah 54:8
696 Psalm 89:1
697 Psalm 30:5

I am blessed to have a loving wife whom I love dearly. The battle that I face in my ministry is not one in my home. I have wonderful children—my battle is not there either. I have friends around the country who appreciate my ministry—nor is my battle there.

I have never loved or desired the Lord more than now. And the more that I pray for young men and women to be reached through this ministry, the more that I say, "God use me, put your hand on me and open my eyes so I can see your power and your glory," the more I can feel myself being crushed under the weight of forces weighing against me.

Like Jesus, I have cried out, "Lord, I cannot take it. Take this cup of pain!"

There have even been times when I have wanted to run from the cup of pain brought on by these heavy forces, to get on a plane and go hide someplace like David, who said, "Oh that I had wings like a dove! I would fly away and be at rest."[698]

Still, I know what it is like to hear Jesus lead me every step of the way. I know what it is to get a pad and a pencil out and to ask God questions and then have him give me the answers. I know what it is like to stand before city officials and men in the government and prophecy as the Spirit comes, giving them the word that God was giving to me.

I also know what it is like to face nights of confusion where I do not know which way to turn, when I make multiple mistakes that cause me to despair and cry out, "Oh God! Where are you?"

During those times, I can feel nothing but death and aloneness. But through it all, there still is a sense of destiny, a sense that God is at work. And in the midst of the storm, I can hear the Spirit whispering, "Ride out the storm; just hold steady. Hold steady because when the enemy comes in like a flood, I will raise up a standard against it."[699]

You may know what I am talking about, praying and feeling like you are facing brass heavens. You bathe your couch in tears. You know the cup of pain. You know the night of confusion. You know what loneliness and isolation are when nobody can touch that pain in your heart.

---

698 Psalm 55:6
699 Isaiah 59:19

I believe that when a man or woman of God is in the making, these forces will come against you with all their fury and terror. But you can stand up and say, **"Though I be tried, though I be tested, though all these forces be raised against me, I know in whom I believe. I know that he is able to keep that which I have committed unto him against that day."**

═ ═

As God refines you, there will also be fiery darts of the enemy, so put on the armor of God so you can withstand them. Those who want to be a man or woman of God have to face the flood when, without any warning, you find yourself with everything hell has thrown at you.

If you are drinking from your cup of pain in this season, **I do not pray that God will deliver you from your cup of pain. Instead, I pray that your faith will not fail.** That is the way Jesus prayed. He said, "I have prayed for you, that your faith should not fail."[700]

This is God's way of strengthening your faith so you can face even bigger tests when they come. For there are tests in life, and there are trials. And these little tests you face prepare you for the big trials in life.

---

700 Luke 22:32

44

The Ministry of Beholding God's Face

The apostle Paul, in his letter to the church in Corinth, describes a ministry to which every single believer is called. "Now the Lord is the Spirit; and where the Spirit of the Lord is, there is liberty," he said. "But we all, with unveiled face, beholding as in a mirror the glory of the Lord, are being transformed into the same image from glory to glory, just as by the Spirit of the Lord. Therefore, since we have this ministry, as we have received mercy, we do not lose heart."[701]

This is not the way we typically view ministry. Our modern-day concept of ministry is not biblical. We tend to think of ministry as the career of ordained men and women who have gone to seminary or Bible college. They pastor churches. They build and maintain institutions. We say they are "in the ministry."

Instead, Paul describes the ministry of beholding the glory of the Lord. The Holy Spirit is the one who invites you into this ministry of spending time in the presence of Jesus, gazing upon the face of Christ, looking at him in focused worship. In doing so, you are being transformed—the Spirit forms Christ in you[702] so you take on the character of Christ.

This word *behold* does not merely mean to take a look. It means to fix your gaze. It means that you make a decision not to move from your position of beholding

---

701 2 Corinthians 3:17–4:1
702 Galatians 4:19

knowing that before you do anything else, before you attempt anything for God, you have to spend time in his presence, then come from there having received something that has changed you. You have been changed by beholding the glory of God in the face of Jesus Christ.

This is not about looking in a mirror. Jesus is not a mirror and you a reflection. Instead, because of the transforming power of the Holy Ghost, you behold his glory as if you are looking into glass, studying, fixing your gaze, and taking on Christ's very nature and character.

Out of this practice of beholding the glory of God, all other godly endeavors or ministries are birthed. And it is not for a select or ordained few but for all of us. It is for you. You have been invited into this ministry.

When you spend time focused on the Lord, he becomes the center and the obsession of your life. What you get from the time spent with him, you cannot get from any other place or person. Being with him transforms you, and while you or others may not see the change right away, a metamorphosis is taking place. The glory of the Lord is being manifest in you.

When you spend time looking at God's glory, you begin to see how short of that glory you have become and how blind you have been to your striving to please God, striving to overcome sin. But Paul reminds us that where the Spirit of the Lord is, there is freedom. **As the Spirit transforms you, your life becomes one of surrender rather than striving. It becomes one marked by freedom rather than captivity.**

This naturally leads to worship. Find a place where you can regularly worship God uninterrupted—your holy of holies where you meet face-to-face with Jesus. Wherever it is, look for someplace you can regularly return, where you can give the Spirit of the most high God the freedom to shape and mold you.

Paul reminds the church that "God has given us the light of the knowledge of the glory of God in the face of Jesus Christ. But we have this treasure in earthen vessels, that the excellence of the power may be of God and not of us. We are hard-pressed on every side, yet not crushed; we are perplexed, but not in despair; persecuted, but not forsaken; struck down, but not destroyed—always carrying about in the body the dying of the Lord Jesus, that the life of Jesus also may be manifested in our body."[703]

Do not miss this! You have the treasure of the knowledge of the glory of God, but you carry this treasure in the fragile vessel of humanity, lest you think it is of yourself. Yet you carry the treasure of having seen God's glory through the ministry of beholding his face.

That is what allows you to go through trials and suffering yet not be crushed.

———

When we were told our granddaughter Tiffany had terminal cancer, my first thoughts were of my daughter Debi. How would Debi take it if God took Tiffany?

But Debi and her husband, Roger, were solid as a rock because she had spent so much time shut in with God, beholding the face of God and reading whatever she could to help her know Jesus more.

What a metamorphosis. She was able to minister to so many people, even at the funeral. Since then, she would tell you, she has had times of sorrow, but she has such peace, rest, and strength.

In the same way, any suffering you go through is a call to ministry. You see, **I am convinced that all suffering, all pain, and all trials that come into the life of a child of God is a call to ministry.** This is why Paul could say, "I thank Christ Jesus our Lord who has enabled me, because he counted me faithful, putting me into the ministry..."[704]

Paul is referring to his conversion on the road to Damascus. Three days after he was blinded, he was in a house by himself, and Ananias was sent by the Holy Spirit to commission him for the ministry. God told Ananias to go and baptize Paul—then still known as Saul—"for he is a chosen vessel of mine to bear my name before gentiles, kings, and the children of Israel. For I will show him how many things he must suffer for my name's sake."[705]

Ananias was not sent to tell Paul of the great things he would do, but that he would suffer for the sake of God's name.

---

703 2 Corinthians 4:6–10
704 1 Timothy 1:12
705 Acts 9:15–16

I believe the reason why Paul said, "Christ enabled me, counting me faithful" before he talked about God laying this ministry of suffering upon him is to say, "I have God's promise that he will give me the strength to be faithful through it all."

Paul was no superman. He knew what few other men knew about despair. There were times he thought he could not make it. He suffered, was imprisoned, persecuted, beaten, stoned, and shipwrecked.[706] He talked about being pressed down beyond all strength and at the point of believing it was all over but in his most trying time he remembers his ministry.[707]

But then Paul remembered the ministry that God had entrusted him with, and he cried out in so many words, "Live or die, I am the Lord's, and I trust in God who raises the dead."[708]

With that, Paul told the Corinthian church that it was their prayers that helped him to make it through. (This is a good reminder not to take lightly the ministry of praying for those in need!)

$$\equiv\equiv$$

In his letter to Timothy, Paul reminds Timothy that there will be a time—*I believe that time is now*—when men will be so given over to their lusts that instead of sound doctrine, they will have teachers who will preach only the kind of messages they want to hear. Nevertheless, he told Timothy to preach the Word. But then will come a time when no amount of preaching, no amount of doctrine will get through to their hardened hearts.[709]

So, what ministry will be able to reach them? What ministry will have an impact?

I believe it will be the ministry of those who had been through the fire, who had endured pain and suffering because they beheld the face of the Lord. They beheld his glory.

$$\equiv\equiv$$

---

706 2 Corinthians 11:23–28; Galatians 5:11; 2 Timothy 3:10–11
707 2 Corinthians 1:8–11
708 2 Corinthians 1:8–9, paraphrased
709 2 Timothy 4:1–5

When you go through the fire, the world will watch how you respond. You will be changed by your suffering. **Whatever captivates your heart, whatever your eyes are fixed upon, the thing that you most yearn for, that will shape your character.**

I have seen time and again on the streets of New York how sexual perversions of all kinds—including pornography—change people. What once they were hiding they now flaunt proudly. And the more entrenched they get, the more they walk in their sin without shame, without one iota of conviction, blinded, and changed by their appetite. They think they have freedom, but instead, they are enchained by sin.

This I have seen to be true: **Whatever you are feeding your soul on, it changes you. It affects you. Your obsessions shape your soul.**

Like Paul, I urge you to surrender to the transforming power of the Holy Spirit so you may find true freedom in being transformed by beholding God's glory. That is your primary ministry, your primary call. And from it flows endurance, so you do not lose heart—no matter what you face!

45

The Path to Hope

You hear a lot about hope. The whole world is crying, "Somebody, somewhere, give me hope!" The word *hope* means an expectation of something good. How many times have you expected something good only to have your hopes dashed before your eyes? Life can become like a roller coaster of hope and despair, hope and despair.

The Bible says that while the world may have lost hope, God's people have a hope that is set before them—hope that is firm to the end.[710]

Where does this hope come from? The apostle Paul says, "Now may the God of hope fill you with all joy and peace in believing, that you may abound in hope by the power of the Holy Spirit."[711]

Because of the power of the Holy Spirit, you should be overflowing with hope. But due to the events around you, you may sometimes run low on hope. Where then do you go to get hope? Paul's letter to the Colossians speaks of "Christ in you, the hope of glory."[712] That is it! Christ *in you* produces hope. He is your hope.

---

710 Hebrews 6:11
711 Romans 15:13
712 Colossians 1:27

In his letter to the church in Rome, Paul shows us a path to hope. "Therefore, having been justified by **faith**, we have **peace** with God through our Lord Jesus Christ, through whom also we have access by faith into this grace in which we stand, and rejoice in hope of the glory of God. And not only that, but we also glory in **tribulations**, knowing that tribulation produces **perseverance**; and perseverance, **character**; and character, **hope**. Now hope does not disappoint, because the love of God has been poured out in our hearts by the Holy Spirit who was given to us."[713]

According to Paul, the path of hope begins by being fully assured that you are right with God—having peace with God through Christ.

Now, this may sound like elementary teaching, but you will not last where the world is headed unless you know that you have an unshakable faith that your sins are covered and no matter how many lies the devil tells you, no matter how your faith may be attacked, you know that Jesus reckons you righteous before the throne of God.

When you sin, the Holy Spirit will convict you, but never in anger. He is not mad at you, no matter what. He will woo you back to him.

Even though David had committed adultery and murder, because of his brokenness about what he had done, because of his contrite heart, God did not despise him. David was even called a man after God's own heart.[714]

Pride could have gotten in the way of David being restored, but he chose to turn to God, broken. As a result, Paul describes David as *blessed*, saying, "David also describes the blessedness of the man to whom God imputes righteousness apart from works: 'Blessed are those whose lawless deeds are forgiven, and whose sins are covered.' "[715]

Once you confess your sin and forsake your ways, God says he will never bring them to count again. Knowing you are forgiven, you can be at peace with God.

Next, the path to hope goes through tribulation and affliction. Paul said you not only rejoice in the hope of the glory of God (having been forgiven), you also glory in tribulations. The apostle Peter says the same: "But rejoice to the extent that you partake of Christ's sufferings, that when his glory is revealed, you may also be glad with exceeding joy."[716]

---

713 Romans 5:1–5
714 2 Samuel 11:2–5; Psalm 51:17; 1 Samuel 13:14
715 Romans 4:6–7
716 1 Peter 4:13

Both Paul and Peter are saying **you can rejoice in suffering because on this path to hope, affliction produces perseverance.** You likely know something about suffering and affliction, and being told to *rejoice* when you suffer is no easy word to accept. But to get to having hope that cannot be shaken, God will shake you. **And being shaken builds in you this lasting, unshakable hope so that it becomes a testimony to the world.**

You and I have access to God by seeking his face. You can choose to approach God complaining, asking, "God, what are you doing? How will you get me out of this?"

Or you can do what the author of Hebrews said, "Let us therefore come boldly to the throne of grace, that we may obtain mercy and find grace to help in time of need."[717]

In approaching God's throne of grace seeking mercy, the path to hope goes through suffering, which allows you to rejoice in the hope of glory, meaning that you know this suffering will end one day and you will be in paradise.

In the meantime, Paul said, tribulation produces patience. In other words, tribulation accomplishes something. It accomplishes you having more patience.

＝＝

The Lord intends that we edify one another, that we build one another up, that we are patient with one another. When somebody says something hurtful to you or about you, you do not carry the hurt. You do not pray, "God get even with them." Instead, ask "the God of patience and comfort [to] grant you to be like-minded toward one another, according to Christ Jesus."[718]

Can you say your thoughts and words are toward (for) your brother or sister— no matter who they are? It is easy to go to church seeking only for God to bless you. But at church, when you glance across the aisle and you see somebody who seems to be struggling, is there something in your heart that says, "God, is there something I can do?"

Sometimes, people share stories with me about a terminal diagnosis. At times like those, if I do not have any words for them, I just give them the biggest hug and cry with them.

---

717 Hebrews 4:16
718 Romans 15:5

When you go to church, tell God, "Help me to edify others today." Knowing how to edify others requires patience, though. The Bible says, "Patient endurance is what you need now, so that you will continue to do God's will. Then you will receive all that he has promised."[719]

Next, the path to hope goes through character. Perseverance brings about character.[720]

Whenever I go through something and I need a word of hope, I do not call just anybody. I would only turn to someone who has been through the fire, who has been tested, someone who will be honest with me. I do not want somebody to simply tell me, "Brother Dave, just hold on. You know the Scriptures—so just hold on."

I am tired of hearing "Just hold on." It is a flippant answer, a cheap answer. There is no experience behind it, no character.

A man from Indonesia emailed me saying, "Brother Dave, I get your daily devotions. I have to go to the hospital every day and watch my wife in pain, dying of a hopeless disease. But," he said, "God has been faithful. He has been meeting us."

I would want to talk to someone like that man. He is not just saying empty words; he is talking out of an experience that he has had with God as he faced tribulations. Or I would want to talk with the woman who emailed me saying, "I have been through so many surgeries. None of them have worked, and I have been in constant pain. But I know my Redeemer lives. I know who I am in Christ. God will bring me through the fire."

I once talked to another man who told me, "Life has been rough. It has been horrible—but oh, let me tell you what the Holy Spirit revealed to me." He took me to the Scriptures and showed me things I had never seen!

As Paul says, tribulation produces perseverance; and perseverance, character; and character, hope. Let me tell you what hope is. **Hope is about wanting to live.**

---

719 Hebrews 10:36 NLT
720 Romans 5:4; the King James Version uses *experience* instead of *character*.

It is an expectation that God will answer your prayers and deliver you. In the meantime, God is doing something deeper in your soul.

Some tell me, "I cannot endure this anymore. I have had all I can take, and I do not see any way out. I do not see any hope. I want to go be with Jesus."

What if God took everybody who had the character produced by suffering? The apostle Paul speaks of being in a storm, and "all hope that we would be saved was finally given up."[721]All hope was gone. And in his letter to the Philippians, he said, "For to me, to live is Christ, and to die is gain…. For I am hard-pressed between the two, having a desire to depart and be with Christ, which is far better. Nevertheless to remain in the flesh is more needful for you."[722]

"I am needed here," Paul said. As are you. God put you where you are. You are in a situation that God had arranged. The enemy may be a factor, but God has allowed you to be in the position you are.

In Christ, you are the hope of the world by being able to tell the world, "Yes, there is pain and suffering, but I know who I know, and his arm is not too short to save me."[723]

"For we were saved in this hope, but hope that is seen is not hope; for why does one still hope for what he sees? But if we hope for what we do not see, we eagerly wait for it with perseverance," Paul said.[724]

Your faith, your peace, your perseverance in the midst of tribulation, your character, it produces the kind of hope that allows the world to see the source of your hope. For that, the world needs you.

---

721 Acts 27:20
722 Philippians 1:21, 23–24
723 Isaiah 59:1
724 Romans 8:24–25

46

The Private War of a Saint

Have you ever gone through something so intense, a time where affliction, adversity, trouble, and trials come one after another, and it does not seem to stop? Whether it is financial, children, grandchildren, friends, health, these are wars of the flesh.

My son Greg went through more than two years of hell on earth dealing with pain. No medication helped. Greg finally had surgery and, thank God, he is doing fine. But there were times he was in such pain, he wanted to take his life.

Greg was experiencing something so profound, no one could reach the depths of his pain. **The physical pain he was going through was so intense; it was a private war between him and God.**

Perhaps you can relate. You might grit your teeth and say, "I can fight this!" You put on a facade and say that everything is all right even when it is not. **God does not want you to put on a front. He knows what you are going through, and he—only he—can help.**

When my daughter was being treated for cancer, nothing anyone could say would make me believe I was going to make it through watching my daughter suffer. When I felt like my world was falling to pieces, God met me and reminded me, "Your daughter has two fathers. You and me. Which one knows what is best?"

I admitted, "You do."

Again, the Lord reminded me, **"Put your family in my hands, trust me, and hold steady. I am not mad at you. Get the fear out of your system. Cry it out; put it in my hands. I will do what is right. Trust that I am a father to you."**

God was doing a deep work in me, and he was doing something supernatural in my daughter's life.

Some of us face a private war that the Bible suggests is a season of heaviness. Peter challenged his readers with these words, "I know you are now rejoicing and that you love God, but there are times of adversity and heaviness ahead. It will only be for a season."[725]

Those seasons can drag out, feeling like it will never end. As the struggle drags on, so does the resulting heaviness, resulting in depression. And when you are facing depression due to the day-to-day battle, it can feel like it is too much to bear.

King David knows what that is about. Worn out, he said, "My soul melts from heaviness."[726]

In other words, you can love God, you can love and help people, and you can do what is right before God—yet you can still be weary, facing a battle with depression.

I recently read the story of a godly man, greatly admired and righteous, a charitable man who had served the Lord faithfully for many years. This man was an intercessor and a famous worship leader.

But then one day, he took and impregnated another man's wife. In his panic, this man made arrangements for a hit man to kill the husband. His world came crashing down as he waged this horrible, private war.

The man was stricken with a disease. His friends and family forsook him. His soul was flooded with grief. God chastened him, and he could not sleep.

So the man said, "My burden is intolerable, my sins have caught up with me. My body is racked with pain. I have been overcome with shame for having reproached

---

725 1 Peter 1:5–6, paraphrased
726 Psalm 119:28a

God's name. I have been a fool; I have been a hypocrite. My sins overwhelm me. All I do is groan. My God, why have you forsaken me?"[727]

Of course, this man is King David. He had sinned, not only by taking Uriah's wife, but also by using the enemy to kill Uriah.[728] **He was waging a private war due to lust.** This war comes as a full-on attack.

James talked about this lust attack that comes against God's people. "Where do wars and fights come from among you? Do they not come from your desires for pleasure that war in your members?"[729]

We have a concept that if you are a praying person and you love the Lord, you cannot be tested, you will never be enticed to sin. But that is not true.

The Holy Spirit gave me a burden for those of you who are being enticed at work, to warn you that the enemy has tried to bring an attraction on the job. This can even happen at church.

If that is you, be warned. You might say you are not looking with lust, you are simply being enticed a little but you have not been responding. If you do not outright reject these temptations and stand strong in the Spirit to resist the enemy, he will come in like a flood.

Perhaps you know what I am talking about.

＝＝

Whether you are in a private war dealing with heaviness, financial difficulties, lust, addictions—whatever it may be, there is a way to have victory. Let us look at what David did.

First, David cried out in agony, "Make haste, O God, to deliver me! Make haste to help me, O Lord!"[730]

Like David, you can cry out to God, "Deliver me, Lord. Bring me out of this. I am weary from the battle." It does not mean God will take you out of your battle right away. It may be that God is doing a deeper work in you, preparing you for something down the road where you will need to have a greater understanding of

---

727 Psalms 38 and 69, paraphrased
728 2 Samuel 11–12:25
729 James 4:1
730 Psalm 70:1

the war that is being waged against believers. It may be that God is strengthening you through the storm. The first step is always to call on him.

Next, David determined to magnify the Lord despite everything he was going through, saying, "Let all those who seek you rejoice and be glad in you; and let those who love your salvation say continually, 'Let God be magnified!' "[731] David had decided, live or die, he would magnify the Lord in his battle.

If God does not take you out of the battle, cry out, "Jesus, give me the grace to endure." The Lord's goal is not just to get you out of one crisis and have you declare, "I have been delivered. God has healed me!" **His goal is for you to come out of it totally dependent on Christ, for the trial to make you more Christlike so you are more compassionate toward people.**

God is doing something greater in you so you can finally say, "Yes, God has delivered me. I am at peace, and I trusted God, but I know there is another battle coming. It may get worse, but I will still set my heart to trust God through it."

In the good times and the bad, set your heart and your mind to trust God through whatever may come.

Finally, David learned that he had to have faith that his distress would not overwhelm him. Like David, you can have the faith to declare, "My problems will not take me down. By faith and by God's grace, I will not be overwhelmed!"

The devil wants to put fear into your heart that your faith will fail, that you will give up and quit. No, you will not quit. Why? You have the Holy Ghost living in you. God will quicken you by his Spirit.

⸻

The apostle Paul said that Satan sent a messenger to harass and bombard him. He said, "I prayed three times, and the Lord said, 'I will allow this because I have enough grace for you. I will give you abundant grace to cope with it.' "[732]

I often wonder if this "messenger of Satan" was a hounding in Paul's mind of the saints he had cast into prison. We do not know what exactly it was, but it was not something small.

---

731 Psalm 70:4
732 2 Corinthians 12:7–9, paraphrased

I know from experience that the devil sends principalities and powers of darkness to lie to those who walk close to God. I know that not because I am holy, but I know that I know God, and I know there has been an assignment on my life for several years.

Powers and principalities have come, being sent on assignment, and they have stayed with me night and day so that in the middle of the night, I would be bombarded by lies. I know I have the mind of Christ in me, and I know God has given me a renewed heart. I have total confidence in my walk with Jesus Christ.

Still, when I walk the streets, when I walk to or from church, when I get up to preach, I often hear lies from the devil saying, "You are a hypocrite. You do not have an anointing!"

I am no longer afraid of those voices. When the lies come, I say, "Devil, I know where that is coming from, and you are just going to get tired one of these days and will have to leave because I am not going your way. I am not listening to these lies. I am covered by the blood of Jesus."

Determine to listen only to God speaking through his Word. Get the Word in your heart. That is what Jesus did. When the devil quoted Scriptures and tempted him, Jesus refuted the enemy with the Word.[733]

The Word of God is the sure voice. Study it. Memorize it. Then wield it when the enemy wages a war against you.

---

733 Matthew 4:1–11

47

A Call to Anguish

All true passion for Christ comes out of a baptism of anguish—extreme distress. Search the Scriptures and you will find that when God is determined to recover a ruined situation, he seeks out a praying man and takes him down into the waters of distress, baptizing him in anguish.

In the book of Nehemiah, you find that Jerusalem was in ruins. God's Holy City and its people were full of iniquity, and the temple was polluted.

I believe we face a similar situation, except ours is worse. The church is defiled. The nation is in a moral landslide inundated with violence and pornography brought to every home through television and the Internet. And Christians take it all in without thinking twice about the filth they are feeding their minds.

Now, you know I believe in the love of God. I have preached mercy, grace, and covenant love. **I believe in preaching about the goodness and patience of Christ, but multitudes are turning the grace of God into something it is not.**

We are much like the children of Israel. "Then the Lord heard the voice of your words when you spoke to me," Moses told them, "and the Lord said to me: 'I have heard the voice of the words of this people which they have spoken to you. They are right in all that they have spoken. Oh, that they had such a heart in them that they

246

would fear me and always keep all my commandments, that it might be well with them and with their children forever!' "734

God was telling Moses, "My people have the right words—they sing the right songs—but their hearts are not right with me."

Sadly, that did not change during the exile. When Hanani and a delegation from Judah came to report to Nehemiah regarding the state of the nation, they said, "The remnant that are left of the captivity there in the province are in great affliction and reproach, the wall of Jerusalem also is broken down, and the gates thereof are burned with fire."735

Hanani and his men had no concept of what God was going to do. All they could see was ruin and despair. But Nehemiah had a different approach. He mourned the condition of Jerusalem and its people, and he sought God in prayer.

God found a praying man in Nehemiah, and he took him into a baptism of anguish so Nehemiah would declare, "I pray day and night confessing the sins of the children of Israel. We have all sinned against thee."736

Nehemiah was not a preacher, he was a king's cupbearer. Still, he was a man of prayer. And the anguish he felt was neither a flash of emotion nor a burst of concern. He broke down and wept. He mourned and fasted. And then he began to pray night and day.

== ==
== ==

Hanani and his men had witnessed the destruction. Why did God not use them in the restoration of Jerusalem? **They had seen the ruin but were not moved to prayer.**

Does the condition of the nation and the church move you to intercession? So many folks slide into passivity, the signs of ruin slowly draining their passion and spiritual power. They are unaware of their spiritual blindness.

Have you, like others, lost your fight? All the devil wants to do is get the fight out of you so you will no longer labor in prayer; you will not wait before God. Instead, you sit and watch television, you spend hours on the Internet while the world around you is heading to hell.

---

734 Deuteronomy 5:28–29
735 Nehemiah 1:3 KJV
736 Nehemiah 1:4–6 KJV, paraphrased

Do these words even convict you at all? Like Nehemiah, Daniel dropped to his knees over the state of God's people, saying, "We have sinned and committed iniquity, we have done wickedly and rebelled, even by departing from your precepts and your judgments. Neither have we heeded your servants the prophets, who spoke in your name to our kings and our princes, to our fathers and all the people of the land. O Lord, righteousness belongs to you, but to us shame of face…because we have sinned against you."[737]

Daniel continues, "All this disaster has come upon us; yet we have not made our prayer before the Lord our God, that we might turn from our iniquities and understand your truth. Therefore the Lord has kept the disaster in mind, and brought it upon us; for the Lord our God is righteous in all the works which he does, though we have not obeyed his voice. And now, O Lord our God, who brought your people out of the land of Egypt with a mighty hand, and made yourself a name, as it is this day—we have sinned, we have done wickedly!"[738]

Could you say this about our nation?

Let me be clear: There is a great difference between anguish and concern. You have concern for something that you have an interest in. But anguish comes from being driven to your knees, such as when I first came to New York from a little country town in Pennsylvania where I pastored a small church. There, I had cried out to God, "I am empty. There has to be more to it than this!" I was desperate for God. I spent weeks calling on the name of the Lord, confessing my own deadness and dryness.

When I finally came to the city for street rallies, when I walked these streets and saw the depravity, I remember breaking down. I sat and wept. I was in anguish. I did not care that people walked by looking at me.

I was not looking for a ministry. I was not looking to build a new church. All I knew was that I was feeling God's pain for a lost city. It was the same agony I felt years before when I started Teen Challenge.

In all my years, I never had any ministry worth pursuing that was not born in anguish. Never. Otherwise, it is but flesh. It is just a program, a dream. **But when**

737 Daniel 9:5–8
738 Daniel 9:13–15

you seek God from a place of anguish, fasting, and praying, he will come and share with you his heart.

He will show you the condition of his church. He will show you the condition of your heart and ask you, "What is it to you?" You will have to decide whether you are okay with being a Christian like so many others around you, or if you are willing to carry the burden God places before you and be an instrument of restoration.

If you choose the latter, it will bring you to your knees. That is where God will speak to you, giving you a word of direction. You can choose that, or you can walk away and go back to your passivity. It is up to you.

"But I do not have a history of prayer," you might object. I would encourage you to tell God, "Lord, I want to step out and come to know your heart in prayer." When you begin to seek his face, allow him to break your heart for the things that break his. God will stir you to pray to bring your city out of ruins, restore your family—whatever it may be, God will show you.

Just as God took you into the waters of anguish, he will bring you out like he did with Nehemiah. He had been fasting, praying, and mourning, and it left a mark on his countenance. King Artaxerxes noticed and asked, "Why are you sad?"[739]

Likely afraid he might lose his job, Nehemiah did not have time to go and seek God for an appropriate response. He had to have direction on the spot. Knowing God's voice from his baptism of anguish, Nehemiah knew how to respond, explaining that the city of his ancestors lay in waste and that he wanted to go to Jerusalem to rebuild the city. Not only did King Artaxerxes approve Nehemiah taking time to go to Jerusalem, but the king also gave him letters in support of the work.

The servant who willingly takes on the mantle of God's pain is the servant who has the authority to hold God to his covenant promises.

Please do not tell me you are concerned about your unsaved loved ones when you are spending hours in front of the television or on the Internet. If God is speaking to you deeply, speaking to your heart like he has been speaking to mine, then go do whatever God has been telling you.

---

739 Nehemiah 2:2, paraphrased

Do it quickly. Cut off whatever keeps you from knowing God's heart, whatever is keeping you from the kind of passion that comes out of a baptism of anguish.

When you see the ruin and lukewarmness around you—in your family, your city, your nation—set your heart to seek God. Then hold God to his covenant promises. "Here is what you promised, God…" It may be that you realize you have wanted it easy, just to be happy. Confess that, keeping in mind that **true joy comes out of anguish, when you see the results of God laying hold of your heart, when he gives you direction, and you see lasting results.**

That is what happened to Nehemiah. After the people were moved by the reading of God's Word, he stood up and said, "Let the joy of the Lord be your strength."[740]

That joy came out of seeing the victory that came out of the anguish. *That* is the result of allowing God to baptize you in anguish for the world around you.

---

740 Nehemiah 8:10, paraphrased

48

The Victory of the Cross of Christ

Mere hours before the crucifixion of Jesus Christ, he gathered his disciples in a private room. He brought a basin with him, and a towel with which he girded himself. Then Jesus washed the feet of the disciples.

If a stranger walked in, they would have thought Jesus was a servant in a wealthy host's home. They would not have recognized him as the Son of God. Through this act, Jesus was trying to prepare his disciples for the bloody day ahead.

Jesus said in so many words that the wicked were going to crucify him. The disciples were going to be hated and cast out of the synagogue. Some would even be killed.[741] Jesus told them, "This is the hour I have been talking about. Prepare your hearts."[742]

When Jesus told them, "I am going to leave you now and I am going to the Father,"[743] it is clear the disciples did not understand what lay ahead for Jesus was the cross.

They told Jesus, "Now, master, you are speaking plainly. You are not speaking in proverbs. By this we believe you came forth from God. We believe now. We think we have got this faith thing figured out."[744]

---

741 John 15:18–16:11, with emphasis on 16:2
742 John 16:25, paraphrased
743 John 16: 10, 17, 28, paraphrased
744 John 16:29–30

So, Jesus turned to them and said, "Are you ready to drink from the cup I am going to drink from? What are you going to do when you see me hanging helpless?"[745]

= ≡ =

What do you think you would do if you were there at the foot of the cross? What would you do if you saw the man who testified to be God in the flesh cry out, "God, why have you forsaken me?"[746]

Surely, the disciples must have thought, "If Jesus were indeed the Messiah, how can the Father allow this suffering?" So, the disciples forsook Jesus. They all fled. **I believe you and I would have done just the same.**

How Satan must have gloated seeing Peter deny Jesus and all the disciples fleeing. "This is the way the church of Jesus Christ is going to end up when the pain comes and when their own personal cross comes," he may have thought. "They are going to fold!"

But there is one thing about our God the devil has never understood. **God never gives up on anybody—even those who fold under pressure.**

= ≡ =

I talked to a young minister going through great hardships. He told me, "Through it all, when I cannot pray and when I do not understand the pain and the suffering, I feel like there is an umbilical cord from heaven, and I am being fed, being filled with the Holy Ghost."

Your house may be shaken. You may fail God. Your faith may come to the place where you think it is absolutely gone and then the lies of hell come, saying, "You see, you thought you had it and you testified about it, but it is gone."

Still, you can tell yourself *and* the devil, "I am *not* going down!"

= ≡ =

---

745 Mark 10:38–39, paraphrased and conflated with John 16:31–32 where Jesus declares that they would scatter when the moment came.

746 Mark 15:34; Matthew 27:46; each quoting Psalm 22:1

At the time it occurred, Jesus's death on the cross may not have looked like a victory. **But here is what I see in the victory of the cross: the forgiveness of all past sins.** This may sound elementary, but this really is the foundational truth to keep you in the last days, the days when hard things come your way.

No matter what comes, you can know you are right with God. John's epistle reminds us, "But if we walk in the light as He is in the light, we have fellowship with one another, and the blood of Jesus Christ His Son cleanses us from all sin. If we say that we have no sin, we deceive ourselves, and the truth is not in us. If we confess our sins, He is faithful and just to forgive us our sins and to cleanse us from all unrighteousness."[747]

I encourage you to stand on these words. You are justified, freely. You are redeemed by grace through faith in the blood of Christ. You are declared his righteousness for the remissions of sin that are past. All guilt, all condemnation, is lifted when you come to the blood of Jesus Christ and you believe what he promised.

Paul tells us through his letter to the church in Rome, "There is therefore now no condemnation to those who are in Christ Jesus, who do not walk according to the flesh, but according to the Spirit....And we know that all things work together for good to those who love God, to those who are the called according to His purpose."[748]

God made provision for you to be reconciled with him. "But God demonstrates his own love toward us, in that while we were still sinners, Christ died for us. Much more then, having now been justified by his blood, we shall be saved from wrath through him. For if when we were enemies we were reconciled to God through the death of his Son, much more, having been reconciled, we shall be saved by his life."[749]

<hr />

The victory of the cross is the end of *all* regrets. A Puritan author from long ago said that to his knowledge, the greatest regret among the Puritan preachers of the day was wasted time.

In their dying days, after spending their life serving God and sharing the gospel, they were still saying what you might be thinking now. "I have wasted so much time. I could have been more than I am. I could have done more."

---

747 1 John 1:7–9
748 Romans 8:1, 28
749 Romans 5:8–10

When I think back, I endure the same thing—thinking of regrets from the past. It is not only how you start the race, but how you finish it. Yet God does not want us to live in the past. That is what the cross is all about. He nailed all of those issues to the cross so that you can sit in his presence now and declare, "That is in the past."

Christ's blood has cleansed you. You have had victory. There is no wrath of God upon you.

At the cross, mercy and peace took on a human face—the face of Christ Jesus who came to bring peace to his people. He made a covenant that his blood would bring everlasting peace and so you could see his glory.[750]

That is not just about being in heaven someday. Today, you can see some of that glory in the peace of God that comes from knowing you have been forgiven.[751]

Jesus *chose* to take the way of the cross.[752] He could have called it quits at any time. He could have chosen a different path in the Garden of Gethsemane after he shed bloody sweat.[753] He could have chosen another route. When they pierced him with the first nail, he could have called down a host of angels, and said, "There has to be another way."

But he did not. Jesus never said, "This is too much for me."

I certainly have. Have you? You might be there right now, asking "How can God be in what I am going through?"

Jesus laid down his life for us, his friends.[754] And he said, "By this all will know that you are my disciples, if you have love for one another."[755] There has never been a needier hour in all of history when we need people who will lay down their lives for the needs of others.

Here is how the world may know love—in that we lay down our lives for others. The world sees God's love in you not by your shouting about God's love but by loving others, even sacrificially.

---

750 John 17:24
751 Romans 15:13
752 John 10:17–18
753 Luke 22:44
754 John 15:13; John 3:16
755 John 13:35

The victory of the cross, too, is that he bore all our griefs and all our sorrows. The prophet Isaiah said of the Messiah, "He is despised and rejected by men, a man of sorrows and acquainted with grief. And we hid, as it were, our faces from him; he was despised, and we did not esteem him. Surely he has borne our griefs and carried our sorrows; yet we esteemed him stricken, smitten by God, and afflicted."[756]

Because of the cross, Christ understands your pain, your weakness, your weariness, your sickness, and your sorrows. He has been through it all. And because of his Spirit in you, you can stand strong, no matter what happens. You can even be willing to be a martyr, should it come down to that, declaring, "Oh God, I will trust you in the fire, and though you slay me, yet will I trust you."

Without the Holy Spirit, this is not possible, though. You cannot simply set your heart and decide to lay down your life for the sake of the gospel. You cannot build your own faith. This kind of faith comes from the Holy Ghost.

The Bible says the Holy Ghost is given to those who ask.[757] Today, cry out to the Spirit of God, "You were sent to comfort me. You were sent to heal me. You were sent to take me through my grief and my sorrows. Holy Spirit, come down!"

---

756 Isaiah 53:3–4
757 Luke 11:13

49

We See Jesus

In the book of Hebrews, the writer quotes the psalmist, declaring, "But one testified in a certain place, saying: 'What is man, that you are mindful of him, or the son of man that you take care of him? You have made him a little lower than the angels; you have crowned him with glory and honor, and set him over the works of your hands. You have put all things in subjection under his feet.' "[758]

These writers are referring to the first chapter of Genesis, where God commanded mankind to "rule over the fish of the sea, over the birds, the cattle and over all the earth. Be fruitful; multiply. Fill the earth and subdue it and rule over all the sea and the birds of the sky and all that is created."[759]

The One who had created all things had made mankind the caretakers of his creation. But instead of taking care of this world, we seem to have trampled upon that which God has asked us to steward. As a result, when we look around us, instead of order, we see brokenness and chaos.

The passage from Hebrews reminds us, though, that we—the church, the body of Christ—do not have to focus on the brokenness and the confusion. "Now we do not yet see all things put under him," he says. "But we see Jesus…"[760]

---

758 Hebrews 2:6–8a, quoting Psalm 8:4, 6
759 Genesis 1:24–28, paraphrased
760 Hebrews 2:8b–9a

Instead of fixating on the chaos, if we fix our eyes on Jesus, he can bring us through any situation, any trial—no matter how difficult it is.

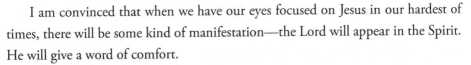

I am convinced that when we have our eyes focused on Jesus in our hardest of times, there will be some kind of manifestation—the Lord will appear in the Spirit. He will give a word of comfort.

Take, for example, the apostle John on the Island of Patmos. John was isolated, and a guard was likely the only person he could talk to. Yet in his hardest moment of isolation and loneliness, Jesus appeared to him.

"When I saw him, I fell at his feet," John says. "He laid his right hand upon me saying, 'Fear not, for I am the first and the last, I am he that lives and was dead and behold I live forevermore. Amen, I have the keys of hell and heaven.' "[761]

In essence, Jesus was telling John, "Nothing can touch you, John. Take my hand."

When you walk with Jesus, when you keep your focus on Jesus, you will hear him say, "Do not be afraid." For no matter what you are facing, Jesus is there.

Do you believe God is with you in your battle? If you do, you can call out to him in times of distress. "Jesus, I know you are here. Speak, Lord. I am listening."

Without fail, whenever I have done that, God has spoken a word that has brought peace as he reminded me that he is my strength.

The apostle Paul would allow nothing in the world to rob him of his message that Jesus Christ is Lord. When he was abandoned by his friends, he said, "All men forsook me, but the Lord stood by me and gave me strength."[762]

He told the church, "I determined to know nothing among you except Jesus Christ and him crucified."[763] Paul would not get involved in the religious controversies of his day, even when he was imprisoned. His message was, "Christ is alive. Christ is the answer to the problems of the world."

---

761 Revelation 1:17–18, paraphrased
762 2 Timothy 4:16–17
763 1 Corinthians 2:2

Paul refused to get involved in the political battles of his day. They tried to trap Paul into getting either on the Jewish side or on the Roman side, but he would not be moved.

To Timothy, he essentially said, "Do not be entangled in the affairs of this life. We are in a war; we are soldiers, and you cannot be taken away from your mission and your message and from the centrality of Jesus Christ."[764]

This is an area where the devil will launch major attacks against the church. He will try to get us off message and entangled in politics. There is such political anger—I do not care whether it is right or left. **There is bitterness that is growing into hatred until people—even Christians—are screaming at the news. God told me to lovingly warn the church against such insanity.**

It does not mean you should not be involved in political issues. What Paul says is not to become *entangled* in it. In other words, do not go to meetings and places where your anger is being stirred like a hot poker and the coals are getting hotter until it consumes you; until that is all you talk about rather than talking about Jesus and what God is doing in your life.

You will not be able to face what is coming unless your soul is at rest and at peace with no anger, no bitterness, no rebellion in your heart.

≡ ≡

As for you who are on the brink of falling into a pit of despair—it may be that you are struggling with a situation in your family or life at large, but you have hit a wall. You are overwhelmed, having faced one battle too many.

My wife Gwen and I can certainly relate to feeling that way. During the time I was preparing this sermon, somebody called me to share Psalm 143. Gwen had found yet another mass. I had no words to pray, and she, too, had lost her fight. But the words of this psalm gave us strength.

In this psalm, David is fleeing from Absalom. He was running, hiding, tired, and at the end of himself. Meanwhile, the enemy was lying to him and brought him under a spirit of fear.

"For the enemy has persecuted my soul," David said. "He has crushed my life to the ground; he has made me dwell in darkness, like those who have long

---

764 2 Timothy 2:4, paraphrased

been dead.[765] Therefore my spirit is overwhelmed within me; my heart within me is distressed."[766]

I do not know if you have ever been to that place. I do not know if you are on the brink of going to that place of feeling like your heart has become numb. Have you ever been numb at the news you hear and the things that are happening, not even mad at God? That is where David was. And that is how Gwen and I felt when we received yet more bad news.

But then, the psalmist cries out, "Answer me speedily, O Lord; my spirit fails! Do not hide your face from me, lest I be like those who go down into the pit."[767]

I believe David is saying, "I have seen people come to a crisis, and I have seen them lose their faith. I have seen them go down into a pit and they chose that as an option and they cannot get out and now it is worse than ever. I am like those who are about to go into a pit and I feel like I have been buried alive. I have to see you in this, God. Do not hide your face. I want to see you. I need a manifestation. Do not hide from me."

David continues, "Cause me to hear your lovingkindness in the morning…"[768] In other words, "Lord, tomorrow morning I want to hear a word of your lovingkindness."

I believe David is not only speaking about the next day; he is thinking about every day to come, that he wants to hear something from the Word of God about the lovingkindness of his Father, a reminder from heaven that God loves him and is concerned about him.

"…for in you do I trust; cause me to know the way in which I should walk… "[769] David cries out, "Give me direction. Lord, that is what I am asking…"

Then comes his challenge to God. "Deliver me, O Lord, from my enemies. In you I take shelter."[770] With that, David vails himself in Christ.

Why can David say this? The answer is in the opening line to this psalm. "Hear my prayer, O Lord, give ear to my supplications! In your faithfulness answer me, and in your righteousness."[771]

---

765 The Hebrew says, "I feel like I am buried alive."
766 Psalm 143:3–4
767 Psalm 143:7
768 Psalm 143:8a
769 Psalm 143:8b
770 Psalm 143:9
771 Psalm 143:1

That is the basis upon which David can come to God. It is not just based upon what he had heard about God from others. His confidence is rooted in who he has seen God be: faithful, just, holy, unable to tell lies, long-suffering, a God of peace, the God who is his strength.

Reading this psalm, it felt to me as if Jesus were sitting right there with Gwen and me. Like David, I could declare anew:

"I believe what you said about yourself. I am coming on the merits of nothing I have done—no righteousness of my own—but on the promises you told me. You are who you said you are, and from this day on, I will vail myself in you. I will cut myself off from all confidence in my flesh or in people. I will throw myself at your mercy, your grace, your power, your glory. I am veiling myself in you, Christ, shutting my eyes to the foolish controversies of man and angry politics."

Will you come to God today? Will you come to him with your numbness? Will you come to him with everything that plagues your soul, will all your fears? **Stand up against the lies that come out of hell that try to take your focus off Jesus.**

50

A Craving for the Presence of the Lord

When I look into the future, I see dark clouds and hear thunder and lightning, and I hear a shaking. We are approaching midnight. All I have preached about for years, everything we have talked about is around the corner.

Every foolish, frivolous thing in your life has to go. Every ungodly ambition has to end. Every attachment to the things of this world, it all has to go. Things have to change. There has to be a change in your walk with God.

When things get really hard, everything will boil down to a very simple question: What is the most important thing right now?

I found my answer when Gwen and I visited Israel. I spent time alone on Mount Carmel, overlooking the valley where Elijah the prophet built an altar and called fire out of heaven.[772]

I had a wonderful time with the Lord, but nothing profound hit me. Afterward, I was taken to the Garden of Gethsemane, expecting that I might have a sense of release in prayer, but even there, I had none.

I had some wonderful times in prayer. I poured my heart out to the Lord, but it did not hit me until we were heading home and I sensed the longing for the place where I was heading—my prayer room, the place where I crave for the presence of the Lord.

---

772 1 Kings 18

Where I had been in Israel was Elijah's place of prayer and Jesus's place of prayer. Back home was where I communed with Jesus. The first chance I had, I went into that room, shut the door, and raised my hands in prayer. I began to weep, saying, "Jesus, I have been so hungry to get back in this room."

The word *crave* means to long, to earnestly desire, to go after, to pursue. **My craving room is not where I go to get prayers answered; it is a place where I adore Christ, a place where I draw near to him, it is a place where he embraces me.**

And every time I go into that room, the craving gets stronger.

═ ═

As for the difficult times that are ahead, I am convinced that God will protect and provide for his people. After all, Jesus said, "Your Father knows the things you have need of before you ask him."[773]

God will provide food, water, and shelter. And he will give supernatural guidance on how to prepare for what is ahead. This is not about hoarding rice, beans, and water. You can have it all and yet be bitter because you missed the point. That is about wanting God's provision, not his presence.

Jesus said, "Life is more than food, and the body is more than clothing."[774] And he said, "Therefore do not worry, saying, 'What shall we eat?' or 'What shall we drink?' or 'What shall we wear?'... But seek first the kingdom of God and his righteousness, and all these things shall be added to you."[775]

In other words, **your focus should not be on feeling secure but on your relationship with God.**

═ ═

You and I can learn from Moses, who knew well that without the presence of the Lord with them, not he or the nation could make it through the perilous times that had befallen them.

---

773 Matthew 6:8
774 Luke 12:23
775 Matthew 6:31, 33

Moses said this at a time when Israel had corrupted themselves by making and worshipping a golden calf while Moses was up on the mountain with God. God was angered, telling Moses he would consume the nation.[776]

But Moses pleaded with God, so God had mercy on them. He spared Israel, saying he would let them go on to the Promised Land, and that he would send his angel with them to lead them.

That is when Moses pitched his tent far away from the camp and interceded for his people. There, at the tabernacle of the meeting, Moses met with God.

Israel had committed *two* sins, and one led to the other. I believe making a golden calf and worshipping it was the result of an even greater sin—something that is as prevalent now as it was then.

That great sin then and today is a lack of desire for the presence of the Lord in our lives. It is to want his provision and his protection yet not crave for his presence—the very presence that makes the provisions possible.

Someone told you about the new covenant of God, that Jesus died for your sins, and if you believe that, you shall be saved. You did that, and indeed—you are saved according to the stipulations of God's legal contract, his covenant.

But if all you want is a legal contract with God, you have missed the point. It will never lead you to know Christ in his fullness.

God offers you so much more than just breaking you out of the bondage of sin. God wants you to love him with all your heart, your mind, your soul, and strength.[777] That is more than a legal arrangement; it is a love affair.

Some people only want God's promises. They want to know they are not going to hell. Even so, God will keep his word. He will take care of you.

---

776 Exodus 32:1–10
777 Mark 12:30

That is no different from what Israel was dealing with up to the point where they made a golden calf. But now, they were facing the issue of God's presence. Up to that point, they had taken it for granted that God was with them.

This is why God essentially says, "Sure, I will protect you, and I will supply all your needs as I promised. But I am not going with you."

This is when they mourned, taking off all their jewelry they had lugged out of Egypt with them, the baggage they brought with them from Egypt.[778] They mourned; they wept for their sins.

Are you ready to mourn for your sins and get rid of all the baggage from your past? Do not go back to your old ways. Do not weep and then pick your baggage back up. Do not go back to your old way of thinking. Leave it behind.

Moses was different. In Moses, God found the man who was not looking just for God to make good on the promises of the covenant with Abraham and protect them. No, Moses wanted more. He would be found on his face before God.

In those perilous times, Moses turned away from all his activities, from every demand on his time, and sought God's presence.

Do you have that kind of time with God? I am not talking about a five-minute devotion. Do you have a craving room, a place where you get alone with the Lord and say, "Lord, I want to *know* you."

The answer to whatever challenges you face is to be on your face before God, to mourn, and to repent. Out of such a prayer time comes a cry, **"If your presence does not go with us, do not bring us up from here."**[779]

Boy, that is a powerful statement. Moses was saying, "Lord, thank you for your generous, gracious, promise to take care of us. Thank you for your covenant promises to deal with our enemies. Thank you for the promise of the angel. But Lord, unless I can have face-to-face intimacy with you, unless I can come to you and know that you are right there, I do not want to take another step."

---

778 Exodus 33:4
779 Exodus 33:15

When Gwen and I were in Israel, we had the honor of visiting two wonderful sisters at the Evangelical Sisters of Mary, a Lutheran organization. One of the ladies we met was Sister Basileah Schlink, one of the cofounders of the organization.[780]

She and another sister had a house on the Mount of Olives overlooking Jerusalem. They had been there thirty-six years by the time we met them, ministering to Arabs and Jews. You could feel the presence of the Lord when you walked into their home.

Over tea and cookies, they told us about the war and how the Jordanian Army surrounded their compound. Not sure if they should leave, they prayed and the Lord gave them a word, the same word he gave to Gideon. "I will be with you, do not be afraid."[781]

The Lord told them to store up food and water, and they did. They kept it in their basement. When the war erupted, their house was hit by two bombs, and the walls collapsed, but the sisters were safe in the basement where they hid for fourteen days, having sufficient food and water. **Though they praised God for his protection and provision, what they still talk about is God's presence.**

"Those fourteen days were the most precious hours we have ever spent," they said. "Jesus manifested himself to us in a way we have never known." And because of the revelation of the presence of Jesus during those two weeks, they craved more time in his presence.

≡ ≡ —

Life is all about Jesus. It is all about seeking him first and giving him everything in your life.

Moses had such a craving heart that God said he would go with Moses. But having been with God, Moses wanted more, asking, "Please, show me your glory." And God showed Moses his goodness, a revelation of his glory.[782]

---

780 When we met her, Sister Basileah was 94 and still praising Jesus. She passed away in 2001, when she was 96.
781 Judges 6:23, paraphrased
782 Exodus 33:18–19

Having spent time in God's presence, Moses's face shone so brightly, the people could not look at him. God's glory not only appeared *to* him, but Moses reflected God's glory.[783]

May that be true of you, that as you spend time with God, he would reveal himself to the world through you.

---

783 Exodus 34:29–35; 2 Corinthians 3:7, 13–16

About the Author

David Wilkerson was called to New York City in 1958 to minister to gang members and drug addicts, as told in the best-selling book, *The Cross and the Switchblade*. He went on to create Teen Challenge, the largest drug rehabilitation program in the world.

Later, David founded World Challenge, a message and missions organization that is working in fifty nations, ministering to hundreds of thousands each year.

In 1987, David established Times Square Church. As its founding pastor, he faithfully led this congregation, delivering powerful biblical messages that encourage righteous living and complete reliance on God.

David Wilkerson also had a strong burden to encourage his fellow pastors and leaders, conducting conferences in over seventy nations.

His passion to support believers, build up leaders, and care for the poor is still at the heart of World Challenge's ministries to this day.

This book celebrates the fiftieth anniversary of the ministry of World Challenge.

A free ebook edition is available with the purchase of this book.

To claim your free ebook edition:

1. Visit MorganJamesBOGO.com
2. Sign your name CLEARLY in the space
3. Complete the form and submit a photo of the entire copyright page
4. You or your friend can download the ebook to your preferred device

Morgan James
BOGO™

A **FREE** ebook edition is available for you or a friend with the purchase of this print book.

CLEARLY SIGN YOUR NAME ABOVE

Instructions to claim your free ebook edition:
1. Visit MorganJamesBOGO.com
2. Sign your name CLEARLY in the space above
3. Complete the form and submit a photo of this entire page
4. You or your friend can download the ebook to your preferred device

Print & Digital Together Forever.

Snap a photo

Free ebook

Read anywhere